AF504134

ANCESTRAL HOUSES

above *The arms of the Duke of
Somerset in the Marble Hall at
Petworth House, West Sussex.*
endpapers *The Adam ceiling in the
gallery at Harewood House, West
Yorkshire.*
frontispiece *The Palladian bridge at
Wilton House, Wiltshire, in the 1860s.
Leaning against the pillar on the right is
Lady Maud Herbert and in the boat is
the Rev. and Hon. Sidney Meade.*

THE NATIONAL TRUST

ANCESTRAL HOUSES

MARK BENCE-JONES

THE NATIONAL TRUST
WEIDENFELD AND NICOLSON

To
MIRANDA AND SILVIA

First published in Great Britain by
George Weidenfeld & Nicolson Limited
91 Clapham High Street, London SW4 7TA

ISBN 0 297 78445 5

Designed by Joyce Chester and Gillian Riley
Picture research by Caroline Lucas

Filmset by Keyspools, Golborne, Lancashire
Printed and bound by LEGO, Vicenza, Italy

CONTENTS

Alnwick Castle
Wallington House
Raby Castle
Ormesby Hall
Muncaster Castle
Castle Howard
Harewood House
Hoghton Tower
Dunham Massey
Plas Newydd
Bodrhyddan Hall
Penrhyn Castle
Erddig
Haddon Hall
Chatsworth
Holkham Hall
Belton House
Belvoir Castle
Peckover House
Houghton Hall
Blickling Hall
Shugborough
Powis Castle
Burghley House
Elton Hall
Baddesley Clinton
Stanford Hall
Hagley Hall
Althorp
Lamport Hall
Coughton Court
Charlecote Park
Castle Ashby
Sudeley Castle
Rousham House
Woburn Abbey
Audley End
Eastnor Castle
Knebworth House
Blenheim Palace
Hatfield House
Stonor Park
Hughenden Manor
Osterley Park
Ham House
Badminton House
Stratfield Saye
Knole
Stourhead
Wilton House
Petworth House
Glynde Place
Uppark
Goodwood House
Brympton D'Evercy
Arundel Castle
Powderham Castle
Antony House
Lanhydrock
Saltram House
Mount Edgcumbe

AUTHOR'S PREFACE

There is more to an ancestral house than the building and its contents. There is the family history; there are anecdotes and memories of guests, famous people or eccentrics; and there are the guests' own recollections of the house, and of what it was like to live in at various stages in its domestic evolution. It is so much easier to appreciate the more elusive qualities of a house if one can see it not only through one's own eyes but through the eyes of people who knew it in the past. And if these people happen to have been great writers, they may also bring the house to life by using it as the model for a house in fiction.

This book portrays more than sixty country houses in England and Wales by means of anecdotes and memories, family history and literary associations. Its object is to give the reader the feeling of having actually stayed in the houses rather than of having merely been taken round on a guided tour. In former times it would not have been unusual to have met somebody who had stayed in at least half the houses featured in this book, and who would have had a story to tell about almost every one of those. With the decline in country house entertaining from 1914 onwards, such people are now, in the nature of things, a breed that is all but extinct. This book is intended to be in some way a substitute for them. It does not set out to describe the houses in detail, which has been done elsewhere, though a brief account of the architecture and art treasures of each of them is included.

The houses were chosen with a view to striking a balance between the famous and the not so well known. A relatively greater amount of space is devoted to the famous ones for the obvious reason that there is much more material available about them. Houses have been included to present a wide geographical spread and a varied cross-section of families and domestic architecture. Some of them are in private ownership, some in the care of the National Trust or other bodies, the criteria being that they should be regularly open to the public and still lived in by the family with which they are chiefly associated, or at least still contain the pictures, furniture and similar possessions of that family.

In thanking all those who have so kindly provided me with material or illustrations, lent me books and papers, allowed me to quote from unpublished sources or helped in other ways, I must mention in particular the following: the Duke of Richmond and Gordon, the Marquess and Marchioness of Salisbury, Lady Diana Cooper, Viscount Hampden, Lord and Lady Camoys, Lord Egremont, Lord Howard of Henderskelfe, Baroness von Twickel, Alice Lady Fairfax-Lucy, the Hon. David Lytton Cobbold, Major and the Hon. Mrs Hervey-Bathurst, Mr James Hervey-Bathurst, Mrs Richard Grahame Adams, Mrs Michael Browne, Mrs Roger Burden, Mr Charles Clive-Ponsonby-Fane, Mr Thomas Cottrell-Dormer, Mr Daniel Gillman, Mr William Hugonin, Mr Hugh Montgomery-Massingberd, the late Ruth Dorrien Pennyman, Mr Claud Proby, Mr William Proby, Mr Simon Reynolds, Mr John Martin Robinson, the Rev. Henry Thorold, Mr Raleigh Trevelyan, Mr Hugo Vickers, Dr David Watkin, FSA.

A special word of thanks is due to Robin Wright, Gervase Jackson-Stops and other members of the staff of the National Trust for their help and encouragement. I am also grateful to have been able to consult some of the admirable National Trust guide-books. Last, but by no means least, I would like to thank Wendy Dallas and others at Weidenfeld, and Caroline Lucas for her excellent picture research.

ALNWICK CASTLE
NORTHUMBERLAND

Alnwick, the great medieval stronghold of the Percys, passed to the Seymours, Dukes of Somerset, through the marriage in 1682 of the 6th Duke of Somerset to Elizabeth, daughter of the last of the original Percy Earls of Northumberland (*see* PETWORTH HOUSE). When the 7th Duke of Somerset died leaving no son the great Percy inheritance was divided between his nephew and his daughter, another Elizabeth, whose share included Alnwick. This Elizabeth was married to Sir Hugh Smithson, a Yorkshire baronet, who caused some raising of eyebrows when he changed his name to Percy and inherited a new Northumberland earldom which had been conferred on his father-in-law with remainder to him. In 1757 he solicited and was given the Garter, and in 1766 he was made Duke of Northumberland.

'They live by the etiquette of the old peerage, have Swiss porters, the Countess has her pipers . . .', Horace Walpole remarked of Elizabeth and her husband soon after their metamorphosis from Smithson to Percy. 'In short, they will very soon have no estate.' He called the buxom, quick-tongued Elizabeth 'a jovial heap of contradictions . . . the blood of all the Percies and Seymours swelled in her veins and in her fancy, her person was more vulgar than anything but her conversation, which was larded indiscriminately with stories of her ancestors and her footmen . . . she was familiar with the mob, while stifled with diamonds.' For all her vulgarity, she was a lady of taste and an indefatigable visitor to country houses, which she viewed with the eye of a connoisseur. Her preference was for the Gothic, to which she was able to give a free rein in her building works at Alnwick, where in 1770 she and her husband entertained the King's brother, the Duke of Cumberland. As the royal guest entered the castle gate, he was saluted with twenty-one guns. On Sunday he went to Alnwick church to hear a sermon preached by the Reverend Dr Thomas Percy, author of *The Reliques of Ancient Poetry*, after which he returned to the castle where the Mayor and Corporation of Newcastle, the local MPs – including Sir Walter Calverley Blackett (*see* WALLINGTON) – and other gentlemen of the county, presented their compliments. Then followed a dinner of 177 dishes exclusive of dessert. 'In short, the magnificence and hospitality display'd on this occasion at Alnwick Castle by its present illustrious possessors gave a striking picture of the state and splendour of our ancient barons', Elizabeth wrote with some complacency in her diary. To the cynical Walpole, her affectation of baronial display, with 'the pipers and drummers and obsolete minstrels of her family and her own buxom countenance at the tail of such a procession' was more like 'an antiquated pageant or mummery'.

Portraits by Reynolds of Elizabeth, Duchess of Northumberland, the heiress of the Percys, and her husband the 1st Duke of Northumberland, formerly Sir Hugh Smithson.

The 2nd Duke of Northumberland, a soldier who distinguished himself at the Battle of Lexington and rose to be a general, was succeeded in turn by his two sons, of whom the elder was described by the diarist Charles Greville as 'a very good sort of man, with a very narrow understanding, an eternal talker and prodigious bore'. The younger son, the first of several Dukes of Northumberland to be a scientist and a Fellow of the Royal Society, carried out an extensive remodelling of Alnwick, replacing Duchess Elizabeth's Georgian Gothic in the principal rooms with a rich Italian Renaissance-Revival. When criticized for putting these sumptuous interiors into a medieval fortress, he said: 'Would you wish us only to sit on benches upon a floor strewn with rushes?' He died in 1865 and was succeeded by a cousin. His widow, known as 'Eleanor the Good', was staying at Alnwick on both the occasions when the writer and country house visitor Augustus Hare came here as the guest of the 6th Duke, and spoke to him of her attachment to the castle and of how much she had hated having to leave it.

In fact Duchess Eleanor rather overshadowed the reigning Duchess, who at the time of Hare's second visit, which was in 1887, was an invalid in a wheelchair. 'The Duke looks wiry, refined, rather bored, and some people

Alnwick Castle in the eighteenth century, by Canaletto.

would find him very alarming', Hare wrote of his host, while he considered the Duke's son and daughter-in-law, Lord and Lady Percy, to be 'two of the most silent people in the world'. Father and son and their respective wives were all deeply religious and adhered to the Irvingite sect, of which the Duchess's father, Henry Drummond, had been one of the 'Twelve Apostles': they attended Alnwick church, but the vicar there was also an Irvingite. 'This Irvingite family is constantly waiting and looking out for the millennium', Hare observed of the ducal family at Alnwick. 'It is terribly anxious work. But their faith is most simple and touching ... it is curious to hear members of this family say casually, "The angel was here on Monday, and will be here again on Friday."'

On the first evening of Hare's visit to Alnwick in 1887 an after-dinner game of whist was interrupted by prayers in the chapel, read by the Duke. This was the first time for fifteen years that Hare had encountered evening prayers in a country house. One member of the party did not stay up long enough to attend these devotions – Lady Emma McNeill, 'a violent Radical who went to bed at once when the Primrose League became the topic of conversation'.

Architecture and Contents

The great Border stronghold of the Percys, dating largely from the fourteenth century, Alnwick was remodelled in Georgian Gothic by Robert Adam for Elizabeth, Duchess of Northumberland. A more extensive remodelling was carried out in the 1850s by the 4th Duke of Northumberland, whose architect was Anthony Salvin. The castle became more consciously baronial in its exterior and was given the interior of an Italian palace of the High Renaissance, Italian decorators being employed to supervise the British craftsmen who did the work. With their elaborately coffered ceilings, their damask hangings and their monumental chimney-pieces, the rooms constitute a rich background to an art collection that boasts no fewer than three Titians, together with works by Tintoretto, Palma Vecchio, Canaletto and Turner and portraits by Van Dyck, Dobson, Gainsborough and Reynolds. The furniture, some of which came from Northumberland House in London, includes a pair of *pietre dure* cabinets that once belonged to Louis XIV, while two splendid Meissen dinner services have pride of place among the porcelain.

Alnwick today.

ALTHORP
NORTHAMPTONSHIRE

'MY LORD, when these things were doing your ancestors were keeping sheep,' the Earl of Arundel (*see* ARUNDEL CASTLE) said to the 1st Lord Spencer during a Parliamentary debate in 1621 – to which Lord Spencer riposted: 'When my ancestors were keeping sheep, Your Lordship's ancestors were plotting treason.' Lord Arundel's not very polite remark alluded to the fact that the Spencer family fortunes were founded at the beginning of the Tudor period by a wealthy grazier, Sir John Spencer, who acquired large estates in Warwickshire and Northamptonshire, including Althorp, which he bought in 1508. Sir John's grandson appears to have been the first of the family to make his home here. Around the nucleus of an existing hall he built an Elizabethan house with a courtyard which is now occupied by the grand staircase made in about 1655 by the celebrated Sacharissa Sidney, widow of Henry Spencer, 1st Earl of Sunderland, who fell at the first Battle of Newbury fighting for the King. The house was remodelled soon after the Restoration by Sacharissa's son, the politician Sunderland, a man in whom, as Macaulay puts it, 'the political immorality of his age was personified in the most lively manner', so that he was able to serve three monarchs of varying beliefs, Charles II, James II and William III.

In 1669, not long after the house had been transformed, Cosimo de' Medici, Hereditary Prince of Tuscany, was regally entertained at Althorp. His secretary thought it 'the best planned and best arranged country seat in the kingdom'. The fact that the principal rooms were on the first floor, in the old-fashioned Elizabethan manner, appealed to him as being like an Italian *piano nobile*, and he also admired Sacharissa's grand staircase which, except that its massive balustrades are of wood rather than of stone, certainly puts one in mind of the staircase in an Italian *palazzo*. Another visitor full of admiration for Althorp was John Evelyn, who wrote after a visit in 1688:

The Halle is well, the Staircase incomparable, the roomes of State, Gallerys, Offices and Furniture such as becomes a greate Prince: It is situated in the midst of Gardens exquisitely planted and kept . . . and what is above all this, Govern'd by a Lady, that without any shew of solicitude keepes every thing in such admirable order both within and without, from the Garret to the Cellar; that I do not believe there is any in all this nation or any other that exceeds her: all is in such exact order, without ostentation, but substantially greate and noble. The meanest servant lodged so neate and cleanly, The Services at the several Tables, the good order and decency, in a word the intire Oeconomie perfectly becoming.

Evelyn wished that the 2nd Earl of Sunderland were 'as worthy' of his 'wise and noble' Countess 'as by a fatal Apostacy, and Court ambition, he has made himselfe unworthy'.

The next Sunderland, a powerful statesman under Queen Anne and
George I, married a daughter of the Great Duke of Marlborough, by whom
he had, with other children, a son who succeeded to the Marlborough
dukedom as well as to the Sunderland earldom, and a daughter, Diana
Spencer, afterwards Duchess of Bedford (*see* WOBURN ABBEY), who was
considered as a possible bride for Frederick, Prince of Wales. When the son
who became Duke of Marlborough inherited BLENHEIM PALACE in 1744,
Althorp passed to his younger brother Jack Spencer, but before that he lived
here, and built the present stables as well as giving the hall its splendid
plasterwork and its hunting pictures by Wootton. Hunting was, at that time,
his ruling passion. 'I hear their recreations all day were galloping and
hollowing', Lord Hervey reported in his *Memoirs* of a house party at Althorp
in 1731. 'And their pleasures all night stale beer and tobacco ... How
essential riches must needs be to happiness, when people with twenty
thousand pounds a year take the same pleasures with those who carry chairs
and burdens for two or three shillings a day.'

During most of the second half of the eighteenth century Althorp was
somewhat neglected. When, in 1755, a large party assembled in the house for
the marriage of Jack Spencer's son, the future 1st Earl Spencer, the bride's
mother remarked on its 'melancholy appearance: about two lighted billets in
each chimney with tin fenders and neither carpet nor screen'. It was the 2nd
Earl Spencer, brother of the fascinating Georgiana, Duchess of Devonshire
(*see* CHATSWORTH), who after succeeding in 1783 rescued Althorp from the
state of dilapidation into which it had by then fallen. At first he intended to
confine himself, as he said, to 'making the apartments we live in weather-
proof and saving the house from tumbling down', but his architect, the
fashionable Henry Holland, eventually persuaded him to embark on a much

more ambitious scheme to bring the house up to date. Lord Spencer had difficulty in finding the money to pay for these alterations, so Holland offered to finance the work, though in the end he was unwilling to advance more than £1,713 out of a total cost of over £20,000. The family borough of Oke-hampton in Devon and a manor in Surrey had to be sold.

The 2nd Earl Spencer was First Lord of the Admiralty during the French Revolutionary War and afterwards Secretary of State. He lived until 1834, by which time his eldest son, Lord Althorp, had been Chancellor of the Exchequer in Lord Grey's Reform Bill Cabinet. In contrast to his eldest son, a Whig patrician statesman like himself, was his youngest son George, who became a Catholic and a Passionist Father who worked among the poor. The political tradition of the Spencers was continued in the Victorian and Edwardian periods by the 5th and 6th Earls: the former held office in several Liberal administrations and was twice Viceroy of Ireland. He was known as the Red Earl on account of his luxuriant red beard which, during the courts held at Dublin Castle – when it was customary for the Viceroy to kiss the debutantes as they were presented to him – would turn white with face-powder by the end of the evening.

The 6th Earl's youngest daughter has written a charming account of her life at Althorp just after the First World War when she was about thirteen. There was then nobody between her and her elderly widower father, the rest of the family having grown up and left.

No conscious loneliness marked the child. The house and park took her over: she became part of them and they part of her ... But life was not all solitary. There was hide-and-seek in the dark all over the house, with a lot of little girls in gym tunics. There was syrup of figs every Friday night, administered by the butler who arrived upstairs in his shirt-sleeves, having finished his more important duties elsewhere. There was skating on the Round Oval, where chestnuts roasted on an enormous bonfire. Jam-making in the stillroom went on the whole summer long, and the warm, delicious smell seemed to spread to the farthest bedrooms. Every evening, waiting in the nursery passage for Fred Manning, whose job it was to lower the flag, meant a long chat and a bag of sweets. Every morning he was meant to hoist it again, but he usually forgot until it was afternoon.

Other inhabitants of the house included Tom Irons, who 'shifted coal in trolleys onto primitive lifts' and Mary Chowler, the 'old parrot maid of 50 years' service' whose collection of parrots was too large 'for hygiene or for comfort – even for the parrots'. She 'slept in a suite set aside for her, to confine the terrible parrot smell. Draped in her eccentric, flowing clothes, she was still able to scream her way across the park, hobbling unreliably but with surprising speed.'

Then there were 'the child's special ghosts ... the sound of turtle doves in June, the blather of rooks the whole year, and, above all, the roof on summer evenings. There lay the jewels of solitude. The child sat there in her dark blue knickers and sweater, no one knowing her whereabouts, listening to the contented, silly hiccuping of the fallow deer, looking at the vivid green fading into the gentle sky, knowing that she belonged for ever to this deep and changeless silence.' One wonders if another daughter of Althorp, whose life as Princess of Wales now affords so little silence or solitude, once felt the same.

The picture gallery.

Althorp, January 1923 : Lady Margaret Spencer (now Douglas-Home) who wrote the account of her childhood at Althorp, with her brother, the 7th Earl Spencer, grandfather of HRH The Princess of Wales, and her young niece Lady Anne Spencer (now Wake-Walker).

Architecture and Contents

An Elizabethan house with a courtyard, which was roofed over in about 1655 to contain the present grand staircase. The house was further remodelled and refaced in red brick after the Restoration. The lofty entrance hall with its stucco ceiling was formed in the 1730s, and in the 1780s the 2nd Earl Spencer employed Henry Holland to restore and modernize the house, the exterior being at this time refaced with white 'mathematical tiles'. A more comfortable series of reception rooms was also made on the ground floor in place of the old state rooms upstairs, of which, however, the splendid oak-panelled picture gallery remains unaltered. Althorp contains one of the finest collections of pictures still in private ownership, with portraits of members of the House of Habsburg by Rubens, beauties of Charles II's Court by Lely, and a whole room full of works by Gainsborough and Reynolds. There is also a wealth of splendid furniture, some of it from Spencer House in London.

ANTONY HOUSE
CORNWALL

*Richard Carew, the historian of
Cornwall and great-grandfather of the
builder of Antony, in a portrait of 1586.*

CAREWS have lived at Antony, on the western side of the ferry between
Devon and Cornwall, since the end of the fifteenth century. Richard
Carew, the Elizabethan poet and historian, refers to Antony modestly as 'the
poor home of mine ancestors' and describes the fishpond which he made here
with sluices to fill it at high tide, telling of how it was looked after by an 'old
fellow, whom I keepe for almes and not for his work'. He planned to build 'a
little wooden banqueting house' on an island in the pond, with four corner
turrets so as to look like a toy MOUNT EDGCUMBE, but this apparently never
got further than the design.

In the seventeenth century, Antony was owned successively by two ill-
fated brothers, grandsons of the historian. The elder, Sir Alexander Carew, a
Roundhead commander, was executed in 1644 for parleying with the
Cavaliers. The younger, John Carew, suffered a similar fate at the Restoration for being a republican and a regicide. 'This morning Mr. Carew was
hanged and quartered at Charing Cross', Pepys wrote laconically in his diary
on 15 October 1660. 'But his quarters, by a great favour, are not to be hanged
up.' They were in fact given a decent burial by a third brother, whose son, Sir
William Carew, went the other way and in 1715 was arrested as a Jacobite.
This did not prevent him from building the present house at Antony, with its
dignified elevations of grey stone and its panelled rooms, which he completed
in 1721.

After the male line of the Carews died out in 1799, Antony passed to a
descendant of Sir William's half-sister, the Right Hon. Reginald Pole-
Carew, a minor politician who by his two marriages fathered no fewer than
fifteen children. His first wife was a granddaughter of Lord Chancellor
Hardwicke, his second a daughter of a Lord Lyttelton (*see* HAGLEY HALL).
Of his second brood, a daughter, Juliana, married the 1st Lord Robartes
(*see* LANHYDROCK), while the elder son, William Henry Pole-Carew, was
Augustus Hare's host when he came to stay at Antony in 1874. To get here
from Plymouth, Hare had to drive through a labyrinth of dockyards and then
cross the ferry, which that day was very rough. It was rougher still that night,
when the family crossed to a ball, but Mr Pole-Carew said that he was glad to
have an arm of the sea between him and 'such a population as that of
Plymouth'.

The roughness of the crossing did not take away from Hare's enjoyment of
his visit. 'The house is perfectly charming', he wrote. 'The old hall and its
pictures, the oak staircase, the warm tapestried sitting room – all, as it were,
typical of the broad Christian kindness and warm-hearted cordiality of its
inmates. It is a house in which no ill is ever spoken, and where scandal sits

The perfectly proportioned Queen Anne exterior of Antony House.

A portrait of Sir Alexander Carew and a view through to the library.

dumb; where, with the utmost merriment, there is the most sincere religious feeling and yet an entire freedom from cant and what is called "religious talking".' On the Sunday night the family sang hymns 'beautifully' in the hall. 'No horrid Gregorians', observed Mr Pole-Carew's daughter, Julia. 'The old monks only sang those by way of penance – so why should we sing them?'

Architecture and Contents

A dignified mansion of grey stone, consisting of a pedimented central block flanked by pavilions, built between 1710 and 1721 to the design of an unknown architect. A *porte-cochère* was added to the entrance front in the nineteenth century. The interior keeps its early eighteenth-century panelling of Dutch oak and pine and contains furniture contemporary with the house, together with a series of family portraits including works by Lely, Kneller, Reynolds, Allan Ramsay and Gilbert Stuart. Sir John Carew Pole, the present baronet, gave Antony to the National Trust in 1961; he and Lady Carew Pole continue to live here.

ARUNDEL CASTLE
WEST SUSSEX

ARUNDEL Castle, the medieval stronghold of the Fitzalans, came to the Howards through the marriage in 1556 of Lady Mary Fitzalan to Thomas Howard, 4th Duke of Norfolk. It was here that their son, Philip Howard, Earl of Arundel, decided in 1583 to become a Catholic (he was to spend the last ten years of his life as a prisoner in the Tower of London on account of his religious beliefs and was recently canonized as one of the Forty English Martyrs). Though the Howards of the Norfolk line are now regarded as England's premier Catholic family, their Catholicism has not been unbroken. The 4th Duke, who lost his head for intriguing with the Catholic Mary Queen of Scots, was a lifelong Protestant, and the ancestor by his second marriage of the Protestant Earls of Suffolk and of Carlisle (*see* AUDLEY END; CASTLE HOWARD), while several of the later Dukes of Norfolk

William Daniell's view of the quadrangle at Arundel in the early nineteenth century.

The library in 1858, with the children of the 14th Duke of Norfolk : a watercolour by Catherine Lyons.

abandoned the Catholic faith. Among the latter was the talented but raffish 11th Duke, known like his fifteenth-century forebear as 'Jockey'. A crony of the Prince Regent, he was so nearly a republican that he drank to the sovereignty of the people and named some of his farms in honour of the American revolutionary leaders. In 1791 he began rebuilding Arundel in the Gothic style which he associated with the ancient liberties of England, the castle having been more or less deserted by the family after being severely damaged in the Civil War.

The work was still unfinished in 1806 when Lord and Lady Ailesbury, on a visit to Worthing, came to see the castle, which was then 'only shown twice a week besides on Sundays after Divine Service'. Lord Ailesbury thought the old keep 'hideous – a place to hang oneself in'; Lady Ailesbury thought it 'charming, an ivy-mantled tower full of moping owls'. She heard that the Duke had deliberately left it as it was: 'Woe betide the person who injures a leaf of ivy, Jockey would never forgive it.' In the dining-room they saw the vast new painted window in which Jockey was portrayed as King Solomon with a buxom Queen of Sheba – 'Queen Solomon', said the housekeeper, who took them round. There was as yet no furniture in most of the rooms: 'Jockey lives in a parlour like one at an inn', Lady Ailesbury observed, and 'sleeps in a bed, the curtains of which were worked by his mother.'

In 1815 Jockey gave a housewarming in his new Barons' Hall to celebrate the 600th anniversary of the signing of Magna Carta. Six months later he died, and was succeeded by a Catholic cousin, Bernard Howard, the friend and patron of the diarist Thomas Creevey, who refers to him as 'Barney' or 'Scroop' and mentions the 'six-year-old mutton' served at his table. Creevey came to Arundel in 1828 and found it in sad contrast to GOODWOOD, where he had just been staying; 'that horrid, dismal benighted castle', he called it, 'with a gallery in it 190 feet long of the most dingy oak'. The 'dingy oak' was in fact mahogany, but the gallery, lit only by a window at each end, was certainly dark. A fellow guest remarked to Creevey that it would be a more suitable place for the owls to live in than the keep. These owls, enormous birds of a breed imported from America, were named after eminent judges. 'Lord Thurlow has laid an egg', the butler announced on one occasion.

Despite various additions and alterations – including the removal of the Queen of Sheba window lest it should offend Queen Victoria – the castle was still very much as Jockey left it when the young 15th Duke brought his bride here in 1877. To celebrate the homecoming a ball was held in the Barons' Hall. The tall and smiling Duchess opened the dancing with the short and stout Mayor of Arundel 'who was literally perspiring with nervousness'; the little Duke danced with the Mayoress, 'a tall, solemn and stately lady, covered with scintillating bugles, from whom even her cheery host failed to extract a smile'. The young Duchess was to die after less than ten years of marriage, leaving an only child, a son who was blind and mentally retarded. As a distraction from his domestic sorrows the Duke had what became a lifelong interest: the rebuilding of Arundel on a larger scale and in a style more convincingly medieval than Jockey's Regency Gothic. The work began in 1875 and continued almost until the outbreak of the First World War. 'Yes,' said the Duke, with a twinkle in his eye, as he showed his guests the last bit of masonry being built into the curtain wall; 'it will be finished this week; and after that the castle will be absolutely impregnable – against bows and arrows.' 'Will it *really* all be finished soon, Uncle Henry?' asked a small nephew. 'And what will you do with it when it is?' 'Well,' replied the Duke, with mock portentousness, 'it really will be finished by Sunday; and next week I am going to hand it over to the Sussex County Council for a lunatic asylum!'

That gregarious Benedictine abbot Sir David Hunter-Blair was not alone in thinking that the castle had been more comfortable before it was transformed, but the simple friendliness of the Duke made up for the chill of his baronial halls. The Arundel house parties in his time were always enjoyable and noted for the diversity of the guests. Hunter-Blair remembered one which included an inspector of fisheries, an extremely Low Church peer and his Quaker wife, the Secretary of the Post Office, several soldiers and young ladies, and Lord Salisbury's clever and eloquent youngest son Lord Hugh Cecil (*see* HATFIELD HOUSE), who spent almost a whole evening discussing the sacramental views of the Zwinglians with the family chaplain. On an earlier occasion, when it was not the time of the year for hunting or shooting, the Duke took his male guests on a 'jumping party', a cross-country run with poles for leaping obstacles. In an attempt to jump a ditch, he fell in almost up to his neck and walked back covered with mud

The park at Arundel in about 1870.

through the town of Arundel, 'acknowledging the respectful salutations of the inhabitants with his usual unembarrassed cheerfulness'. Few men worried less about their appearance than the 15th Duke of Norfolk; with his shabby clothes and shaggy beard he was sometimes mistaken for one of his own gardeners. He is said to have argued that as everybody at Arundel knew who he was, it did not matter how he dressed there, and that as nobody in London knew who he was, it did not matter how he dressed there either. The latter contention was hardly true, for he was a well-known public figure, premier duke and leader of the English Catholic laity, in which capacity he was instrumental in obtaining a cardinal's hat for Newman. As Hereditary Earl Marshal he organized the funeral of Queen Victoria and the coronations of Edward VII and George V. On the night of Edward VII's coronation, the town and castle hill at Arundel were illuminated, but the great pile of the castle itself was in darkness because the Duke was mourning the death of his handicapped son. A year or two later, at the age of fifty-six, he married again, and another son and heir, the late 16th Duke, was born to him in 1908.

Architecture and Contents

The great castle of the Fitzalans consists, like Windsor, of two wards or enclosures separated by a central mound from which rises a keep. Like Windsor, it was heavily restored in the late eighteenth and nineteenth centuries, so the domestic apartments, which extend round three sides of the more southerly enclosure, are virtually a late-Georgian and Victorian rebuilding. Of the late-Georgian work, carried out by the 11th Duke of Norfolk largely to his own design, little now remains apart from the Gothic library in the eastern range, more than a hundred feet long and with everything made of carved mahogany. The rest of the domestic quarters were rebuilt by the 15th Duke over a period of years from 1875, on a larger scale and in a style intended to be more evocative of a real medieval castle than what had existed before. The Duke and his architect, Charles Alban Buckler, aimed at what a contemporary called 'the assimilation of the spirit of the past' rather than 'the sterile reproduction of its letter', so that their rooms, though uncomfortably large and with detailing that is relentlessly medieval, are nevertheless designed for late-Victorian living – the exceptions being the vast Barons' Hall and the exquisite, shrine-like domestic chapel. At the same time as he reconstructed the castle, the 15th Duke collected sixteenth- and seventeenth-century furniture of superb quality, mostly Continental, to which has now been added the splendid eighteenth-century English furniture formerly at Norfolk House in London. Arundel is also noted for its armour and for its magnificent series of family portraits, many of them dating from the sixteenth century, others by later artists ranging from Van Dyck and Daniel Mytens to Lely, Gainsborough and Lawrence.

AUDLEY END

ESSEX

'BY MY troth, mon, it is too much for a king, but may do for a Lord High Treasurer', James I said pointedly of Audley End, then nearing completion. It was in fact a palace larger than any other private house in England, and cost its builder, the Lord High Treasurer Thomas Howard, Earl of Suffolk, as much as £200,000, for those days an incredible sum. Suffolk, a younger son of the 4th Duke of Norfolk (*see* ARUNDEL CASTLE), who had inherited the estates of his maternal grandfather, Lord Chancellor Audley, ruined himself building his vast house and was obliged to resort to corruption to meet his debts, which led to his downfall. He was relieved of his office in 1618 and in the following year was charged with embezzlement; his wife, a former beauty now notorious for her rapacity, was charged with him, being regarded as more guilty than he. The two of them were committed to the Tower. They were soon released, however, and Suffolk eventually got away with no worse a punishment than a £7,000 fine, but there was now no question of his being able to keep up the princely state for which he had intended Audley End to be a suitable background.

For the next two Earls of Suffolk Audley End was a white elephant, and after the Restoration the 3rd Earl offered it to Charles II, who at that period did not possess a suitable residence in the country. The King agreed to buy it for £30,000 cash and a £20,000 mortgage. Suffolk kept most of the surrounding estate and was appointed 'Keeper of the King's House at Audley End', which left him virtually in control of the palace, though he no longer had to pay for its upkeep. Samuel Pepys, who had a connection with Audley End through Magdalene College, Cambridge – refounded by Lord Chancellor Audley, whose heirs enjoyed the privilege of appointing its Master – came here in 1667, when the negotiations between the King and Suffolk were in progress. He had been here before, and this time was not so impressed as on the previous occasion. 'A great many pictures and not one good one in the house but one of Henry VIII done by Holbein', he noted in his diary. 'And not one good suit of hangings in all the house, but all most ancient things, such as I would not give the hanging up of in my house, and the other furniture, beds and other things accordingly. Only the gallery is good, and above all things the cellars, where we went down and drank of much good liquors. And indeed the cellars are fine; and here my wife and I did sing to my great content. And then to the garden, and there did eat many grapes, and took some with us.'

Having acquired Audley End, and renamed it the New Palace, Charles II came here for an occasional visit. While staying here in 1670, the Queen and her ladies went, as a 'frolick', to the local fair, disguised as 'country lasses in

red petticoats, wastcotes, &c'. Unfortunately they overdid their disguise so that people thought they were strolling-players and crowded around them; then the Queen was recognized and everybody came to stare at her. The royal party got back on to their horses and beat a hasty retreat, 'but as many of the Faire as had horses got up with their wives, children, swete-harts, or neighbours behind them, to get as much gape as they could, till they brought them to the Court gate.'

After Charles II had restored Windsor Castle there was no longer such need for Audley End as a country palace and it became neglected. Eventually, in 1701, William III handed it back to the 5th Earl of Suffolk who in return surrendered the £20,000 mortgage which had not yet been cleared. By then the vast building was in decay: the 5th Earl never lived in it, and the 6th Earl's plan to have it restored by Sir John Vanbrugh came to nothing on account of his death. On Vanbrugh's advice, the house was reduced in size, the buildings of the great outer court, which had fallen into ruin, being demolished. After the death in 1745 of the 10th Earl – son of George II's mistress, Henrietta, Countess of Suffolk (*see* BLICKLING HALL) – there were plans to demolish what remained or to sell it for conversion into a silk factory. By now the windows were broken and the local schoolchildren played in the derelict long gallery which had once been the admiration of all visitors.

But though in the late 1740s the house was in a poor way, rescue was at hand. The 10th Earl left no direct heir and the kinsman who succeeded to the earldom did not inherit the Audley End estate, which was divided between two descendants of the 3rd Earl. One of them, the forceful Elizabeth, Countess of Portsmouth, was determined to save Audley End for her family, so she bought the house and park from the other heir for the knock-down price of £10,000, which included the entitlement to appoint the Master of Magdalene College.

The work of restoration started by Lady Portsmouth was completed after her death in 1762 by her nephew and heir, Sir John Griffin Griffin, a distinguished soldier who rose to the rank of Field Marshal. It entailed the demolition of the range containing the long gallery, which was ruinous, and the house, as restored, was further reduced in size. The derelict seventeenth-century palace became a comfortable mansion for an eighteenth-century magnate, while keeping its Jacobean character. Sir John spent £100,000 on the house and its surroundings, transforming the latter into a typical eighteenth-century romantic landscape with seven miles of walks requiring twelve gardeners to maintain; a total of fifty gardeners were employed by him. Inside the house his staff was not excessive by the standards of the time. In 1784 there was a house-steward or butler paid 60 guineas a year, a French cook paid £50, a valet and a groom of the chambers, each paid £30, an under-butler and two footmen receiving £16 each, and two boys who each received £4 8s. There were various maids, each of whom was paid £8 or £9, a lady's maid who was paid £12 and at the top of the female hierarchy, a housekeeper who received £30.

A few years earlier, the housekeeper suddenly went mad. When the sixteen-year-old Hester Grenville, whose sister married Sir John's heir, came into her room to tell her something, she shut the door and said: 'Now you must say your prayers at once, for I have a commission from Heaven to kill you.' 'Oh, you cannot do that,' Hester replied, taking up a white napkin and giving it to her, 'for here is a reprieve.' And the unhappy woman gave in at once.

In 1784 Sir John succeeded in obtaining the barony of Howard de Walden, which had been held by the Suffolks but had fallen into abeyance on the death of the 3rd Earl. When he died in 1797 without leaving any children, the Howard de Walden title again fell into abeyance, but the barony of Braybrooke, which had been conferred on him in 1788, passed under a special remainder to a great-nephew of Lady Portsmouth's first husband, who was the heir to Audley End.

The 3rd Lord Braybrooke, soon after his succession in 1825, made a new and grander series of reception rooms, opening out of the first-floor saloon. In this he was reverting to the original Jacobean arrangement, the eighteenth-century restoration having brought the reception rooms down to the ground floor, which was now turned into bedrooms. The work cannot have caused much disruption, for Prince Pückler-Muskau, who came here when it was progressing, does not allude to it. The peripatetic German princeling was allowed to see over the house even though Lady Braybrooke was in residence. He regarded this as an 'uncommon' privilege, having been refused admission to not a few of the country houses on which he descended. He does not seem to have minded not being actually received by her ladyship. He comments on the lack of paths in the park – 'the English ladies are not so afraid of setting their feet on wet grass as ours are' – and on the fact that Lord Braybrooke read Divine Service himself in the chapel when his chaplain was absent.

It was characteristic of the 3rd Lord Braybrooke that he should, when necessary, have turned lay reader, for he was a man of varied accomplishments. He played a part in politics, he hunted, shot, and bred racehorses, including the famous Sir Joshua, but his first love was scholarship, as witnessed by the magnificent library, finest of his new rooms, and his editing of the original published version of Pepys' Diary. There was a tradition of scholarship in the Braybrooke line; the Mastership of Magdalene was held continuously from 1813 to 1904 by two members of the family, uncle and

The great hall.

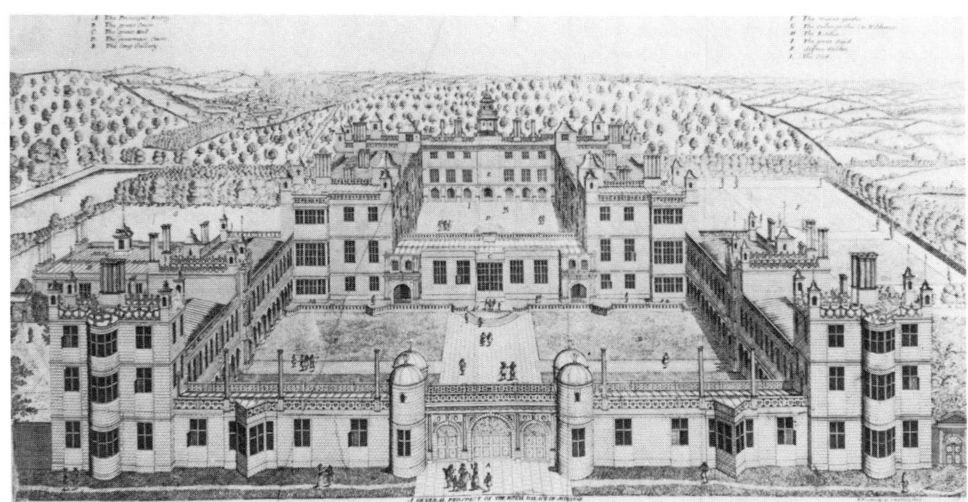

Winstanley's view of Audley End in 1676.

nephew, of whom the latter succeeded in 1902 as the 6th Lord Braybrooke. After his death, Audley End was let for some years to the 8th Lord Howard de Walden, the then holder of the title historically associated with the estate, from which it passed away in 1797. The 7th Lord Braybrooke came back here in 1914, but the family suffered such heavy estate duty on account of the death in action of his two sons during the Second World War that Audley End was sold to the nation.

Architecture and Contents

The 1st Earl of Suffolk's prodigious Jacobean palace was greatly reduced in size early in the eighteenth century, having fallen into disrepair, and it was further reduced during the course of the restoration carried out later in the century by Elizabeth, Countess of Portsmouth, and her nephew and heir, Sir John Griffin Griffin. What remained was a very large mansion by normal standards, of cream-coloured stone with great oriels and copper-roofed towers and turrets: two balancing wings joined by the original hall range with its twin Renaissance porches. The hall is on a scale in keeping with Audley End's original grandeur, and has a tremendously ornate wooden screen carved by Italian craftsmen in about 1605. The saloon, on the first floor, is the original great chamber and has a Jacobean pendant ceiling and a rich armorial chimney-piece, but its frieze, by the younger Joseph Rose, and its panelling incorporating full-length paintings of Audley End's former owners, date from the eighteenth-century restoration. Three of the downstairs rooms have decoration by Robert Adam, whose work elsewhere in the house was lost in the early nineteenth-century remodelling, when a series of grand Jacobean Revival reception rooms was formed opening out of the saloon. In the park, which was landscaped by Capability Brown, stand buildings by Adam. The house is now in the care of the Department of the Environment, and still contains its original furniture and pictures, including works by Lely, Reynolds and Canaletto.

BADDESLEY CLINTON
WEST MIDLANDS

THE moated manor house of Baddesley Clinton, with its medieval gatehouse tower, its courtyard and its interiors of panelling and armorial glass, is, like COUGHTON and STONOR, the archetypal recusant house. The Ferrers, who acquired Baddesley in 1517 through marriage to an heiress, and were themselves descended from the medieval Lords Ferrers of Groby and Earls of Derby, adhered constantly to the Old Faith. A tunnel in the footings of the western range, originally a medieval sewer, is almost certainly the hiding-place where the Jesuits Henry Garnet, Robert Southwell and John Gerard, together with four other priests, were concealed in October 1591; there is also a hiding-place dating from the same period in the roof of the range opposite. At that time, Baddesley was let to two sisters of the Vaux family who were closely involved in the activities of the missionary priests, its owner, the antiquary Henry Ferrers, having been obliged for financial reasons to live in London, where in 1590 he was imprisoned for debt. Though himself a devout Catholic, Ferrers managed to avoid the graver consequences of recusancy, and achieved considerable standing among the antiquaries of his time, one of whom was Camden who wrote of him as 'a man both for parentage and for knowledge of antiquity very commendable, and my especiall friend; who . . . hath at all times courteously shewed me the right way when I was out, and from his candle, as it were, hath lighted mine.' For most of his long life he lived in peaceful retirement at Baddesley, devoting himself to heraldry, genealogy and antiquities, collecting material which was to form the basis of the monumental *Antiquities of Warwickshire*, written after his death by his son's friend and neighbour Sir William Dugdale. Having lost his wife in 1586 when she was only twenty-three, he lived quietly and frugally. 'I dined in my dyning roome and had butter basted turneips and a roasted eg, and did eat browne bread and drink water', he wrote in his diary in February 1629, while a fortnight later he recorded that he had eaten a meal of 'bread, two herrings and two apples'.

Though he clearly had little money to spare, Henry Ferrers was able to adorn the house with some new chimney-pieces. His son Edward, who succeeded him in 1633, carried out more improvements, encouraged no doubt by the fact that, when he inherited, things were looking up for the English Catholics. But it was a false dawn, and before his death in 1651 he was to suffer heavy losses at the hands of the Parliamentarians. From then onwards the Ferrers of Baddesley were chronically poor. In the later seventeenth century the house may even have been abandoned, for Edward's son Henry was obliged to let the park, and he and his son George appear to have gone to live at Sutton Coldfield. In 1739 the estate was worth less than

The moated medieval manor house of Baddesley Clinton.

£600 a year. Although the house was restored and made more convenient by one or more of the eighteenth-century Ferrers (who showed such a respect for the earlier work that it is still hard to believe that anything was done later than the middle of the seventeenth century), the family fortunes continued to decline to such an extent that, in the 1830s, the widowed Lady Harriet Ferrers came near to being imprisoned for debt, as Henry the Antiquary had been in 1590.

Lady Harriet's son, Marmion Edward Ferrers, the last of the original male line, was a man of great kindness and charity. (He once found an old woman stealing his wood, and instead of scolding her merely said, 'That load of wood is a great deal too heavy for you, you must let me carry it home for you.') But he was not the sort of man who could have rescued a heavily mortgaged estate. By 1867 when, at the age of fifty-three, he married Rebecca Dulcibella Orpen, known as Pysie, a bride much younger than himself, it seemed that Baddesley would soon have to be sold. The situation was saved by Pysie's aunt Georgiana, Lady Chatterton, and her second husband Captain Edward Heneage Dering, who was much younger than her and well-off: they came to live with the Ferrers at Baddesley. For the nine years that followed, these two childless couples lived together in their moated grange in an atmosphere of Catholic piety, romantic affection and nostalgia for the past. They read the works of Tennyson to each other; Pysie painted and Georgiana wrote novels, as did Edward Dering, who was also musical. The two bearded gentlemen and their two ladies dressed in a way that was as much Elizabethan as Victorian. Then, in 1876, Georgiana died, and in 1884 Marmion Ferrers followed her to the grave. A year later came the inevitable conclusion to the romance: Edward Dering married Pysie, whom he had clearly long admired.

Pysie lived on until 1923, having been widowed for the second time in 1892. At the turn of the century Baddesley was visited by that sociable Benedictine abbot Sir David Hunter-Blair. 'Its venerable quadrangle and some of the stained glass date from Plantagenet times', he wrote in his memoirs, 'and the quiet Catholic chatelaine who gave us tea in cups centuries old, and who spent her days painting in her studio, or praying in her oratory, looked as if she too had stepped out of the Middle Ages.'

Baddesley caught the imagination of Maurice Baring and seems to have been the inspiration for Alton-Leigh, home of the recusant family of Lacy, in his novel *Cat's Cradle*:

Blanche gave a slight gasp when she first set eyes on the house. The beauty of the place, the warm walls, the flaming creeper on the square tower, the large mullioned windows with the sun glinting on the square panes, the still moat full of water-lilies, in which one swan was proudly swimming, affected her with a pang of pleasure that was almost painful in its sharpness. ... Inside the house nothing, as Walter Troumestre had told Blanche, had been touched; additions had been made, but nothing had been taken away, improved, restored or spoilt. ... The small rooms downstairs were full of furniture of every epoch: old pictures, old china, old chests, old chairs (on which the *petit-point* seemed fresh and bright), tapestry, musical instruments, harpsichords, harps, great majolica vases, bowls of potpourri, and wide stone fireplaces with wood logs. The whole house was aromatic with the smell of wood and faded spices.

The great hall at Baddesley Clinton in the 1870s, with Marmion Ferrers on the left, Edward Heneage Dering and his wife, Georgiana Lady Chatterton, sitting on either side of the fire, and Rebecca Dulcibella ('Pysie') Ferrers standing.

Architecture and Contents

A moated manor house built around a courtyard with a fifteenth-century gatehouse tower. The present great hall, replacing one demolished in the early or mid-eighteenth century, contains a splendid armorial chimney-piece of carved stone. It dates from the time of Henry Ferrers, who died in 1633, as do most of the other armorial chimneypieces of carved wood and much of the panelling and armorial glass in the house. Baddesley Clinton, now in the care of the National Trust, has remained almost entirely unchanged since the time of the Civil War.

BADMINTON HOUSE
AVON

Bᴜᴛ for the illegitimacy of their early Tudor ancestor, the 1st Earl of Worcester, the Somersets, Dukes of Beaufort, who have lived at Badminton since the seventeenth century, would rank higher than any other family in the English aristocracy, being by blood Plantagenets descended in the direct male line from Edward III's son John of Gaunt. Through the 1st Earl of Worcester's marriage to an heiress of the great Norman–Welsh family of Herbert (*see* POWIS CASTLE; WILTON HOUSE), the Somersets acquired what was virtually a kingdom in the Welsh Marches with Raglan Castle as their principal stronghold. Owing to the damage suffered by Raglan during the Civil War, when it was gallantly defended for the King by the 1st Marquess of Worcester, it was abandoned as the principal family seat by the Cavalier Marquess's grandson, the 1st Duke of Beaufort, who established himself at Badminton, a manor bought by the family in 1608, across the Severn from his main territory. As a young man, the 1st Duke courted Cromwell and sat in the Rump Parliament as 'Mr Herbert', Lord Herbert being then his courtesy title. In this way he recovered the family estates which the Roundheads had confiscated from his father. Before the Restoration,

Badminton: the staircase and landing lined with pictures in the eighteenth-century fashion.

however, he made his peace with Charles II, who eventually created him Duke of Beaufort. He later showed his loyalty to the deposed James II by refusing to take the oath of allegiance to William III. For the rest of his life he lived in retirement at Badminton, where he transformed the old manor house into a palatial mansion with avenues radiating from it in all directions. These even extended beyond the boundaries of his own land, for according to the late seventeenth-century lawyer and writer Roger North, the neighbouring gentry 'cut their trees and hedges to humour his vistas'.

North gives us an account of the 1st Duke's 'princely way of living' which he reckoned to be 'above any other, except crowned heads' that he had ever seen. In some respects it was a way of life modelled on the feudal past rather than on the palaces of contemporary Europe, which Badminton, in its architecture and setting, so greatly resembled. Thus the men of the Duke's household, some two hundred in number, dined together in a hall 'with a sort of alcove at one end, for distinction'. There were nine tables, 'properly assigned'; at one sat the chief steward with the gentlemen and pages, at another the master of the horse with the coachmen and grooms, at another, an under-steward with bailiffs and some husbandmen, at another, the clerk of the kitchen with bakers and brewers, while at other tables again sat 'more inferior people'. The women had their own dining-room and 'were distributed in like manner'. According to this account:

The method of governing this great family was admirable and easy, and such as might have been a pattern for any management whatever. For if the Duke and Duchess (who concerned herself much more than he did, for every day of her life in the morning she took her tour and visited every office about the house, and so was her own superintendent) observed anything amiss or suspicious, as a servant riding out or the like, nothing was said to that servant; but his immediate superior, or one of a higher order, was sent for who was to enquire and answer if leave had been given or not; if not, such a servant was straight turned away.

For the Duke and Duchess and their friends, the day began with breakfast in the Duchess's gallery which opened into the gardens; 'then, perhaps, a deer was to be killed . . . or the gardens and parks to be visited.' In the afternoon –

when the ladies were disposed to air, and the gentlemen with them, coaches and six came to hold them all. At half an hour after eleven the bell rang to prayers, so at six in the evening; and, through a gallery, the best company went into an aisle in the church (so near was it), and the Duke and Duchess could see if all the family were there. The ordinary pastime of the ladies was in a gallery on the other side, where she had divers gentlewomen commonly at work upon embroidery and fringe-making; for all the beds of state were made and finished in the house. The meats were very neat, and not gross; no servants in livery attended, but those called gentlemen only; and in the several kinds, even down to the small beer, nothing could be more choice than the table was . . . the Duchess, with two daughters only, sat at the upper end. If the gentlemen chose a glass of wine . . . many a brisk round went about; but no sitting at a table with tobacco and healths, as the too common use is.

The children of the family were, according to the same writer, 'bred with a philosophical care. No inferior servants were permitted to entertain them, lest some mean sentiments or foolish notions and fables should steal into them; and nothing was so strongly impressed upon them as a sense of

honour.' It may have been this sense of honour, and a desire to atone for the 1st Duke's defection to Cromwell, which gave the next three Dukes of Beaufort their Jacobite leanings: for much of the eighteenth century there were portraits of the Pretender and his wife prominently displayed at Badminton. The art-loving 3rd Duke, who employed William Kent to carry out many improvements to the house and to design the exquisite Worcester Lodge at the northern end of the park, may even have had dealings with the Pretender when he was in Rome as a young man on the Grand Tour. It is significant that in acquiring works of art he was helped by Cardinal Alberoni and made many of his purchases from Cardinal Alessandro Albani, both of whom were closely connected with the exiled Stuarts. The tutor who accompanied him on his tour managed to purloin a large part of his collection, which he offered for sale by public auction in London. That he could have been so blatant might be attributed to the fact that he knew about transactions which the young Duke did not wish him to reveal.

The 3rd Duke, who was divorced from his wife, had no children and was succeeded by his brother, another great patron of the arts, who was instrumental in bringing Canaletto to England. After the death of the 4th Duke in 1756, the family at last became reconciled to the House of Hanover. The 5th Duke entertained Queen Charlotte at Badminton and in anticipation of her visit the portraits of the Pretender and his wife were moved to a less conspicuous place. The 5th Duke had five sisters, including the beautiful Isabella, Duchess of Rutland (*see* BELVOIR CASTLE), but no brothers. Had he failed to produce a son, he would have been the last of the Somersets, for there were then no collateral branches living, but in fact he had seven sons of whom the youngest was the unfortunate Crimean War general who became Lord Raglan. His eldest grandson, the 7th Duke, who as a very young man was involved with the notorious Harriet Wilson, married a niece of the great Duke of Wellington (*see* STRATFIELD SAYE). She died a few years later and as his second wife he chose her half-sister. They had to elope, being thought to be within the prohibited degrees of affinity, though afterwards an Act of Parliament was specially passed to ensure that the son of the marriage could succeed to the dukedom. He eventually did so in 1853 and reigned until the end of the century, one of the best-loved grandees of his time. During those years life at Badminton was mainly centred on hunting and racing. The arts were largely neglected, and the Duke and Duchess were not much interested in the house and its treasures. They once used a priceless old Worcester service for a picnic with Queen Victoria and did not mind when, on the way back, most of it was broken. And when their two little granddaughters had whooping-cough and were liable to be sick, the bowl which the Duchess provided for this contingency was of the most exquisite Crown Derby. One of these granddaughters gives us several glimpses of life at Badminton during the late Victorian period: the games of cricket, in which W. G. Grace, whose brother was the family doctor, frequently played, and the Sunday attendance in the church, which was still connected to the house as it was in the 1st Duke's time. The family occupied a spacious gallery at the back, with comfortable armchairs and a roaring fire in winter. From its inner recesses the Duke and the other men of the party were able to slip out unobserved before the sermon, leaving their womenfolk to sit through it, for 'in those days it was always considered that "women should be religious"'. Then there was the annual servants' ball on the Duke's birthday, which was held in the great ballroom at the end of the enfilade. Once, when the Duchess was in here on her own, she was attacked by a lunatic cook who threatened to kill her with a kitchen knife, but by giving him the 'extraordinary dominating look in her eyes' which she used on her grandchildren when they were naughty, she made him go quietly.

Another incident which disturbed the peace of late-Victorian Badminton was the departure without warning before breakfast of Lady Henry Somerset (*see* EASTNOR CASTLE), a daughter-in-law of the Duke and Duchess, who proceeded to accuse her husband of homosexuality. Although nothing was actually proved against him, and he continued to be a member of the Privy Council – to which, as a rising young politician, he had been appointed a few years earlier – he was obliged to spend the rest of his life abroad. Whatever the truth about Lord Henry's inclinations, there is no doubt about those of the Duke his father, who had affairs with numerous women, though he and the Duchess were devoted to one another.

The 10th Duke of Beaufort, who was the doyen of the equestrian world and a great huntsman, and who died in February 1984, was the grandson of this amiable Victorian ducal pair. His widow is a niece of Queen Mary, who spent the war years at Badminton, arriving in October 1939 with more than fifty servants and some seventy pieces of personal luggage. She occupied the whole house except for two bedrooms and a sitting-room which were retained by the Duke and Duchess, who had their meals at her table. During the years she was here the old Queen occupied her time sorting papers in the

The Duke of Beaufort's Hounds in the early 1920s. The late Duke, then Marquess of Worcester, leads the field; his father, the 9th Duke of Beaufort, watches from the back seat of a car.

muniment room, clearing ivy off walls and leading her entourage in amateur forestry operations. With her passion for order, she sometimes cut down shrubs which the Duke and Duchess valued; they only just managed to prevent her from felling the great cedar tree outside the drawing-room window in which Lord Raglan of the Crimea had played as a boy.

Sir Osbert Sitwell tells of a sad occurrence during a wartime Christmas spent at Badminton as Queen Mary's guest. Before dinner on Christmas evening the old courtier Sir Richard Molyneux invited him to his room to share a bottle of champagne which he had brought in his luggage, adding that he did not expect they would get any at dinner owing to the stinginess of Lord Claud Hamilton, Queen Mary's Comptroller. But when Sir Richard tasted the champagne 'a look of complete tragedy came into his eye. "It's corked," he shouted, "and the only bottle!"' At dinner they were in fact given champagne; but as Sir Richard tasted it Sir Osbert 'saw a look in his eye that I had seen before. "It's corked", it stated as plainly as possible. A second bottle was produced, but proved to be similarly afflicted.' After dinner, Sir Richard kept on saying plaintively to Sir Osbert, 'I don't mind about the champagne, but I'm *so thirsty*.' But when he remonstrated with Lord Claud, 'he received an answer which made him still more angry. "The champagne was getting old, and I wanted to see if it was still fit to drink – and we're all old friends, so it doesn't matter."' However, Sir Richard forgot his grievance at the sight of Queen Mary leading the way from the room, a magnificent figure in silver, 'blazing and sparkling' with sapphires, pearls and diamonds. He turned to Sir Osbert and 'said in his loud, deaf voice, like that of a man shouting from a cave into a strong wind, "I wonder if you realise it, but after that old lady has gone, you'll never see anything like this, or like her, again!"'

Architecture and Contents

A late seventeenth-century house enlarged and altered in about 1740 by William Kent who gave it the pediments, cupolas and rusticated pavilions which make its principal front so impressive. Kent also designed the hall, with its Corinthian columns and doorcases and its baroque plasterwork. The dining-room is as it was in the late seventeenth century, with carvings by Grinling Gibbons. The gilded great drawing-room (also known as the ballroom), and the library were redecorated early in the nineteenth century by Sir Jeffry Wyatville. The pictures include portraits by Reynolds and Lawrence, hunting scenes by John Wootton and two famous views of Badminton by Canaletto. Although the park was landscaped by Capability Brown, it still keeps some of the formal layout of avenues planted by the 1st Duke of Beaufort; the principal axis extends in a straight line for nearly three miles from the house to Kent's domed Worcester Lodge.

BELTON HOUSE
LINCOLNSHIRE

RICHARD Brownlow, who was appointed Chief Prothonotary of the Court of Common Pleas in 1590, made a fortune which he invested in Lincolnshire land, including Belton, where his great-grandson Sir John Brownlow built the present house in the 1680s. The newly built house is the subject of a late seventeenth-century view, believed to have been painted by Sir John Brownlow's porter Henry Bug, who features in the picture: a tall, imposing figure holding a silver-topped staff which is still to be seen in the house. Bug's finest hour must have been in 1695, when William III visited Belton and was 'mighty nobly entertained' to dinner by Sir John who 'killed 12 fat oxen and 60 sheep besides other victuals for his entertainment and made the most of him and his followers that can be imagined.' The entertainment seems to have been rather too noble, for the normally dour Dutch monarch became 'exceeding merry' and by the time he reached Lincoln could 'only eat a mess of milk'.

After Sir John's death in 1697, his formidable gout-ridden widow, Alice, lived on at Belton. She had no son, but made the most of her four daughters, for as her epitaph in Belton church records, 'three of them she married to noble peers of the realm and the fourth to her husband's nephew out of respect to his memory'. The 'noble peers' included two great magnates, the Duke of Ancaster and the Earl of Exeter (*see* BURGHLEY HOUSE); the least illustrious of her sons-in-law, her husband's Brownlow nephew who eventually came into Belton, was himself raised to the peerage of Ireland as Viscount Tyrconnel. He fancied himself as a patron of the arts and sciences, but seems to have been rather a bore: Mrs Pendarves, whom he wished to marry as his second wife, told a friend that she would not tie herself to 'such a companion for an empire'. After a long but undistinguished political career in which he failed to obtain the English peerage he coveted, he retired to Belton, where his chief occupation was boring the local parson, who would be summoned to the house every afternoon and compelled to listen to him until midnight. 'Sickness, thank God, will restore me to myself for a while', the unfortunate clergyman once remarked. 'I was ill last night, I have taken Physick this morning and so shall enjoy my liberty all this Day.' In between his monologues, Tyrconnel found time to make various improvements to the house and park, planting avenues, enlarging the forecourt, and adorning some of the rooms with tapestries and fine new furniture. Nevertheless, Mrs Lybbe Powys, who came here in 1757 three years after his death, was not much impressed. ''Tis nothing more than a good family house', she wrote dismissively.

Since Lord Tyrconnel was childless, he was succeeded at Belton by his

The formal garden at Belton from the roof of the house.

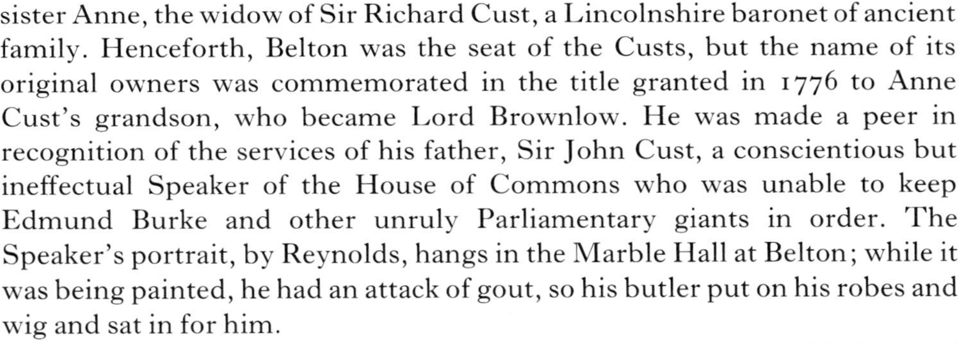

sister Anne, the widow of Sir Richard Cust, a Lincolnshire baronet of ancient family. Henceforth, Belton was the seat of the Custs, but the name of its original owners was commemorated in the title granted in 1776 to Anne Cust's grandson, who became Lord Brownlow. He was made a peer in recognition of the services of his father, Sir John Cust, a conscientious but ineffectual Speaker of the House of Commons who was unable to keep Edmund Burke and other unruly Parliamentary giants in order. The Speaker's portrait, by Reynolds, hangs in the Marble Hall at Belton; while it was being painted, he had an attack of gout, so his butler put on his robes and wig and sat in for him.

The 1st Lord Brownlow made some changes to the exterior of Belton and redecorated some of the principal rooms. His architect was James Wyatt, who was probably recommended to him by his brother-in-law, Philip Yorke (*see* ERDIGG). Further alterations were carried out for the 1st Earl Brownlow, who inherited in 1807, received an earldom in 1815, married three times and lived until 1853 – an ultra-Tory who would not allow *The Times* into his house but who built comfortable three-bedroomed cottages for his workmen. His third wife, who was a daughter of the 2nd Earl of Mount Edgcumbe (*see* MOUNT EDGCUMBE), thought Belton a 'handsome, gentleman-like house'. Its air of squirearchical reticence, which Mrs Lybbe Powys had found disappointing, clearly appealed to her.

The Cust family was soon to acquire a second country seat which surpassed Belton in grandeur though not in beauty. This was Ashridge in Hertfordshire which, together with estates reckoned to be worth a couple of million pounds, was bequeathed to the 1st Earl Brownlow's son, Lord Alford, by his maternal great-uncle, the penultimate Earl of Bridgewater.

There was, however, an impossible condition in Lord Bridgewater's will to the effect that Lord Alford should somehow contrive to be made a duke, or at any rate a marquess. It took a *cause célèbre* to set aside this condition, by which time Lord Alford was dead, so the Bridgewater inheritance eventually went to his young son, the 2nd Earl Brownlow. His widow, Lady Marian Alford, a daughter of the 2nd Marquess of Northampton (*see* CASTLE ASHBY), was one of the *grandes dames* of Victorian society: extravagant, witty, renowned for the beauty of her hands and feet, fond of power yet always ready to do good. She was also the first woman to make a study of English needlework, the wealth of which at Belton benefited greatly from her knowledge.

On the death of the 3rd Earl in 1921 the earldom became extinct and a kinsman, Adelbert Cust, succeeded to Belton and the Brownlow barony. He was the father of the late Lord Brownlow who was a friend of Edward VIII and played a part in the Abdication drama. Adelbert's elder brother was the legendary Harry Cust, one of the most brilliant, amusing and attractive men of his generation and a man whom women found irresistible. Perhaps because everything came too easily to him, his career did not fulfil his early promise. As a final sadness, he failed to survive the 3rd Earl, though he was almost twenty years his junior; had he done so he would have become Lord Brownlow and inherited Belton. The profusion of Cust monuments in Belton Church is said to have inspired one of those witticisms for which he was famous, which was that the Church was 'dedicated to the Memory of God and the Glory of the Cust family'.

The Red Drawing-Room, which may have been redecorated by Wyatville.

Architecture and Contents

A pleasing late seventeenth-century house of warm-coloured stone, with a pediment and a high-pitched roof crowned with a balustrade and cupola. From the quality of the building, which dates from the 1680s, it would seem that one of the leading architects of the day was employed in its design: William Winde, perhaps, or possibly even Wren. Much of the original interior survives, with bolection-moulded panelling and carving in the manner of Grinling Gibbons; there are also rich plasterwork ceilings by Edward Goudge. Some of the rooms were, however, redecorated in about 1776 by James Wyatt, whose nephew Sir Jeffry Wyatville carried out further alterations early in the nineteenth century. The roof balustrade and cupola were removed in the second half of the eighteenth century by the 1st Lord Brownlow, but the former was replaced by the 1st Earl and the latter by the 3rd Earl. The pictures at Belton include Tintoretto's *Entombment* and a Lely State portrait of Charles II which faces a splendid Reynolds of Speaker Cust in the entrance hall. Belton was recently acquired by the National Trust.

BELVOIR CASTLE
LEICESTERSHIRE

THE spectacular hilltop castle of Belvoir now seems entirely a creation of early nineteenth-century romanticism, but it rises from the foundations of the Norman stronghold of the Lords de Ros, whose heiress married Sir Robert Manners at the time of the Wars of the Roses. Thomas Manners, 1st Earl of Rutland, rebuilt the castle from 1528 onwards, and it was in this Tudor Belvoir that Prince Rupert stayed during his first visit to England in 1636, acquiring when out hunting a knowledge of the surrounding country that was to stand him in good stead nine years later in his adventurous dash to Newark after the collapse of the Royalist cause. By then, the 7th Earl of Rutland, the Prince's host in more peaceful times, had been succeeded by a cousin whose sympathies were with Parliament, though this did not prevent Parliament from ordering the demolition of Belvoir in 1649, since during the war it had been held for the King.

It was rebuilt after the Restoration, becoming in appearance a rather plain late seventeenth-century mansion. The rebuilding is said to have been at the behest of the 8th Earl's wife. Her husband preferred to live at HADDON HALL in Derbyshire which had been his home before he succeeded to the earldom. However, the 8th Earl's son, Lord Roos, who caused a sensation by divorcing his wife for adultery and marrying again, established himself at Belvoir where in 1671, the year of his second marriage, a strange occurrence was said to have taken place. At Christmas, when he kept open house, his former wife turned up disguised as a gentleman 'in splendid and becoming attire' and played at dice with him, only to be recognized by a servant on account of a mark on her hand. According to the story, when the new Lady Roos heard about this she was so upset that she went into a decline; certainly she died after being married for only a few months.

Lord Roos, who succeeded his father as the 9th Earl in 1679 and became the 1st Duke of Rutland in 1703, was famous for his hospitality, which was of the old English sort – 'all was hearty and substantial at his board'. During the buck-hunting season his vast retinue was clad in green, and this green hunt livery continued to be used for foxhunting by the 3rd Duke, whose love of Belvoir earned him the nickname of 'the Old Man of the Hill'.

The 3rd Duke's son, the popular Marquess of Granby, who commanded the British troops in the Seven Years War and had so many inns named after him, did not live to succeed to the dukedom, and it was the Old Man of the Hill's grandson who became the 4th Duke. A great patron of the arts, he was a friend of Reynolds and made the poet Crabbe his chaplain at Belvoir. He died in 1787 at the age of thirty-three when he was serving as Viceroy of Ireland. His beautiful wife Isabella (*see* BADMINTON) was in England at the time of his death, but he declared himself 'content to die with her image before his mind's eye'. Duchess Isabella survived her husband by more than forty years, and when she was no longer so young became known as 'Duchess Was-a-Bella', despite her efforts to preserve her looks. There is a story told of how her granddaughter met a country girl in the park at Belvoir who would have been lovely but for the loss of a front tooth. When she asked how it happened, the girl replied: 'Oh, the Duchess had lost one of hers, so she forced me to have mine taken out to replace it.'

In 1789, when the 5th Duke was still a minor, the diarist John Byng, afterwards Lord Torrington, visited Belvoir, where he found 'everything ... in neglect and Ruin'. There were only four servants; a housekeeper 'of a very drunken dawdling appearance' took him round and he saw 'no Furniture (Pictures excepted) that a Broker would think worth the carrying away; Nor one Chair, Table, Carpet or Curtain of use or comfort.' The pictures, on which the late Duke had spent most of his money, were 'all tost about in confusion'. This depressing state of affairs was probably due not so much to neglect as to the fact that the 4th Duke had been about to start work on remodelling the castle when he was appointed to Ireland. Owing to his untimely death the work had to be postponed until 1800, after his son had come of age and married Elizabeth Howard (*see* CASTLE HOWARD). But then the remodelling was far more radical than anything that the 4th Duke had contemplated. Elizabeth, another beautiful Duchess of Rutland, is said to have been disappointed when she first saw Belvoir and found that it did not look like her idea of a castle. Her husband shared her romantic tastes and commissioned James Wyatt to transform the seventeenth-century mansion into a golden vision of Camelot above the tree-tops. The vision was realized by 1813 when the Prince Regent came to Belvoir and was presented with the key of the castle by the Reverend Dr Staunton of Staunton, a manor which his medieval ancestors (after whom the Staunton Tower, at the south-eastern corner of the building, was named) held of the Lords de Ros by performing the feudal service known as 'castleguard'. In honour of the royal visit the grandest room in the castle was named the Regent's Gallery. While it was meant to re-create the feudal past, the castle as transformed made use of the technology of the Industrial Revolution: the coal for heating it was brought from the Grantham Canal by a railway laid specially for the purpose in 1815.

A year later the Duke's and Duchess Elizabeth's romantic vision all but went up in smoke when two sides of the castle, together with nearly half the 4th Duke's picture collection, were destroyed by a fire which only just stopped short of the Regent's Gallery. The work of rebuilding was supervised by the Duke's talented chaplain, the Reverend Sir John Thoroton, who was knighted at the time of the Regent's visit. Thoroton designed the massive eastern tower which contains the sumptuous Elizabeth Saloon, conceived and planned by Duchess Elizabeth but barely finished by the time of her death at the age of forty-five in 1825; it became her shrine, dominated by her life-size statue in marble.

Duchess Elizabeth's second son, Lord John Manners, was a romantic like his parents; a poet and a leader of that group of high-minded young politicians of the 1840s known as Young England, who brought a new sense of purpose to the Tory party, standing to maintain an England that was traditional and aristocratic, while at the same time advocating social reform. The group included the young Disraeli (*see* HUGHENDEN MANOR) who depicts Lord John as Lord Henry Sydney in his novel *Coningsby*, with Belvoir as Beaumanoir. Lord John was to hold office in almost every Conservative administration from 1852 until 1892, by which time he was seventy-four and had succeeded his brother as the 7th Duke. Augustus Hare stayed at Belvoir during his reign and was delighted by what he called 'the mediaeval ways': the trumpeters who walked up and down the passages and sounded the dressing time; the watchman who called the hours through the night; the ballroom always ready in the evenings for those who wanted to dance; the band, in uniform, which played soft music from an adjoining room during dinner, at which all the hunting men appeared in their red coats, adding 'brilliancy and colour to the immensely long table with its glorious old silver ornaments'.

The Young England Duke lived on until 1906. His granddaughter, that timeless beauty Lady Diana Cooper, remembers him as 'a beautiful bent old man ... walking down the endless corridors of Belvoir, wrapped warmly in a thick black cape buttoned down the front, for these passages in winter were arctic – no stoves, no hot pipes, no heating at all. He would unbutton his cape at the drawing-room door and hang it on a long brass bar with many others.' He often took his granddaughter with him for an afternoon drive in the landau, the barouche or the victoria, and she remembers how, on the days when the castle was open to the public (which were then almost as frequent as

John, Marquess of Granby, afterwards 9th Duke of Rutland.

Lady Marjorie Manners, eldest of the three beautiful daughters of the 8th Duke of Rutland and Violet Duchess of Rutland, the youngest being Lady Diana Cooper. In 1912 Lady Marjorie married the 6th Marquess of Anglesey (see PLAS NEWYDD).

they are now, the only difference being that there was then no charge for admission) he 'would uncover his head and bow very slightly with a look of pleasure and welcome on his delicate old face' as he passed the crowd of tourists gathered on either side of the approach. 'He loved his tourists. They represented to him England and liberty and the feudal system, and were a link between the nobility and the people.'

Lady Diana remembers the night-watchman calling the hours, but the trumpeters who had so impressed Augustus Hare had disappeared by the time of which she writes and been replaced by an ancient gong-man, with a loose-hanging livery and a white beard to his waist. There were other archaic functionaries in the Belvoir household at the turn of the century: the lamp-and-candle men, who filled and tended the oil-lamps and snuffed the candles which were still the only form of lighting; the upholsterer, 'exactly like a Hans Andersen tailor'; the huge, powerfully built water-men, who carried gigantic cans of hot and cold water up to the bedrooms for the jugs and hip-baths; the sinister coal-man, 'much like his brothers of the water, but blacker far and generally more mineral'.

All the staff and dependants – all two hundred of them – were given presents at Christmas. The housemaids' presents were rather dull; each of them customarily received a length of stuff for a new uniform. When Lady Diana's mother became Duchess, she livened up these parcels of material by slipping something nice into each of them. This, like bathrooms, central heating and motor cars, was one of the many innovations at Belvoir after the new Duke and Duchess took over in 1906. The Duchess was beautiful, charming and a highly talented artist. As Lady Granby she had been prominent in that coterie of the 1880s known as the Souls, which also included the charming Harry Cust (*see* BELTON HOUSE) – with whom she is generally believed to have had an affair – and Lady Elcho, whose son subsequently married the Rutlands' daughter Violet. As well as Violet and Diana, the Rutlands had an eldest daugher, Marjorie, who became Marchioness of Anglesey (*see* PLAS NEWYDD), and an only surviving son who succeeded in 1925 as the 9th Duke. From then until the outbreak of the Second World War, the 9th Duke (whose wife, a niece of several of the Souls, is yet another in the long line of beautiful Duchesses of Rutland) kept up considerable state at Belvoir. Even when there was only a small family party the men were required to put on white ties and tails for dinner. Somebody once asked the Duke whether he ever made do with a dinner jacket in the country. 'Yes,' he replied, 'when I dine alone with my wife in her bedroom.'

Belvoir, seat of the Dukes of Rutland, in its present guise as a dramatic Regency castle designed by James Wyatt for the 4th Duke and Duchess.

Architecture and Contents

A spectacular Regency castle by James Wyatt, Belvoir was built on the foundations of a Norman stronghold which had been rebuilt after the Restoration. It was restored after the fire of 1816 under the supervision of the Reverend Sir John Thoroton. Of the interiors which survived the fire, the finest is the vast Regent's Gallery, hung with rose-coloured Gobelin tapestries and with busts by Nollekens ranged along the walls. Of the post-

1816 rooms, the most magnificent is the Louis XIV-Revival Elizabeth Saloon by Matthew Wyatt, which has panelling from a château of Madame de Maintenon. Also dating from after the fire is the impressive Gothic Guard Room, with its high vaulted ceiling, vistas through arches, and displays of weapons. The picture gallery contains a Stuart bed with hangings of Venetian velvet, together with a collection of pictures that includes works by the younger Teniers and the younger Van de Velde, Gainsborough landscapes, a contemporary version of Holbein's portrait of Henry VIII, miniatures by Cosway and Isaac and Peter Oliver and three of the five outstanding Poussins in the castle, the other two being in the chapel, where there is also a Murillo.

BLENHEIM PALACE
OXFORDSHIRE

The 1st Duke of Marlborough and his Duchess, Sarah, with their five children: from left to right, Elizabeth, Mary, Henrietta, Anne and John, who died young. This family portrait was painted by Closterman, c. 1696, before the palace was built.

BLENHEIM Palace, that monument built by a grateful nation to the glory of John Churchill, the Great Duke of Marlborough, was started in 1705 but not completed for many years owing to the feud between the hero's wife, the quarrelsome Duchess Sarah, and the architect, Sir John Vanbrugh. Like most people, Sarah regarded Vanbrugh's plan as inconvenient. This is not really fair, for he was in advance of his time in providing a series of comparatively small rooms for the family in the east front which constitutes a self-contained apartment, quite distinct from the great rooms of state. And such was his and his assistants' attention to detail that it is possible to look from one end of the state rooms to the other through the line of keyholes.

By the 1730s Blenheim, though completed, was deserted and neglected, for Sarah could not bear to live in it. Horace Walpole, who came to see it at that time as an undergraduate from Cambridge, found it inhabited only by 'a cross housekeeper and an impertinent porter'. The palace was never occupied by the Great Duke's eldest daughter who was Duchess of Marlborough in her own right, and only intermittently by the 3rd Duke, a somewhat ineffectual character who was appointed to command the British forces in Germany during the Seven Years War but died on campaign soon after his appointment. The 3rd Duke was the son of another of the Great Duke's daughters, his father having been the statesman Charles Spencer, Earl of Sunderland (*see* ALTHORP) whose magnificent library came to Blenheim and was housed in the long gallery.

It was not really until the time of the 4th Duke, who succeeded his father in 1758 and reigned for nearly sixty years, that Blenheim came into its own as a family home. The 4th Duke, though inclined to be haughty and overbearing, was upright, generous and a connoisseur. He employed Capability Brown to make the great lake – which gives point to Vanbrugh's heroic bridge – and also, unfortunately, to sweep away the formal gardens in accordance with the prevailing fashion. He built up a famous collection of gems, and he made a theatre with seating for two or three hundred people, where amateur performances were held, to which not only the locals and the county neighbours but also the town and university of Oxford were invited. The Duke's hospitality was not confined to theatre parties; when his wife, a daughter of the 4th Duke of Bedford (*see* WOBURN ABBEY) was safely delivered of their second son, he celebrated by giving a supper at which the food consisted of roast beef, mutton and pork, loin and fillet of veal, pork and mutton pies, chicken, ducks, geese, tongues, boar's head, two dishes of soused herrings, an apple pie and two plum puddings. As he grew older, the Duke became less sociable. He did not feel up to receiving Nelson and Sir

Blenheim Palace. The lawn was originally a formal parterre.

William and Lady Hamilton when they called during the summer of 1802, but simply sent out refreshments to them in the park. These were indignantly refused, and Emma declared that if she were Queen, Nelson would have been given a principality such as would make Blenheim Park seem like a kitchen garden, a remark which reduced the victor of the Nile to tears. On a later occasion, when the Duke was told that he had another distinguished caller in the person of Madame de Staël, he moaned: 'Take me away! Oh, take me away!'

The 4th Duke died a couple of years after Waterloo, and it was probably in order that those earlier military glories associated with the name of Churchill should not be forgotten that the 5th Duke, on his accession, took Churchill as a surname in addition to his patronymic of Spencer, which the two previous Dukes and their descendants had borne by itself. This was perhaps the one worthwhile act in a life of wanton extravagance. He brought himself close to bankruptcy, and the palace was even invaded by bailiffs, who were fortunately prevented by the entail from seizing its treasures. By 1824 the

43

spendthrift Duke was doing everything he possibly could to raise money, even exploiting a source of revenue of which all too many twentieth-century landowners are obliged to take advantage, but which to Mrs Arbuthnot seemed the ultimate in degradation: 'People may shoot and fish at so much per hour!' she recorded with horror after visiting Blenheim that year in company with the Duke of Wellington (*see* STRATFIELD SAYE). A few years later, Prince Pückler-Muskau found the palace sadly run down. On his arrival, 'some very dirty, shabby servants' went to fetch the housekeeper, who, wrapped in a Scotch plaid and so majestic that she might have been mistaken for the Duchess, showed him 'many chill and faded rooms'.

Shortage of money continued to be a problem for the Marlboroughs throughout the nineteenth century. Their income of £40,000 a year was not great by ducal standards, certainly not with Blenheim to maintain. The 7th Duke – a Victorian statesman and the grandfather of Winston Churchill, who was born at Blenheim – had to sell the Sunderland library and the Marlborough gems. Worse was to come; in 1886 the pictures – the Rembrandts, the Rubenses, the Van Dycks and the rest of the Great Duke's collection, almost everything except for the family portraits – was sold by the 8th Duke, who spent the proceeds on modernizing his farms, putting up orchid houses, installing electric light in the palace and converting some of the bedrooms into laboratories for his chemical and electrical experiments, for he had a brilliant scientific mind and is said to have anticipated at least one of Edison's inventions. But along with scientific genius went a strange, unhappy nature like that of his younger brother, Lord Randolph Churchill. He expressed his grudge against life by inscribing the bedroom mantlepieces with sentiments such as 'Dust. Ashes. Nothing.' Having been divorced in rather scandalous circumstances, he came to be regarded as wicked, and after his sudden and premature death in 1892 there were said to have been unpleasant psychical manifestations in the rooms at Blenheim which he had used as laboratories. There is a story of how a certain gentleman, on hearing that these rooms had a bad reputation, insisted for the hell of it on spending the night in one of them, though his host, the young 9th Duke, tried hard to dissuade him. He emerged next morning shattered, having had a terrifying experience. 'I was in bed with a corpse,' he said, 'and it was giving me electric shocks.'

The 9th Duke resembled his father in being gifted but unhappy. His first wife, the American heiress Consuelo Vanderbilt, whom he married in 1895 and from whom he parted in 1906, has described the bleak dinners alone with him at Blenheim.

They were served with all the accustomed ceremony, but once a course had been passed the servants retired to the hall; the door was closed and only a ring of the bell placed before Marlborough summoned them. He had a way of piling food on his plate; the next move was to push the plate away, together with knives, forks, spoons and glasses – all this in considered gestures which took a long time; then he backed his chair away from the table, crossed one leg over the other and endlessly twirled the ring on his little finger. While accomplishing these gestures he was absorbed in thought and quite oblivious of any reactions I might have. . . . As a rule neither of us spoke a word. I took to knitting in desperation and the butler read detective stories in the hall.

The 9th Duke of Marlborough outside Blenheim in the 1920s, with one of his wife's Blenheim spaniels.

A Blenheim house party watching the Yeomanry Sports, May 1911. Winston Churchill is under the umbrella.

We have a glimpse of the 9th Duke from a different angle in the memoirs of the Benedictine abbot Sir David Hunter-Blair, who brought a party of Oxford undergraduates to Blenheim in 1899 on a day when the palace was open to the public. In the saloon 'the big glass doors suddenly opened, and the little Duke in khaki (he was encamped with his Yeomanry in the park) rushed in, and seeing the mob of tourists, rushed out again with a loud and forcible expletive. We all stared at this unexpected apparition, but the butler who was escorting us (looking like a duke himself) merely announced, with no sign of emotion, "His Grace, the Duke of Marlborough"!'

The interests of the 9th Duke were artistic rather than scientific. He was passionately devoted to Blenheim and did what he could to make good the depredations of his father and grandfather, buying pictures and furniture, and building up a collection of books to take the place of the Sunderland Library. He also employed the French garden architect Achille Duchêne to re-create part of the original formal layout. A sphinx on one of his water terraces had the head of his second wife, the fascinating Gladys Deacon, an American who had spent much of her life in France and Italy and was a friend of Proust. During the 1920s she invited many writers to Blenheim including H.G. Wells and Lytton Strachey – 'There is a bridge over a lake which positively gives one an erection', the latter wrote admiringly after his visit. Her life at Blenheim ended with the break-up of her marriage early in the 1930s, a cause of dissent between the Duke and Duchess being her army of Blenheim spaniels, which she kept in pens in the great hall and even in some of the state rooms. The Duke would spend hours looking for stains on the carpets and curtains, and would be disappointed if he failed to find any.

The Great Marlborough's palace can all too easily be represented as a vast mausoleum of a house in which its occupants rattled and found little happiness. Yet it had its sublime moments such as during the last summer before the Second World War when, as Sir Sacheverell Sitwell recalls –

the whole of Blenheim was floodlit for the ball, from panoramic court and scenic portico to the dark cedars on the lawn and the bust of 'Le Roi Soleil', a prisoner, upon the pediment; from the powdered hair and 'Padua' scarlet of the state liveries, through the crowded ballrooms, down to the room hung with 'Indian' papers that look out upon Bernini's fountain; to the shelves of water and the deep lake that seemed to move and flow. That was a galaxy of light upon this theatrical, but heroic building, upon this private monument that is a Roman triumph and a public pantomime; and amid those lights it was possible to admire Vanbrugh's architecture as it may never be seen again.

Architecture and Contents

This wonderfully dramatic masterpiece of the English baroque, with its massive Corinthian centre, its corner towers crowned with flaming bombs in stone, symbolic of Marlborough's military genius, its colonnades and its courts, is largely as it was originally conceived early in the eighteenth century by Vanbrugh in collaboration with Hawksmoor. The great hall, with giant Corinthian columns and a painted ceiling by Thornhill, leads into the saloon, with its marble doorways by Hawksmoor and its walls and ceiling painted by Laguerre. This is the centre of an enfilade of state rooms along the south front, some of them hung with tapestries woven in Brussels by Judocus de Vos depicting Marlborough's campaigns. Running the full length of the west front is the long library, originally a picture gallery, decorated by Hawksmoor and dominated by Rysbrack's statue of Queen Anne. Some of the rooms were redecorated in the second half of the eighteenth century by the 4th Duke, while in the 1890s the 9th Duke employed French craftsmen to adorn the state rooms with gilded woodwork. The 9th Duke to some extent made good his father's depredations by acquiring fine French furniture, Savonnerie carpets and pictures. The family portraits, which escaped the 8th Duke's sales, include works by Van Dyck, Kneller, Reynolds and Romney, to which the 9th Duke added the well-known Sargent group of himself and his family. His bust by Epstein has also been added to the sculpture in the great hall. Blenheim now has an exhibition dedicated to the memory of Winston Churchill, who was born in a small room between the great hall and the long library and is buried in Bladon churchyard on the edge of the park. As a worthy setting for the palace, Capability Brown, working for the 4th Duke, created his finest landscape.

BLICKLING HALL
NORFOLK

Blickling Hall : the south or entrance front. The towers are capped by ogival cupolas, similar to those which originally adorned HATFIELD, which was also designed by Robert Lyminge.

THE estate of Blickling, which had once belonged to the family of Anne Boleyn, was bought in 1616 by Sir Henry Hobart, Lord Chief Justice, who proceeded to build the present great Jacobean mansion. The Lord Chief Justice's grandson, Sir John Hobart, was a staunch Parliamentarian who sat in Cromwell's Upper House, though like so many other former Roundheads he managed to make his peace with Charles II at the Restoration. He married a daughter and eventual co-heiress of John Hampden, 'The Patriot', whose estate was in Buckinghamshire, giving the Hobarts a link with that county which Sir John's grandson and namesake commemorated by taking Buckinghamshire as his title when he was made an earl in 1746. The earldom, and the barony which preceded it, were obtained by the younger Sir John through the influence of his sister Henrietta, Countess of Suffolk (*see* AUDLEY END).

The 2nd Earl of Buckinghamshire held the important posts of Ambassador at St Petersburg and Viceroy of Ireland. He was sent to Russia because it was thought that his pleasant face and agreeable manners would appeal to Catherine the Great; and while Horace Walpole nicknamed him 'The Clearcake' after a confection which was 'fat, fair, sweet and seen through in a moment', he acquitted himself well during the three years of his embassy. The Empress presented him with a vast tapestry of Peter the Great at the Battle of Poltava and Lord Buckinghamshire formed the neo-classical Peter the Great room at Blickling specially for it. This was part of the 2nd Earl's very extensive remodelling of the house, towards the cost of which his first wife left him her jewels when she died in 1769. A year after her death he married again, to a sister of Thomas Conolly, a great Irish magnate. A well-known story of how the Devil appeared to Conolly at Castletown, his home in County Kildare, is also told of Blickling, where the Prince of Darkness is said to have appeared to the second Lady Buckinghamshire's cousin, Lord Rockingham, who threw an inkstand at him which marked the wall, just as Conolly is reputed to have got rid of his unwelcome guest by getting the local priest to throw a breviary at him, which cracked a pier glass. One would like to know which of the two houses Old Nick really visited; possibly the story originated in something that Lord Buckinghamshire heard in Russia.

The great gallery with its ceiling of Jacobean plasterwork and its nineteenth-century bookcases and painted decoration by John Hungerford Pollen. The photograph was taken early this century before the removal of the nineteenth-century chimneypiece.

Two years after Lord Buckinghamshire's second marriage, Lady Beauchamp-Proctor, whose home was on the far side of Norwich, called at Blickling with her husband and three young ladies. She had been once before, when Lord Buckinghamshire was away on his Russian embassy, and had not admired the house; now she liked it no better, though her judgement may have been coloured by the fact that while the Buckinghamshires were on this occasion at home, they did their best to make themselves scarce. 'We were afraid of being too soon,' Lady Beauchamp-Proctor wrote, 'but on sending in our names were admitted. We found they had breakfasted, and My Lord's horses stood at the door, though the servant told us he was gone out. We saw no other traces of Her Ladyship than two or three workbags and a tambour; I believe we drove her from room to room, but that we could not help. We saw only the old part of the house, over which a very dirty housemaid with a duster in her hand conducted us.' But as they were leaving, Lord Buckinghamshire appeared and 'made a thousand courtier-like speeches, but they were so little worth attending to that they went in at one ear and out at t'other; one thing, however, I could not help remarking – he said he was mortified beyond expression that he happened to be out when we came, and you know I have mentioned his horses being at the door when we went in.'

On the death of the 2nd Earl, who left no son, the earldom went to his brother, but Blickling was inherited by his daughter Lady Suffield, one of whose sisters married the 6th Marquess of Lothian and another the 2nd Earl of Mount Edgcumbe (*see* MOUNT EDGCUMBE). In the nineteenth century the estate passed to the Lothians, whose interests were principally in Scotland. For many years Blickling was the home of the charming Constance, Lady Lothian, widow of the 8th Marquess, with whom Augustus Hare stayed in 1887 when the house party also included the wealthy philanthropist Baroness Burdett-Coutts. Hare wrote down what he heard about Blickling's ghosts.

Anne Boleyn was said to walk in the drawing-room with her head in her hand, though the house had not been built until nearly a century after her execution. Then there was a large black dog, said to have come out of the mouth of an enormous fish caught in the lake, which had gone round and round in circles in the house until it had been confined by the putting up of a partition across its path. But Lady Lothian and her husband, when they first came to live here, had taken down the partition to enlarge a room. 'I wish these young people would not pull down the partitions', an old woman in the village had said to the local parson; 'they will let the dog loose again, and there's not a wise man in all London who could lay that dog now.'

Constance, Lady Lothian, died in 1901, after which Blickling ceased to be regularly inhabited by the family and was frequently let. It was eventually left to the National Trust by the 11th Marquess, a brilliant but erratic politician who died in 1940 as Ambassador to Washington, having refused to see a doctor on account of his Christian Scientist beliefs. James Lees-Milne, who came to Blickling on behalf of the Trust in 1943, wrote in his diary when he first arrived: 'It is a sad, lonely, unloved house with a reproachful air. I dare say it will be burnt down before long.' Later he grew to love the house, and enjoyed writing his letters at a table in the long gallery, 'surrounded by 12,000 calf bound books, looking on to the beautiful but unkempt, unmown garden.' He also tells of a visit in the summer of 1945 to the mausoleum in the park where lie the bodies of the 2nd Earl of Buckinghamshire and his two Countesses. While he and his companion were exploring the interior there was a flash of lightning and, lest the great iron doors should be struck, they retreated into one of the empty niches. 'The thunder was deafening as it rolled and echoed round the reverberating dome of the mausoleum. We agreed that nothing could be more dramatic or eerie. The Buckinghamshire coffins remained motionless on their shelves.'

Architecture and Contents

A great Jacobean mansion of red brick with corner turrets, a cupola and curved gables, Blickling was built in 1616–25 by Sir Henry Hobart to the design of Robert Lyminge, the architect of HATFIELD. The two houses have certain similarities. The interior was largely remodelled in the eighteenth century by the 2nd Earl of Buckinghamshire, his architects being the father and son, Thomas and William Ivory. Some Jacobean features remain, notably the ceiling of the long gallery, which in the nineteenth century was fitted with ornate bookcases by John Hungerford Pollen to contain the very important library acquired by the 2nd Earl. Blickling's other treasures include tapestries and portraits by Mytens and Gainsborough. The house, with its contents and estate, was left to the National Trust in 1940.

A portrait by Gainsborough of Caroline Conolly, the second wife of the 2nd Earl of Buckinghamshire.

BODRHYDDAN HALL
CLWYD

THE ancient family of Conwy, descended from William the Conqueror's High Constable Sir William Conias, has been at Bodrhyddan since the late fourteenth century, having probably come to Wales with Edward I's invasion. The house has grown gradually round a medieval core. In the sixteenth and seventeenth centuries the Conwys were recusants; one of them translated an anti-Protestant tract into Welsh. Henry Conwy joined Charles II in exile abroad and at the Restoration was made a baronet, but on the death of his son, Sir John – who carried out one of the several remodellings of the house – the baronetcy and also the male line of the Conwys became extinct.

When Doctor Johnson came to Bodrhyddan in 1774 and pronounced the house 'pretty' with 'pleasant shades about it' – as well as remarking on 'a constant spring that supplies a cold bath' – it was owned by Sir John Conwy's descendants in the female line, and during the course of the next hundred years it was to pass by way of a couple more heiresses. One was the wife of William Shipley, Dean of St Asaph, who lived at Bodrhyddan for many years after her death in 1789. In the words of his great-nephew Augustus Hare, Dean Shipley –

was devoted to hunting and shooting, and used to go up for weeks together to a little public-house in the hills above Bodrhyddan, where he gave himself up entirely to the society of his horses and dogs. He had led a very fast life before he took orders, and had a natural daughter by a Mrs Hamilton . . . but after his ordination there was no

The entrance front of Bodrhyddan, as remodelled by W.E.Nesfield.

A photomontage of 1870, showing members of the family assembled in the drawing-room. William Shipley-Conwy, with a high forehead and white whiskers, sitting in the left foreground, is included though he had died a year previously. The subsequent owner of Bodrhyddan, Conwy Rowley-Conwy, sits at the right of the picture, behind his wife Marian and her dog. His mother sits behind him, and his father, Colonel Richard Thomas Rowley, is the man in the armchair in the centre. Standing to the left of Colonel Rowley is his future son-in-law, Admiral Leveson Somerset. A cousin of the family, Lady Williams-Wynn, sits immediately to the left of Mrs Rowley. The figures are out of proportion to the room, making it seem very much larger than it actually is.

further stain upon his character. As a father he was exceedingly severe. He never permitted his daughters to sit down in his presence, and he never allowed two of them to be in the room with him at once, because he could not endure the additional talking caused by their speaking to one another.

In addition to his three daughters (one of whom married Reginald Heber, the first Bishop of Calcutta, who wrote 'From Greenland's Icy Mountains' and other well-known hymns) the Dean had five sons; the second youngest was a gallant naval officer killed in action in 1808. Bodrhyddan eventually passed to the Dean's grandson, another William Shipley, whose sense of the past caused him to assume the additional surname of Conwy and to make the house more like what he imagined it to have been in former times, notably by introducing a quantity of old woodcarving.

Augustus Hare has left an evocative description of Bodrhyddan in William Shipley-Conwy's time:

Under an old clock-tower one entered upon a handsome drive with an avenue of fine elms, on the right of which a lawn, with magnificent firs, oaks and cedars, swept away to the hills. At the end rose the stately old brick house, half covered with magnolias, myrtles and buddleia, with blazing beds of scarlet and yellow flowers to light up its base. Through an oak hall hung with armour a fine staircase led to the library – an immense room with two deep recesses entirely furnished with black oak from Copenhagen, and adorned with valuable enamels collected at Lisbon.

When Hare stayed here, the bachelor William Shipley-Conwy, though still young, was paralysed; his sister, Mrs Rowley, used to feed him at table like a child, one mouthful for him and one for her.

Hare stayed here again in 1876, by which time Bodrhyddan had been inherited by Mrs Rowley's son, Captain Conwy Rowley-Conwy, who had recently commissioned William Eden Nesfield to give the house a new entrance front and a general face-lift, as well as making it more convenient (hitherto, the kitchen and dining-room had been at opposite ends of the building). 'Restored, they call it,' Hare observed with some asperity, 'but though well done in a way, the quaint old peculiar character is gone.' He was also distressed at the lack of interest shown by his host and hostess in the people who had lived here before them. There was a portrait of a little girl with a dog in Mrs Rowley-Conwy's sitting-room; Hare asked her who it was, and she replied vaguely that it was 'some sort of great-aunt', adding that 'the dog was rather nice'. The girl in the portrait was in fact Dean Shipley's most cherished niece. 'One could not help remembering how that child's little footsteps were once the sweetest music that house ever knew,' was Hare's wistful comment. 'And now her very existence is forgotten there, but her picture is preserved because "she had rather a nice little dog".'

Architecture and Contents

Bodrhyddan is a house of many periods, of which the core is probably medieval: it was enlarged in the sixteenth century and remodelled towards the end of the seventeenth by Sir John Conwy, who gave it a more up-to-date appearance by concealing the roof with a parapet wall, adding a cupola and substituting sash windows for some of the original mullions. A dining-room was added to the eastern end of the house in 1810, and finally in 1873–4 a new entrance front was made to the west, the original front to the south becoming the garden front. The architect of these additions and alterations was W.E.Nesfield, who carried them out in a characteristic Victorian 'Queen Anne' style, in sharp red brick with trim white-painted woodwork. The new entrance front has an elaborate central feature incorporating pilasters, a balcony on console brackets and a pedimented doorcase, the whole surmounted by a tall curvilinear gable. The interior of the house contains a great deal of old woodwork, mostly acquired in the 1830s and 1840s by William Shipley-Conwy. A low entrance hall in Nesfield's new front, its walls hung with armour, opens into what was probably the great hall of the medieval house. The dining-room contains an interesting series of family portraits, including works by John Vanderbank, Thomas Hudson and Allan Ramsay. The drawing-room, embellished with some of the most ornate of William Shipley-Conwy's woodcarvings, has recently been redecorated in cream and gold. William Shipley-Conwy's sister married Captain Richard Rowley, second son of the 1st Lord Langford; their descendant, the present owner of Bodrhyddan, succeeded his kinsman as the 9th Lord Langford in 1953.

BRYMPTON D'EVERCY
SOMERSET

THE former seat of the Sydenhams, Brympton D'Evercy is arguably one of the most beautiful houses in England. With its golden-grey seventeenth-century garden front it is like a country cousin of Inigo Jones's Banqueting House at Whitehall. The house was bought in 1731 by Francis Fane MP, a barrister and minor politician whose mother was the heiress of a Bristol merchant. Fane's roots were in Kent, where his family had risen to wealth and power during the sixteenth century, the family of Vane (*see* RABY CASTLE) being of the same stock. In 1624 his ancestor and namesake was given a new creation of the earldom of Westmorland, formerly held by the Nevills from whom he was maternally descended, and in 1762, three years

Brympton D'Evercy : the Tudor west front.

after Francis's death, his brother Thomas, who had inherited Brympton, succeeded to the earldom. For the next two generations Brympton went with the other Westmorland properties, but in the middle of the nineteenth century it passed to Lady Georgiana Fane, the spinster daughter of the 10th Earl by his second marriage – his first wife having been the heiress Sarah Child (*see* OSTERLEY PARK). The second Lady Westmorland, who did not get on with her husband, set up her own establishment at Brympton with Lady Georgiana. She and her daughter furnished the house more or less from scratch and introduced the marble chimney-pieces. After her mother's death in 1857 Lady Georgiana allowed the estate to get into debt, for she had a bad head for business, though she did much to enhance the surroundings of the house, planting trees, making the pond and constructing the balustraded terrace along the principal front.

When she died in 1875 Lady Georgiana left Brympton to her nephew Spencer Ponsonby, a son of her half-sister who had married the 4th Earl of Bessborough; he consequently assumed the additional surname of Fane. At the time of her death he was in Ireland, having gone there with his elder brother Frederick for some snipe shooting and also to avoid being called as a witness in a lawsuit, for which reason the two brothers had left no address. But the post boy, carrying a telegram announcing her death, managed to track them down, and gave it to Frederick; he and Spencer were at first uncertain as to which of them it was meant for, and may even have tossed as to which of them should take on the burden of Brympton and their aunt's debts. But when Spencer saw Brympton, which he had never set eyes on before, he was so captivated by the beauty of the house that he vowed he would if necessary sell everything else he possessed in order to keep it. In the event he was able to keep it without having to go to such extremes, and without having to give up his career as a courtier – for like his better-known cousin, Sir Henry Ponsonby, he was a prominent member of the household of Queen Victoria, ending up as Sir Spencer Ponsonby-Fane and a Privy Councillor. As well as being a courtier, he was a herald and also a cricketer – a co-founder of the I Zingari club.

Spencer died in 1915 at the age of ninety-one. His son and heir survived him by less than a year and he was succeeded by his grandson Richard. But as Richard suffered from ill-health and chose to live in Japan, his real successor was his granddaughter Violet, whose husband, Captain Edward Clive, was descended from a cousin of Clive of India (*see* POWIS CASTLE). Violet Clive was a redoubtable personage who in her youth played hockey for the West of England and rowed for the Leander Club. She was also a master carpenter, but is chiefly remembered as a gardener; between the wars, Brympton was well known for the garden which she laid out and tended, doing a great deal of the work with her own hands. Her grandson, the present owner of Brympton, has written a memorable description of her:

Granny was . . . the worst-dressed woman I had ever known and many people have remarked that, on first coming across her deep in some shrub, they mistook her for a vagrant. Somehow I doubt it. With her hawk-like, imperious nose and deep, penetrating eyes, there was no doubt that she was in charge. Every day she would dress in the most awful shapeless black creation of no design and even less style. She may have had more than one of these voluminous garments, but if she ever did ring

Violet Clive gardening at Brympton D'Evercy. Behind her is the seventeenth-century garden front.

the changes, the end result was exactly the same – a mess. Around her waist she would bolt on the most monstrous leather belt; from it dangled hooks, spikes, trowels, knives and other accoutrements that made her look like an itinerant ironmonger rather than the lady of the house. On her head was perched a plain black hat, held in place with a large diamond brooch. She wore this family heirloom not as a symbol of authority, nor even to add a little chic to the ensemble, but rather for the practical purpose of keeping the hat on.

Her son, the late Nicholas Clive-Ponsonby-Fane, decided in 1956 that he could no longer afford to live at Brympton and let the house to a school, having sold almost all the contents except the family portraits. The school left in the early 1970s and in 1974 Charles Clive-Ponsonby-Fane made the brave decision to move back into the house, which he and his wife have since gradually restored and refurnished. Their labours are amusingly and at times heart-rendingly recounted in his book *We Started a Stately Home*.

Architecture and Contents

A Tudor house on to which was built, in the 1670s, a garden front of outstanding beauty, consisting of two storeys of mullioned windows crowned with alternate segmental and triangular pediments. The house forms a ravishing group with the church and the detached fifteenth-century chantry house. There is an oak staircase on a prodigious scale and a series of panelled state rooms along the garden front. The rooms contain family portraits, some of them by Lawrence, a collection of watercolours and good English eighteenth- and early nineteenth-century furniture. There is also a display of Victorian costumes and, in the chantry house, a museum of coopering and cider-making.

BURGHLEY HOUSE
NORTHAMPTONSHIRE

BURGHLEY, a palace which surpasses all other surviving Elizabethan mansions in size and grandeur, was built between 1553 and 1587 by William Cecil, afterwards Lord Burghley, who for most of the first Elizabeth's reign was her chief minister and as such the most powerful man in England. Cecil was himself largely responsible for the design which would explain why, for all its sophistication, it is basically old-fashioned and suited to his rather outdated way of life; he was unusual among English magnates of his generation in keeping up the ancient custom of dining in the hall with his entire household.

William Cecil's elder son, the 2nd Lord Burghley, was promoted to being Earl of Exeter in 1605, on the same day as his half-brother Robert, now chief minister to James I, was made Earl of Salisbury (*see* HATFIELD HOUSE). During the minority of his great-grandson, the 4th Earl of Exeter, Burghley was garrisoned by the Cavaliers and besieged by Cromwell, who bombarded it and took it by assault. Cromwell ordered that the house should not be pillaged, but it must have suffered considerable damage, which would explain the very extensive remodelling of the interior carried out by the 5th Earl after his accession in 1678. One doubts, however, if this 'Maecenas' Earl of Exeter, who went three times to Italy and collected pictures in Florence with the help of the Medici Grand Duke, would have needed any such excuse when most of his relations and in-laws were engaging, or had recently engaged, in large-scale building activities – his grandfather the Earl of Rutland at BELVOIR, his brother-in-law the Duke of Devonshire at CHATSWORTH, and the parents of his Brownlow daughter-in-law at BELTON. His work at Burghley is of the utmost splendour, the state rooms painted by Antonio Verrio with a riot of baroque deities and attendant figures which rather shocked the prim Celia Fiennes by their nakedness. 'That was the only fault,' she wrote, after seeing the rooms in 1697, when they were nearing completion, 'the immodesty of the Pictures especially in my lords appartment.' Verrio, together with his family and hangers-on, lived at Burghley almost continuously for ten years, being paid a salary from which was deducted such expenses as the cost of his table: the latter included claret, port, Canary wine and brandy, as well as foreign delicacies such as '*saussissons de boullogne*'.

Lord Exeter's sudden death – through eating too much fruit on a visit to Paris in 1700 – put an end to his work, which remained unfinished for more than fifty years, during which time the house was allowed to fall into a state of disrepair. It was eventually rescued by the 9th Earl who embarked on a programme of restoration.

Lawrence's portrait of the 10th Earl (afterwards 1st Marquess) of Exeter, with his wife Sarah, the 'Cottage Countess', at Burghley.

The 9th Earl was childless and his heir was his nephew Henry Cecil, the hero of the story romanticized by Tennyson in *The Lord of Burleigh*. In 1789, after his first wife had eloped with a curate, the future Lord Exeter sought a new identity as 'John Jones' in a remote Shropshire village. Here he fell in love with the sixteen-year-old Sarah Hoggins, whose father farmed in a small way and kept the village shop. Having contracted a bigamous marriage with her, he married her lawfully in 1791 after divorcing his first wife. Two years later his uncle died and he came into his inheritance, but he did not tell Sarah that she had been metamorphosed into the Countess of Exeter and the mistress of Burghley until, on a winter's night, their carriage drove up to the stupendous front of their new home.

On the whole the 'Cottage Countess' was treated well by her husband's world; even the catty Horace Walpole heard good reports of her, 'especially of her great humility and modesty on her exaltation'. There was an occasion when the Duchess of Ancaster, a former governess, tried to embarrass her in front of a large party of people by addressing her in French which was then much spoken in fashionable circles, but Lord Exeter turned the tables on the Duchess by saying sweetly to his wife: 'My dear, Her Grace says so-and-so, but she forgets you never had the advantage of being one of her pupils.' Yet even with her husband to protect her, the 'beautiful, modest and shy' Sarah who, unlike other eighteenth-century peeresses of humble birth 'was never able to rise to her position either in manners or mode of speech', found the house parties at Burghley sheer misery. Her 'aspirates were not perfect', and she could never get out of the habit of addressing great ladies as 'Ma'am'; letter-writing was 'a torture to her, for her fear of committing some breach of etiquette'. Nor was she able to manage her servants: 'she passed a great deal of time in their company, telling them that it was far more agreeable to her to be with them than in the company of the nobility.' In short, she was far from happy in her new life, which in the event did not last very long, for she died in 1797 after giving birth to her younger son.

The elder son of the Cottage Countess became the 2nd Marquess of Exeter – his father having been given a step up in the peerage in 1801. It was in his time that Prince Pückler-Muskau turned up at Burghley, which he thought showed 'a very corrupt taste in art' on the part of the Elizabethan statesman; one suspects he was influenced by the fact that the housekeeper refused to take him round the house because it was a Sunday. Another nineteenth-century visitor to whom 'the finest house in England' did not come up to expectations was Augustus Hare, who stayed here in 1877 in the time of the 3rd Marquess. 'There is a series of stately rooms, dull and oppressive,' he wrote, 'and a multitude of pictures with very fine names, almost all misnamed.' But as with Pückler-Muskau, his judgement may have been warped, in his case by the fact that he did not find the company very congenial. Lord Exeter, 'with his lank black hair and his wrinkled yellow jackboots high above the knee', looked to him 'like a soldier of Cromwell'; he and the whole family danced all evening to the music of a barrel-organ which they took it in turns to wind. The family worshipped the memory not of the Great Cecil but of a prize bull named Telemachus, whose stuffed head was enshrined in the hall and his statue in silver in the dining-room, among the statues and portraits of 'a whole dynasty of Telemachi'. To add to Hare's

Burghley House.

boredom, his fellow-guests included nobody more interesting than 'a row of elderly baronets of only hunting and Midland-county fame'. He complained of the number of elderly baronets to Miss Fowke, the young lady whom he took in to dinner. 'Yes,' she replied, 'they are old and they are numerous, and the central one is my father.'

Architecture and Contents

An Elizabethan palace of stone built on the traditional late-medieval courtyard plan, with a gate-tower on the side opposite the great hall. It was designed largely by William Cecil, afterwards Lord Burghley, who had a Flemish 'mason' to help him with the Renaissance detail. The interior was extensively remodelled towards the end of the seventeenth century by the 5th Earl of Exeter, who employed Verrio to paint the state rooms and formed a succession of other fine rooms with ceilings of rich plasterwork and panelling carved in the manner of Grinling Gibbons. More work was carried out in the middle of the eighteenth century by the 9th Earl with as his architect Capability Brown, who also landscaped the park. The magnificent picture collection, acquired by the 5th and 9th Earls, includes works by the Carracci, Guido Reni, Carlo Dolci, Luca Giordano and Jan Breughel, as well as a self-portrait by Van Eyck. Among the family portraits are works by Cornelius Johnson, Van Dyck, Lely, Kneller, Gainsborough and Lawrence. The furniture includes a Florentine cabinet of *pietre dure*, a James II state bed with its original hangings, a set of ormolu commodes by Chippendale and a Queen Anne wine-cooler reputed to be the largest in the world.

The Heaven Room, decorated with paintings by Antonio Verrio in 1695–6.

CASTLE ASHBY
NORTHAMPTONSHIRE

THE great Elizabethan mansion of Castle Ashby was built in 1574 by the 1st Lord Compton and enlarged and embellished during the early years of the seventeenth century by his son and grandson, the 1st and 2nd Earls of Northampton. The 1st Earl, when he was still Lord Compton, greatly increased the family fortunes by marrying the daughter of Sir John Spencer, a wealthy Lord Mayor of London. Spencer is said to have disapproved of the marriage and there is a romantic story of how Compton disguised himself as a baker's boy and carried off his intended bride in a basket on his head, meeting Spencer on the stairs who tipped him sixpence, which he afterwards swore would be the only sixpence Compton would see; thanks to the intervention of Queen Elizabeth he relented, however.

The Queen's successor, James I, was entertained twice at Castle Ashby. According to the contemporary letter-writer John Chamberlain, the second of these entertainments was rather mean, which is surprising in view of Northampton's well-known munificence. In 1629, when he rode from London to Windsor for his installation as a Knight of the Garter, he caused a sensation by the brilliance of his cortège, which was almost a hundred strong.

The 2nd Earl, who gave Castle Ashby its Renaissance front, reputedly by Inigo Jones, was a Royalist commander in the Civil War and fell at Hopton Heath. 'He was a person of great courage, honour and fidelity,' Clarendon wrote of him, 'and not well known till his evening, having, in the ease and plenty of that too happy time, indulged to himself with that licence which was then thought necessary to great fortunes: but from the beginning of these distractions, as if he had been awakened out of a lethargy, he never proceeded with a lukewarm temper.' Four of his sons were officers under him and three of them rode in the charge which cost him his life, the eldest, who became the 3rd Earl, being severely wounded by a shot in the leg. The second son, Sir Charles Compton, afterwards led a daring surprise attack on Beeston Castle in Cheshire. The brother of these martial Comptons became Bishop of London, and a leader of the Revolution of 1688. He officiated at the coronation of William and Mary in place of the Archbishop of Canterbury, whose conscience prevented him from taking the oath to the new sovereigns.

Apart from the 3rd Earl's younger son, Spencer Compton, Earl of Wilmington, who was Prime Minister for a brief period after Walpole (*see* HOUGHTON HALL), the Comptons were not very prominent from the end of the seventeenth century onwards, although the 9th Earl was made Marquess of Northampton in 1812. Lady Marian Alford (*see* BELTON HOUSE), a daughter of the 2nd Marquess, was well known in Victoria's reign as a *grande dame*, and also for the beauty of her hands and feet. (For a German nobleman

The young Charles Compton, 7th Earl of Northampton, painted in 1758, the year of his succession, by Pompeo Batoni.

staying at Castle Ashby in 1841, tying her shoelaces for her on a walk to the Home Farm was an unforgettable experience.) Lady Marian's clerical brother, Lord Alwyne Compton, who became Bishop of Ely, was the only nineteenth-century Compton to hold an important office. His wife used to tease him for having too high an opinion of his family: 'He thinks that the Comptons are quite perfect and always have been', she once remarked in his presence. 'When I first married, I hoped to have made a compromise and I told Lord Alwyne that if he would give up to me his great-grandfather I would spare all the rest; but he wouldn't.'

The nephew of this ancestor-worshipping Bishop, the 5th Marquess of Northampton, was host at a memorable week of celebrations at Castle Ashby in the summer of 1906 for the coming-of-age of his son and heir. One of the girls in the immense house party, Lady Cynthia Charteris – the future Lady Cynthia Asquith – has left an account of the festivities in her diary: 'Arrival at this extremely "stately Home of England" somewhat alarming. Descending in hordes, we were greeted by the Birthday Boy and our excellent host, his father, who at once made us the first of his many well-turned speeches, welcoming us under his roof, and charging us all to enjoy ourselves as heartily as he intended to enjoy himself.' Lord Northampton, who was a widower, had imported 'two official chaperons' for the occasion, 'both of whom, poor things, already looked like weary Atlases'. After dinner, everyone repaired to the ballroom, where Lord Northampton 'made yet another little speech telling us that because of the inevitable fatigues of the formidable programme before us, he proposed that on this first night we should not dance later than one o'clock.' Nevertheless, after all the other girls had obediently gone off to bed, Lady Cynthia and her future sister-in-law Violet Asquith stayed on in the ballroom for a few minutes, 'each talking to a MAN'; and they 'overheard the two chaperons' stage-whisper, "most annoying, most annoying".'

It took Lady Cynthia a long time to get to sleep: 'the heavy feet of the night watchman, who for fifty years has patrolled the house every half-hour

A photograph taken at the turn of the century of the 5th Marquess of Northampton looking over the balustrade of the Terracotta Bridge; his son, Earl Compton, afterwards the 6th Marquess, sits in the boat.

through the night, slowly crunched the gravel.' Next morning she had breakfast in Violet Asquith's bedroom, 'down labyrinthine corridors and up several flights of stairs'. They were joined by three other girls, Hilda Lyttelton (*see* HAGLEY HALL), Venetia Stanley and Clementine Hozier, the future wife of Winston Churchill (*see* BLENHEIM PALACE). 'Three "lackeys" staggered in, each bearing an enormous tray laden with good things – eggs, crisp curly bacon, hot scones in napkins, peaches, white grapes.' After breakfast they watched several games of golf and went to see the tents in which the young men of the party were accommodated, there being only room for the girls and older guests in the house, vast though it was. Lady Cynthia thought the tents 'far more luxurious than most bedrooms, each hung with tapestry and rigged up with electric light'.

After luncheon there were 'automobile races (very leisurely. Street speed limit scarcely exceeded).' That night there was a ball for the county neighbours. 'We danced until half past four. Bliss. Violet and I very careful to be amongst the first to go upstairs. Unhappy Duennas much incensed by clandestine 5 a.m. automobile party "mixed" and unchaperoned.'

On the following afternoon there was an entertainment out of doors for the tenants, with speeches, glee-singing and 'an extremely hard-working Funny Man'.

After dinner that night there was more dancing and 'everybody went rather mad, dressed up, and to annoyance of the professional band made hideous noises on improvised musical instruments – dinner gongs, tin kettles and papered combs. Authorities anxious for relatively early break-up, but though they could send us upstairs, they could not send us to sleep, and uproar raged for hours . . . Gradually all the men mustered outside and all the girls leaned out of the windows. Thunderous singing, the Pilgrims' Chorus and the Venusburg music from *Tannhäuser* being the most popular encores.' There was no need for them to worry about making too much noise, because Lord Northampton was himself 'heading the riot', dancing a cake-walk in his shirt sleeves.

An early nineteenth-century watercolour of Castle Ashby.

Architecture and Contents

A great Elizabethan and Jacobean mansion, dominated by a pair of polygonal towers and with a balustrade of lettering, extending round what was originally a three-sided court; this was enclosed in 1635 by the building of a classical range attributed to Inigo Jones. The interior dates largely from the late seventeenth century. The rooms are panelled or hung with Flemish and Mortlake tapestries, the grand staircase is luxuriantly carved with foliage, and two of the rooms are adorned with carving in the manner of Grinling Gibbons. The great hall, the chapel and the long gallery were redecorated in the 1880s by Sir Thomas Jackson. The portraits include works by Kneller, Reynolds, Allan Ramsay, Hoppner and Lawrence.

CASTLE HOWARD
NORTH YORKSHIRE

I N 1700 Charles Howard, 3rd Earl of Carlisle, began building a new and palatial house to replace the partially burnt castle on his Yorkshire estate which his ancestor Lord William Howard, youngest son of the 4th Duke of Norfolk (*see* ARUNDEL CASTLE) had acquired through marrying an heiress of the Dacres. His architect was the playwright Sir John Vanbrugh, assisted by that prolific designer of London churches Nicholas Hawksmoor; together they produced Castle Howard, a house in the grandest manner, but one which combines grandeur and drama with baroque gaiety. This makes it an easier house to live in than Vanbrugh's second and much larger great work, BLENHEIM PALACE, with which it is all too frequently compared. When staying at Castle Howard in 1713, a year after the family moved in, Vanbrugh wrote of how convenient Lord Carlisle was finding his new house. The long passages were 'so far from gathering and drawing wind as he feared, that a Candle wou'd not flare in them . . . He likewise finds that all his Rooms with moderate fires Are Ovens, And that this Great House do's not require above One pound of wax and two of Tallow Candles a night to light it more than his house at London did.' To live at Castle Howard and 'keep the whole house and offices in perfect cleanliness', Lord Carlisle needed only 'three housemaids and one Man' more than the domestic staff he had needed when living in the surviving remnant of the old castle.

Vanbrugh's claim that moderate fires made the rooms at Castle Howard into ovens is not upheld by the Duchess of Northumberland's description of the house, written later in the century, in which she speaks of the saloon as 'a very Cold Room where they dine'. And if the Duchess thought the saloon cold, Horace Walpole was not much impressed by it as a room, despite its splendid wall and ceiling paintings by Pellegrini. Of the garden front he observed, 'There is a scarce a large room in it. No tolerable eating room, Salon, library or chapel.' Walpole came here in 1772 when the long gallery and the other grand rooms in the west wing, which the 4th Earl was in the course of building at the time of his death in 1758, were as yet unfinished; it was not until about 1800 that the 5th Earl completed them. The 5th Earl of Carlisle was an archetypal great Whig magnate of Georgian England. A man of pleasure when young and a companion of Charles James Fox at the card table (though also a great collector and a friend of George Selwyn), he became a patriotic statesman in middle life, a tyrant and a bore when old. Lady Harriet Cavendish, the future Lady Granville (*see* CHATSWORTH), whose sister married his son and heir Lord Morpeth, found him very trying when she stayed at Castle Howard in 1807. When he was in a bad mood, everyone was terrified; when he was in a good mood, he would repeatedly tell the same admittedly quite funny stories at which everyone had to laugh. On a later visit, Harriet wrote: 'The dinners are insufferable – I am promoted to Lord Carlisle's right hand – We none of us speak – He sits like the nightmare upon our powers of articulation, and if Lady Carlisle did not laugh incessantly we should be taken for a meeting of quakers waiting for the spirit to move us.' The Morpeths and their children lived at Castle Howard with the Carlisles; their daughter Harriet is said to have called out, as she drove off in the carriage on her way to her first London season: 'Goodbye Castle Howard, you will never see Harriet Howard again!' Her eagerness to leave home and marry was the result of a desire to escape from her tiresome grandfather – and she did get married only a month after her coming-out ball, to a future duke, thereby doing as well as her aunt Elizabeth Howard who had married the Duke of Rutland (*see* BELVOIR CASTLE).

The 5th Earl appears in a more sympathetic light in his relations with the immortal Sydney Smith, who in 1809 became rector of Foston, a village close to the southern end of the stupendous Castle Howard avenue. Among the earliest callers at his rectory were Lord and Lady Carlisle, but their coach got bogged in his field and Lord Carlisle arrived in a bad temper. The Reverend Sydney, however, soon laughed him out of it, and from then on he and his wife were always welcome at Castle Howard, often being invited to stay for several days at a time.

As a tyrant, the 5th Earl is overshadowed in the history of Castle Howard by that formidable chatelaine of late-Victorian and Edwardian days, Rosalind Countess of Carlisle, a member of the remarkable Stanley of Alderley family and an aunt of Betrand Russell (*see* WOBURN ABBEY). Her husband, the 9th Earl, a highly talented painter who was a friend of Burne-Jones and other Pre-Raphaelites, was happy to leave the management of his estates to her, for she was extremely competent, though obsessed with detail. She liked to make lists: her daughters and the housemaids once had to carry every mattress and every pillow in the vast house down to the tapestry room, where, reclining on a sofa, she listed them. The pillows and mattresses had to be measured, so that their size could be entered, and they also had to be unpicked, in order that their quality could be ascertained.

Her other obsessions included making her children go about barefoot out of doors in the Yorkshire winter – 'I can still revel in the delicious hot feeling of the Castle Howard stone floors as I came in barefoot from the deep snow', her daughter wrote many years later. She was also passionately committed to the cause of temperance, though the oft-repeated story of how she had the wine from the Castle Howard cellar poured into the lake is a myth. What she and her husband, who was also a teetotaller, did throw away when they took over at Castle Howard was a lot of extremely old hock which had turned to vinegar. In fact for many years she actually gave wine to her guests. When the British Association for the Advancement of Science met at York, a large number of the delegates were invited to Castle Howard and given the strong home-brewed audit ale on which, in former times, the tenant farmers used to get uproariously drunk at rent dinners. This had a regrettable effect on some of the eminent scientists who were afterwards found peacefully asleep under various trees and shrubs – with the result that the remaining supply of the audit ale was also thrown away, doubtless furthering the legend of the wine

Rosalind Countess of Carlisle.

being poured into the lake. Rosalind Carlisle finally stopped serving wine after an occasion when a guest who had drunk too deep slipped under the table and the footmen were not sober enough to rescue him. All the men-servants were consequently dismissed and Castle Howard was henceforth staffed entirely by formidable parlour-maids – 'a row of Grenadier Guards-men in skirts', as somebody once described them. All the wine in the house was got rid of by the redoubtable Rosalind at the same time as she sacked the men servants. It did not, however, go into the lake, but was thoughtfully sent by her to the York hospital for the benefit of the patients. Autocratic and difficult though she was, Rosalind Carlisle did have a genuine concern for the underprivileged. She arranged for parties of children from the industrial towns to be given holidays on the Castle Howard estate. She also made a

The great baroque hall under the dome : looking across from one staircase to the other.

guest house in one of the wings of the Pyramid Gate on the avenue, which in former times had served as an inn for tourists; here she would entertain deserving women in batches of twelve throughout the year.

When Rosalind Carlisle died in 1921 Castle Howard was left to her teetotal eldest daughter Lady Mary Murray, wife of Professor Gilbert Murray, the classical scholar, her grandson, who was then the 11th Earl, having inherited Naworth Castle, the family seat in Cumberland. The Murrays were perfectly happy in their house at Boar's Hill, Oxford; so Lady Mary handed over Castle Howard, together with its estate and contents, to her younger brother Geoffrey Howard. His son, the present owner, was in 1983 made a life peer with the title of Lord Howard of Henderskelfe.

Architecture and Contents

Castle Howard consists of a central block, surmounted by a lantern and dome, prolonged by wings on the south or garden side to form an incomparable 300-foot façade relieved throughout its length by fluted Corinthian pilasters. On the north or entrance front, Vanbrugh's original plan was for there to be two similar projecting wings forming an open court, each with a cupola to reflect the great dome in the centre. The composition was to be extended by turreted quadrangles to the east and west, one containing domestic offices, the other stables. The stable quadrangle, however, was never built; nor was the more westerly of the two projecting wings. The existing west wing, which is much larger than its fellow to the east, and has a wide, shallow dome instead of a cupola, was added in the 1750s by the 4th Earl of Carlisle to the design of Sir Thomas Robinson, its interior being completed in about 1800 by the 5th Earl. The house was seriously damaged by fire in 1940 but has since been restored. The interior of Castle Howard is no less magnificent than the exterior. The hall rises into the dome, which having perished in the fire was re-created in 1960, complete with a replica of its original painting by Antonio Pellegrini, whose work in the principal rooms of the south front was also lost in the fire; one of these rooms now has decorative panels by Felix Kelly. The gallery, in the west wing, is 192 feet long.

The house is rich in works of art. The pictures include a Rubens and three landscapes by Gaspard Poussin as well as Holbein's portraits of Henry VIII and the 3rd Duke of Norfolk; there are also portraits by Van Dyck, Lely, Kneller, Hoppner and Lawrence. There are collections of Greek, Roman and Egyptian antiquities, an array of busts, one of them by Bernini, and Soho tapestries woven by Vanderbank after the younger Teniers. The surroundings of Castle Howard are as breathtaking as the house itself: to the north is a great lake, to the south-east are gardens containing numerous statues, a temple and a bridge designed by Vanbrugh, while some distance beyond, on a hill in the park, is Hawksmoor's dramatic mausoleum. The park is bisected by a dead-straight avenue nearly five miles long which passes beneath two arches, one of them framing a spectacular vista to an obelisk. The gardens have been added to and restored in recent years and now include the greatest

Vanbrugh's Castle Howard: the garden front.

collection of old roses in the country, as well as extensive plantings of rhododendrons and many rare shrubs. Castle Howard featured as 'Brideshead' in the recent television dramatization of Evelyn Waugh's novel *Brideshead Revisited*.

CHARLECOTE PARK
WARWICKSHIRE

OF THE select company of English country houses with literary associations, the palm must surely go to Charlecote, which not only knew Shakespeare but features in one of his plays. ''Fore God, you have a goodly dwelling and a rich', Falstaff observes to Justice Shallow in *Henry IV, part II*, and there is no doubt that Shallow is a caricature of Sir Thomas Lucy and that his 'goodly dwelling' is the mansion which Sir Thomas built on the banks of the Warwickshire Avon in the first year of Elizabeth I's reign. Here, according to tradition, the young William Shakespeare was brought one April morning in 1585, after being caught poaching the deer in Sir Thomas's park, to be confronted by the angry Knight of Charlecote in his great hall, where a stained glass window displayed the three white luces or pike which were the arms of Lucy. When Shakespeare came to write *The Merry Wives of Windsor* he gave Justice Shallow as *his* arms 'the dozen white luces', which is not only proof that he had Sir Thomas Lucy in mind, but suggests that he was mildly poking fun at Sir Thomas's pride in his kinship with the medieval Lords Lucy (*see* PETWORTH HOUSE), knowing that this was in fact pretty remote. But if the use of the surname and arms of Lucy by Sir Thomas and his forebears was open to question, they were themselves of ancient enough lineage, being descended from Thurstane de Cherlcote who owned Charlecote in the twelfth century.

Sir Thomas's grandson, another Sir Thomas, was in his younger days a friend of Lord Herbert of Cherbury (*see* POWIS CASTLE) and of the poets Michael Drayton and John Donne. His epitaph says that any good man was welcome at his board, especially if he could talk of theology or poetry. There is, however, no legend of Shakespeare returning to the hall where he had once been had up for poaching to spend a convivial evening talking about poetry with this younger Sir Thomas Lucy, who was a student at Lincoln's Inn when Shakespeare's plays were running at the Globe Theatre.

Although the younger Sir Thomas had thirteen children, most of the Lucys of the next three generations were childless, so that for a time Charlecote passed from one brother to the next or from uncle to nephew. More than one of these seventeenth- and early eighteenth-century Lucys had wives who preferred London to Warwickshire, which meant that Charlecote was at times deserted; nevertheless most of them made some contribution to the house or its surroundings. The Puritan Richard, who was summoned by Cromwell to the 'Barebones Parliament', collected most of the rare books in the library; Captain Thomas Lucy laid out a great formal garden; Colonel George Lucy, a soldier of the Williamite Wars, made a new staircase with a ceiling painted in the manner of Verrio.

A portrait by Kneller of Captain Thomas Lucy.

Meet of the Warwickshire Hounds at Charlecote Park in November 1926, at the invitation of Sir Harry and Lady Fairfax-Lucy.

With a younger George Lucy, who reigned in the middle and later years of the eighteenth century, the male line of the Lucys came to an end. This George, who modernized the house and commissioned Capability Brown to landscape the park, was an elegant valetudinarian bachelor looked after by a housekeeper named Mrs Hayes, to whom he would write almost every day when he was away in London, Bath or Cheltenham. She in turn would send him lists of household wants – finest green tea, powdered loaf sugar, Jordan almonds, Jamaican pepper, pistachio nuts, white paper for lining shelves, French brandy. When she died, the faithful Mrs Hayes left him her small possessions, including her cornelian seal and her 'buff tabby to cover his easy chair'.

George loved entertaining and was in his element as High Sheriff of the county at the time of the Shakespeare Jubilee which David Garrick organized in 1769. A host of fashionable visitors came to Stratford from London, and having heard Garrick discoursing on Shakespeare in the pouring rain and danced in a wooden rotunda on the banks of the Avon, they drove out to Charlecote to see the park gates on which the Bard was said to have hung a rhyme lampooning Sir Thomas Lucy. The deer-stealing legend was naturally embellished for the occasion, and the villagers of Charlecote and Hampton Lucy made a good thing out of selling souvenirs such as snippets of the poet's cloak and fragments of the deer's horns.

Charlecote was bequeathed by George to a cousin, the Reverend John Hammond, who changed his name to Lucy, and was descended through the female line from the younger Sir Thomas. His son, George Hammond Lucy, married a lively Welsh girl, Mary Elizabeth Williams, in 1823. The newly-wed couple arrived at Charlecote after dusk and were greeted by a torchlight procession of tenantry with other dependants standing on the flat roof of the gatehouse holding flambeaux and cheering.

But while Mary Elizabeth fell in love with Charlecote and its Shakespearian associations, she found the house old-fashioned, uncomfortable and dilapidated. She afterwards recalled: 'The Great Hall did indeed look as it might have done in Shakespeare's time, with its old worn paved floor, small panes of glass in its large oriel window, and every window frame creaking and rattling with every gust of wind, and so cold! Oh, so cold! No hot air then as now. No beautiful garden in the Court, only a few large beds with old-fashioned flowers. I soon caused my husband to let me root them all up.' Her husband was in fact even more impatient than she was to get to work on 'the good old house', for he was imbued with the ideas of the Age of Romance and an avid collector of pictures and furniture.

So in the years following their marriage, George Hammond and Mary Elizabeth Lucy not only repaired Charlecote and made it comfortable, but embellished it and greatly enlarged it; so that it lost most of its original character and became to all intents and purposes a large and richly appointed early nineteenth-century mansion in the Elizabethan Revival style. Thus they did not hesitate to remove the screen and minstrels' gallery from the great hall and to replace the flags which Shakespeare may have trodden with a floor of Venetian marble fitted with ornamental grilles to admit the warm air from a boiler in the cellars. To the Lucys and their contemporaries, it seemed that the house had been 'beautified' and sympathetically restored. Sir Walter Scott, who came here in 1828, wrote in his Journal: 'Charlecote is in high preservation. . . . While we were surveying the antlered hall with its painted glass and family pictures, Mr Lucy came to welcome us in person and to show the house. . . . Our early breakfast did not permit out taking advantage of the excellent repast offered by the kindness of Mr and Mrs Lucy, the last a lively Welshwoman. The visit gave me great pleasure; it really brought Justice Shallow freshly before my eyes.'

Mary Elizabeth went on 'beautifying' Charlecote after her husband's death in 1845. It was a severe blow to her when in 1850 the house suffered a burglary – a misfortune more suggestive of our own times than of early-Victorian Warwickshire. Thieves cut a panel out of the garden door while the household was asleep and took all the snuffboxes, miniatures and other bibelots that were displayed on table-tops, including a gold watch given by Charles II to Jane Lane, an ancestress of the family, who helped him to escape after the Battle of Worcester. To make the house more secure in future the garden door was fitted with metal shutters, but in the later years of Mary Elizabeth's long life it was not so much thieves as the depression in farming which constituted a threat to her late husband's treasures. Her son, who was only really interested in his hounds, was obliged to sell some of the pictures in order to keep going. It is said that when an expert came to Charlecote to value them, he had to work early in the morning before Mary Elizabeth was up and could forbid their sale.

During the sixty-odd years leading up to the Second World War a large part of the picture collection was sold, along with most of the estate, and while the old way of life continued at Charlecote until quite recent times – beer was brewed in the house up to the turn of the century – the family eventually decided that the best hope for the future lay with the National Trust. At the handing-over ceremony in 1946 the late Sir Brian Fairfax-Lucy gave the keys of the entrance gate to the Director of the Shakespeare Memorial Theatre, who in turn gave them to the National Trust's Chairman,

Charlecote Park in the eighteenth century: a view attributed to Jan Stevens (d. 1722).

the historian G.M.Trevelyan (*see* WALLINGTON). 'The Muses of Drama and History were thus invoked to preside over the exchange', recalls Sir Brian's wife, Alice, Lady Fairfax-Lucy, herself a representative of the Muses, being a writer and the daughter of novelist John Buchan. To Shakespeare, Scott and Buchan one can add, in the list of Charlecote's literary associations, Henry James, who wrote in *Portraits of Places* of 'Charlecote Park, whose venerable verdure seems a survival from an earlier England, and whose innumerable acres, stretching away, in the early evening, to vaguely seen Tudor walls, lie there like the backward years receding to the age of Elizabeth.'

Architecture and Contents

A turreted Elizabethan mansion of rose-red brick built by Sir Thomas Lucy, approached through an enchanting gatehouse also with turrets and cupolas. Modernized in the eighteenth century by George Lucy and greatly enlarged and altered in the reign of William IV and the early Victorian period by George Hammond Lucy and his wife, who gave the house rich interiors of the period to the design of Thomas Willement. They also acquired much of the present furniture, some of it from the collection of William Beckford (*see* POWDERHAM CASTLE). The dining-room contains the celebrated 'Charlecote Buffet', a vast and highly ornate oak sideboard carved in 1858 by J.M. Willcox and offered as a gift to Queen Victoria who refused it. Charlecote, though administered by the National Trust, is still the home of Sir Edmund Fairfax-Lucy.

CHATSWORTH
DERBYSHIRE

THAT the Tudor royal favourite Sir William Cavendish should have forsaken his native Suffolk and begun building himself a mansion on lands which he had bought in the wilds of Derbyshire is a sign of how much he was ruled by his third wife, the Derbyshire heiress Bess of Hardwick. Bess completed the house, which was the original Chatsworth, after his death in 1557, and a few years later she had as her guest here the captive Mary Queen of Scots, who was in the custody of her new husband the Earl of Shrewsbury. Bess of Hardwick's Chatsworth was transformed into the present baroque palace by her descendant William Cavendish, 4th Earl of Devonshire, who as one of the peers most instrumental in putting William and Mary on the throne was rewarded by them with a dukedom. As well as transforming the house, the 1st Duke of Devonshire laid out the tremendous water gardens, which were admired by Celia Fiennes when she came here in 1697. She was particularly impressed by 'a fine grottoe all stone pavement roofe and sides, that is designed to supply all the house with water besides severall fancyes to make diversion.' Inside was a 'batheing room' with a marble bath. 'You went down steps into the bath big enough for two people; at the upper end are two Cocks to let in one hott the other cold water to attemper it as persons please; the windows are all private glass.'

The eighteenth-century Dukes and their Duchesses lived mostly at Devonshire House in London. Chatsworth was, however, fully maintained, and the 4th Duke, who was briefly Prime Minister and added greatly to the family possessions by marrying the heiress of the Earls of Burlington and Cork, employed James Paine to build monumental stables and Capability Brown to landscape the park. This work was in full swing in 1760 when Horace Walpole came to stay. He reported in a letter to a friend that, despite gout in both feet, he was 'running about with the children and climbing hills'. He remarked on how the windows of the house had gilded glazing bars, and how the Duke, when in residence, received his county neighbours on 'two public days in a week' and made it a rule 'to return no visits in the County'.

Walpole stayed at Chatsworth in August, when the climate of the Derbyshire Peaks would have been at its least rigorous. The 5th Duke and his Duchess, the beautiful Georgiana Spencer (*see* ALTHORP), took to coming here in the coldest months of the year, just as their descendants did in the early part of this century. Instead of making the most of the few short hours of daylight, they had their private rooms in the north-west corner of the house. The room in which they generally sat was high and narrow with one window facing west and 'the door opening to the cold windy passage', as their son afterwards recalled. But while they appear to have put up with

Chatsworth : the west front, which was probably designed by Thomas Archer in 1700.

considerable discomfort, the life here in their time was anything but austere. To supply the house, an average of five bullocks were killed every fortnight and three times that number of sheep every week. There were sometimes as many as 180 people sleeping under the hospitable Chatsworth roof, what with servants, family and guests – the latter often so numerous that Paine's vast stables could not accommodate all their horses, the overflow being stabled at the local inn. Among the celebrities of the times who stayed here were Fox, Burke and Sheridan. Dr Johnson came to Chatsworth in 1784, the last year of his life, when the Duke and Duchess were here on a summer visit; he dined and then sat and talked in the shade of a row of limes afterwards called Dr Johnson's Walk. He was pressed to stay, but refused, saying: 'A sick man is not a fit inmate of a great house.'

A livelier guest was the politician and wit James Hare, who wrote satirically of how the ladies at Chatsworth would 'rise from one o'clock to two' and retire for the night 'as the Housemaids begin to twirl their mops and open the shutters to the sunshine'. Hare also poked fun at the baby-talk which the ladies affected and the way in which they passed their time: they would write innumerable letters and then go out walking in the dark and snow, wearing muslin and thin sandals and bearing 'a long pole with a spike on the end of it to throw over their shoulders or stick into any Gentleman's foot who has the honour of accompanying them.' When dinner was announced, they would pay no heed, and after the food had been spoiling for half an hour they would go off to their rooms to change. While one would be inclined to doubt whether the charmed circle of relations of Duchess Georgiana – the 'Devonshire House set' – could really have been as futile as Hare makes them out to have been, there is little doubt that the morals of some of them were on the easy side. In the nurseries of Chatsworth, along with the other children were the illegitimate offspring of various members of the cousinhood, while the Duke and Duchess formed a *ménage à trois* with Lady Elizabeth Foster, who was the Duchess's best friend as well as being the Duke's mistress.

Duchess Georgiana and her husband more than made up for their shortcomings by being the parents of the Bachelor Duke, one of the most attractive of the Devonshires, a scholar and connoisseur who was a charming mixture of grandeur and humility, melancholy and humour. Since he was also handsome, generous, sociable and enormously rich, it is a mystery why he never married; some said that he was so much in love with George IV's daughter Princess Charlotte that he never wished to marry anybody else. Much of the devotion which he might have shown as a husband and father he lavished on Chatsworth. During the course of his reign, which lasted from 1811 to 1858, he greatly enlarged the house, embellishing it and bringing it into line with early nineteenth-century standards of comfort, while showing a praiseworthy regard for its original character. He also improved its surroundings, repairing much of the damage done by Capability Brown to the 1st Duke's formal layout. To help him with his scheme he had Sir Joseph Paxton, whose genius he recognized after taking him into his service as a gardener. With the Duke's encouragement, Paxton rose in the world, and having adorned the Chatsworth gardens with a conservatory of unprecedented size, went on to design the Crystal Palace.

The Bachelor Duke's love of Chatsworth can be seen in the account of the house which he wrote in the form of a letter to his sister. In it, he reminds her of some of the more remarkable characters employed there in the days of their youth, such as the ladies' maid Mrs Bunting, who was 'passionately fond of horsemanship and a hard rider ... one day she was brought in after a tremendous fall, with her features scarcely to be distinguished and gashes across her face and throat; and I am sure you must remember her exclamation, when she was again able to speak, addressed to you, an unwilling equestrian – "Oh, ma'am, what an encouragement this must be to your Ladyship!"' Then there was M.Caille the confectioner, who when a wooden staircase caught fire 'aggravated the evil when he saw fire through the chinks of the floor under his feet, by pouring into them the contents of the kettle he was carrying, which undoubtedly fed the flame, being melted sugar.' Presumably it was on this occasion that the 5th Duke, as his son tells us, having been awakened with the news that the house was on fire, 'turned round to sleep on his other side, observing that they had better try to put it out.' The Duke sometimes stayed in bed until four in the afternoon.

No less somnolent was the 8th Duke, who as Marquess of Hartington led the Liberal Party from 1875 to 1886 and on three occasions was offered and refused the Premiership; he is said to have admitted to falling asleep in the middle of one of his own speeches in Parliament. He was also notoriously indifferent to his possessions. When an American lady went into raptures over the beauties of Chatsworth, he murmured 'Rummy old place.' When Lord Salisbury (*see* HATFIELD HOUSE), spending a happy afternoon looking at the books in the Chatsworth library, asked his host, who was drowsily ensconced by the fire, how one got up to the gallery which runs round the upper part of the bookshelves, the Duke replied after some thought: 'I'm damned if I know!' Having been single for most of his life, the 8th Duke, when he was nearly sixty, married the widowed German-born Duchess of Manchester, his mistress of long standing, who consequently became known as the Double Duchess. She entertained at Chatsworth on a lavish scale, but the young Raymond Asquith, who was a member of a house party which she gave for Edward VII in 1906, was not impressed. 'How you would loathe this place', he wrote to his fiancée. 'It crushes one by its size and is full of smart shrivelled-up people. There is only one bathroom and that is kept for the King.'

Two years later the 8th Duke was succeeded by a nephew and for the first time since the days of the 5th Duke and Duchess Georgiana there was a Duke and Duchess at Chatsworth with a family of young children. Those of them who had not yet gone to school were taught by a French Mademoiselle and a German Fräulein; the young Cavendishes found that by bringing up the subject of Alsace–Lorraine, they could set these two ladies at each other in a bitter and interminable Franco-German argument which effectively put an end to the morning's lessons. During those years before the outbreak of the First World War, the house was restored and modernized and various alterations were carried out. The war sounded the death-knell of Paxton's Great Conservatory, of which the Bachelor Duke had been so justly proud with the shortage of coal it could no longer be heated, so that all the tropical plants died and, instead of being restocked after the war, it was blown up.

Georgiana, Duchess of Devonshire, and her daughter, painted by Reynolds.

The Bachelor Duke towards the end of his life, sitting with his cousins, great-nephews and great-niece, flanked by a banana tree and some of the other exotic plants grown for him by Paxton. His cousin the Earl of Burlington, who was also his nephew by marriage and who succeeded him as the 7th Duke of Devonshire, sits in the basket chair to the right, and Lord Burlington's sister-in-law, Lady Louisa Cavendish, on the left. Lady Louisa's husband, George Cavendish MP, stands behind the Duke, between Lord Burlington's eldest son, Lord Cavendish, who eventually became the 8th Duke, and his two younger sons, Frederick and Edward. Standing with her hand on her father's shoulder is Lord Burlington's daughter Louisa, afterwards Lady Louisa Egerton.

The loss of the Great Conservatory, though perhaps the most obvious, was only one of many post-war changes at Chatsworth. Yet the life of the house went on much the same as ever during the 1920s and '30s, as Harold Macmillan, who married the 9th Duke's daughter Lady Dorothy, tells us in his memoirs. Every year there was a Christmas house party of which the numbers grew steadily as the children of the Duke and Duchess married and had children of their own. Not only did the daughters and sons-in-law bring children, nannies and nursemaids as well as valets and ladies' maids, they also brought ponies and grooms. This meant an influx of anything up to sixty people, in addition to which there were cousins and other guests, including one or two ancient cronies of the Duke who were invited to spend Christmas at Chatsworth every year as a matter of course. The Duke, in Harold Macmillan's words, 'treated them with more than his usual taciturnity. "Hello Jim", "Hello Walter" he would say when they arrived and "Goodbye Jim", "Goodbye Walter" when they left. So far as I know, no other conversation passed between them.'

During the Second World War, the house was taken over by a girls' school. The 10th Duke and his Duchess – who was a Cecil (*see* HATFIELD HOUSE) – did not return here after the school moved out, and it seemed even more unlikely that Chatsworth would ever again be a family home after the Duke's sudden death in 1950 left his son, the present Duke, with several million pounds to pay in death duties. But while much of the present Duke's inheritance had to go in order to clear this crushing burden, he managed to keep Chatsworth, and in 1959 he and the Duchess and their children came to live here. The house, splendidly done up under the Duchess's supervision, became a family home in a way that it had never really been in the past, when the Dukes of Devonshire had possessed so many great houses that they could only spend part of the year in each.

Architecture and Contents

A Tudor mansion extending round four sides of a court, rebuilt between 1686 and 1707 as a baroque palace with façades of golden stone. The south and east fronts, which are adorned with fluted Ionic pilasters, are by William Talman. The west front, which has a pediment carried on engaged Ionic columns, and the bowed Corinthian north front, are probably by Thomas Archer, assisted by his patron the 1st Duke of Devonshire. The painters Laguerre, Ricard, Verrio and Thornhill and the carvers Samuel Watson, Joel Lobb and William Davis were employed to give the house a splendid interior of painted ceilings and carved and inlaid woodwork, of which a great deal remains more or less unchanged, notably the painted hall, the chapel and the succession of state rooms on the second floor. Various alterations were made to the house and its surroundings later in the eighteenth century, and between 1822 and 1832 the Bachelor Duke built a vast new wing in a restrained classical style running northwards and ending with a belvedere tower. The architect of this addition was Sir Jeffry Wyatville, whose work at Chatsworth also included converting the 1st Duke's gallery on the first floor into a library and redecorating the first-floor reception rooms in the style of the period, with gilded ornament and brocade-hung walls. There are interiors by Wyatville on a grander scale in the north wing, notably the great dining-room, the sculpture gallery and the theatre.

The treasures of Chatsworth include pictures by Veronese, Murillo, Rembrandt, Van Goyen, Frans Hals, Gaspard Poussin, Sebastiano Ricci, Luca Giordano and Landseer, together with portraits by Van Dyck, Lely, Wissing, Kneller, Zoffany, Reynolds, Millais, Watts, Sargent, de Laszlo and Lucien Freud. In the sculpture gallery, among other acquisitions of the Bachelor Duke, are works by Canova and Thorvaldsen. There are Mortlake tapestries in the state drawing-room and elsewhere; there is a collection of antiquities and a wealth of fine furniture, some of it by William Kent, and Sèvres, Meissen and Oriental porcelain.

Chatsworth is spectacularly situated, backed by a steep wooded hill and facing across the River Derwent towards a park laid out by Capability Brown. On three sides of the house there are formal gardens in the grand manner, with terraces, fountains, a long canal, a cascade and a maze.

Spy cartoon of the 8th Duke of Devonshire.

COUGHTON COURT
WARWICKSHIRE

Coughton Court from the west.

COUGHTON, seat of the Throckmorton family, rivals STONOR and BADDESLEY CLINTON as the typical recusant house, with priests' hiding-places and a room in the tall early Tudor gatehouse tower where the wives of the Gunpowder conspirators awaited the outcome. Thomas Throckmorton, the then squire, was related to the chief instigator, Robert Catesby, whose servant rode up to Coughton on that fateful night with news that the conspiracy had failed. Throckmorton himself was, however, abroad at the time so the family were not directly implicated in the Plot. When asked if they had been, a present-day Throckmorton replied laconically, 'No, we had a plot of our own.' He alluded, of course, to the Throckmorton Plot of 1583, named after Thomas Throckmorton's cousin Francis who was an inter-mediary between Mary Queen of Scots and the Spanish Ambassador.

Francis Throckmorton was not the only member of the family to have dealings with the ill-fated Scottish Queen. His and Thomas's Protestant uncle, Sir Nicholas Throckmorton, father-in-law of Sir Walter Raleigh, was Queen Elizabeth's Ambassador to her in France and later in Scotland. Thomas Throckmorton is himself believed to have been involved in the conspiracy which cost Mary Stuart her life, the Babington Plot. Whether or not he was guilty of treason, he certainly suffered for being a Catholic, and was frequently imprisoned and obliged to pay heavy recusancy fines. The family fortunes, which his ancestors had steadily built up since the time of Sir John Throckmorton (who was Under-Treasurer of England in the reign of Henry VI and acquired Coughton by marrying an heiress) had by the end of Elizabeth's reign reached a low ebb. Nevertheless, Thomas and his descendants managed to hold on to at any rate part of their ancestral lands, and Mass continued to be said at Coughton, often in secret. Thomas's grandson Robert was prosperous enough to keep racehorses, thereby incurring the disapproval of his mother, who told him: 'All the contry talketh of it, that Papists hath so much monis that theye run it awaye.'

The racehorse-owning Robert was given a baronetcy in 1642, just after the outbreak of the Civil War in which he was to be a considerable sufferer. Towards the end of 1643, Coughton was occupied by the Roundheads. Royalist troops came from Worcester to dislodge them, but left without doing anything, though there is a legend that they bombarded the house and that the garrison hung out bedding as a form of protection (doubtless quilts and mattresses would have had much the same effect as sandbags). When the Royalists advanced in the following year the Roundheads abandoned the house, having looted it and set it on fire. It was repaired, at considerable expense, after the Restoration by Sir Francis Throckmorton, 2nd Baronet,

*Sir Robert Throckmorton, 4th Baronet,
by Nicolas de Largillière.*

only to suffer further damage during the Revolution of 1688 when a Protestant mob came out from the nearby town of Alcester and wrecked the chapel which Sir Francis's son, another Sir Robert, had made in the eastern range of the courtyard opposite the gatehouse tower.

This younger Sir Robert made the first of two advantageous marriages which were to bring estates in Berkshire, Worcestershire and Devon to the Throckmortons, restoring them to something like their pre-Reformation prosperity. The 4th Baronet, yet another Sir Robert, whose life spanned almost the entire eighteenth century, built a fine new house at Buckland on his Berkshire estate; he also, towards the end of his life, remodelled the west front of Coughton, giving the wings on either side of the gatehouse tower their Georgian Gothic character. As a young man he must have been a considerable swell, judging from his portrait by the French court painter Largillière, who painted no fewer than five members of the family, including his nun sister, Elizabeth. He made a grand though in this case not particularly lucrative marriage to a daughter of the Jacobite 2nd Marquess of Powis, who is portrayed with her sisters in classical dress in one of the painted ceilings at POWIS CASTLE.

Sir Robert's grandson, Sir John, who succeeded him in 1791, opened the east side of the courtyard at Coughton by clearing away what was left of the chapel which had been wrecked by the mob a century earlier, and made a new chapel for the Catholics of the neighbourhood in the southern range with a tribune for the family at first-floor level. His wife Maria was a friend of the poet Cowper, who wrote to her affectionately, before her husband succeeded to the baronetcy, as 'my dear Mrs Frog'; he also wrote verses 'On the death of Mrs Throckmorton's Bulfinch'. Maria Throckmorton had no children so her husband was followed in succession by his two childless brothers. The younger of them, Sir Charles (who, like a number of younger sons of recusant families in the days when the services and other careers were closed to Catholics, was a qualified Doctor of Medicine) handed over Buckland to his nephew after he succeeded and made his home at Coughton. His move, in the early summer of 1827, accompanied by a housekeeper, a cook, an under-butler, a laundry-maid, an under-housemaid and a kitchen-maid, is recounted in his diary:

Left Buckland for Coughton ... arrived within a mile of Alcester abt halfpast 3 p.m. when I was met by most of my Tenants and many of the Tradesmen in Alcester with white scarfs & decorated with Laurel leaves, & all mounted on horseback; they attended me all the way to Coughton through Alcester where they stopped & hurra'd me on coming to the bounds of the Manor, they took the horse off & drew me to the house: over the 1st gate entering the Lawn was inscribed 'May happiness enter with you' & a little further on an Arch decorated with flowers, over which inscribed 'Proceed and prosper' & over the Tower a large flag with 'Long live Sr Charles'.

Eleven years later, to celebrate Queen Victoria's coronation, the eighty-year-old Sir Charles stood in front of the house handing out medals and oranges to the children of the neighbourhood.

In the second half of the last century, the situation was reversed: Coughton was let and Sir William, the 9th Baronet – whose sister Mary spent some years at the Austrian Court in charge of the youngest daughter of the Emperor Franz Joseph and the Empress Elizabeth – lived at Buckland. After

A group at Coughton Court in the 1870s.

selling Buckland in 1908 Sir William came back to Coughton, making a large reception room out of the former chapel which was no longer used as such since his father had built a Catholic church in the grounds. The house was considerably modernized in Sir William's time: even the family ghost, the Pink Lady, was got rid of, though this was done without his consent by the over-pious wife of his land agent, who officiously brought in a priest to exorcise her while he was away. When Sir William returned and heard that he had been done out of his ghost he was furious and never spoke to the agent's wife again.

There was soon to be a supernatural occurrence of a different sort at Coughton. In 1916, on the day that Colonel Courtenay Throckmorton, Sir William's nephew and heir, was killed in action in Mesopotamia, the family arms fell from the gatehouse tower. Colonel Throckmorton and his wife and children had lived at Coughton with Sir William, who was a bachelor, and his widow stayed on as chatelaine after Sir William's death in 1919, her son, the present Baronet, being then a boy of eleven. During those years between the two world wars, Coughton was run very much in the old manner. Milk was brought to the house by a man with two pails hanging from a wooden bar over his shoulder. Meals had to be carried across the courtyard from the kitchen, which was in the northern range, to the dining-room on the first floor of the range opposite; in wet weather they had to go round all three sides of the house. Yet the present Baronet's sister cannot remember a single occasion when the food was cold. The servants' food, except for that of the cook, made almost as long a journey, for the servants' hall was also in the southern range on the ground floor. The cook, who acted as housekeeper, ate in the housekeeper's room near the kitchen. The butler, the lady's maid and the senior laundry-maid had the privilege of eating their pudding with her in the housekeeper's room; so having eaten their main course in the servants' hall along with the footman, the three housemaids, two kitchen-maids, the junior laundry-maid and the boy, they helped themselves to the pudding, which had already been brought across the courtyard from the kitchen to the servants' hall, and then proceeded to carry their plates back across the courtyard in order to finish their meal in more select company.

Architecture and Contents

A flamboyant gatehouse tower built in about 1509, with a two-tiered oriel above its archway, dominates both aspects of Coughton – the entrance front, where the wings on either side were refaced in Georgian Gothic in the 1780s, and the open courtyard at the back, where the ranges to the north and south still display their original sixteenth-century timbering. The house contains many family portraits, two of them by Nicolas de Largillière; other treasures include Jacobite relics and the chemise worn by Mary Queen of Scots at her execution. Sir Robert Throckmorton, the present Baronet, gave Coughton to the National Trust in 1945, though it has been leased back to him and his heirs. He and Lady Isabel Throckmorton still occupy about half of the house.

DUNHAM MASSEY
CHESHIRE

THE family of Booth, which produced an Archibishop of York and a Bishop of Exeter in the fifteenth century and two Mayors of Chester in the reign of Elizabeth I, inherited Dunham Massey in 1453 through marrying into a family descended in the female line from the Masseys, to whom it was granted soon after the Conquest. The medieval manor house here was rebuilt by the second of the two Elizabethan mayors, Sir George Booth, who lived until 1652. Though he was in his seventies when the Civil War broke out, he sided with Parliament; a Puritan pamphleteer wrote of him as 'free, grave, godley, brave Booth, the flower of Cheshire'. He was succeeded by his grandson and namesake, who enlarged the house and threw together two rooms adjoining the great hall to make a chapel. Here his chaplain, who also taught the children mathematics, conducted 'family duty' twice daily in accordance with his Presbyterian leanings, being paid an annual salary that started at £40 but eventually dwindled to £15.

The younger Sir George Booth was, like his grandfather, a Roundhead, but in 1659 he attempted to raise Cheshire and South Lancashire for Charles II. The rising failed and landed him in the Tower of London from which he was released shortly before the Restoration. Charles rewarded him with a peerage and he became Lord Delamer, but by the time of his death in 1684 he was out of favour with the Court as being one of those extreme Protestants who planned to make the King's illegitimate son, the Duke of Monmouth, his successor in place of his brother and rightful heir, the Catholic James, Duke of York.

Monmouth was entertained at Dunham Massey in 1682, and held court here, presumably in the great hall. 'The rabble' were 'suffered not only to gaze into the room, but to come in and view the Duke', and pieces of blue ribbon were handed out to them to wear as a sign of their allegiance to him. Lord Delamer's great-niece Katherine Booth sat at the Duke's feet to 'tell him who everybody was'. 'Many things he asked me', she recorded in her diary, 'and when he danced he made me dance with him (tho' I had never learnt).' The family's dealings with Monmouth made Lord Delamer's son Henry a suspect at the time of the Rye House Plot in 1683, and in 1686, after James's accession to the throne and Monmouth's rebellion and execution, the 2nd Lord Delamer (as he had now become), was tried by his fellow peers for high treason. He was acquitted, and two years later marched with 500 men in support of William of Orange, who in 1690 made him Earl of Warrington.

When, in 1698, Celia Fiennes, a distant cousin of the family, came to Dunham Massey and wrote of 'its old fashion building which appears more

'Good Will', 9th Earl of Stamford, at Dunham Massey early this century, with his wife and their two children, Roger, Lord Grey of Groby, afterwards 10th and last Earl of Stamford, and Jane, now Lady Jane Turnbull.

Dunham Massey : a bird's eye view of the house and park by John Harris the Younger, c. 1751.

in the inside and the furniture, old but good gardens walled in', the 2nd Earl of Warrington had inherited. He was to live until 1758, 'the stiffest of all stiff things', as a contemporary called him; his wife, the daughter of a London merchant, was described as 'a limber dirty fool'. The two of them 'quarrell'd and lived in the same house as absolute strangers to each other at bed and board', causing Lord Warrington to publish a pamphlet advocating divorce for incompatability of temper, even though his wife had brought him £40,000 which repaired the somewhat depleted family fortunes. His wife's money also enabled him to remodel the house at Dunham, which, when he inherited it, was in his own words 'so decayed . . . it could not have lasted safe another generation'.

The house as transformed did not impress the diarist John Byng, afterwards Lord Torrington, who visited Dunham Massey in 1790. 'The park is very verdant' he wrote, 'and every kind of tree grows to a wonderful stature. But judge of my astonishment, when fancying and hoping that I was to see an old magnificent mansion ... I approach'd a modern, red brick, tasteless house, which I had not a wish to enter.' Instead, Byng sat at a 'most sequester'd spot' in the park, and listened to the cries of the herons – than which, in his opinion, 'nothing cou'd be more transcendently gloomy or gratifying'.

At the time of Byng's visit Dunham was owned by George Grey, 5th Earl of Stamford, a grandson, through his mother, of the 2nd Earl of Warrington, whose titles had died with him. The Greys were a much more illustrious family than the Booths, descended from a brother of Henry Grey, Duke of Suffolk, whose daughter was the ill-fated Lady Jane Grey. Like the Booths, they had been Roundheads at the time of the Civil War: Lord Grey of Groby, the son of the 1st Earl of Stamford, was actually a regicide, but fortunately for the family he died before the Restoration and also before his father. Until the death of the 7th Earl in 1883, the Stamfords possessed seats in Staffordshire and Leicestershire as well as Dunham, which became only an occasional residence of the family, and was eventually let. The 7th Earl was well known as a cricketer, a racehorse owner and a Master of Foxhounds. As an undergraduate at Cambridge he fell in love with the daughter of the Trinity College bootman and married her. She died after a few years and he married as his second wife a beautiful and fascinating circus rider whose father was a farm labourer and whose mother was a gipsy. The 7th Earl's cousin and successor chose an even more exotic lady as his third wife: a Hottentot, who had presented him with a son before he married her. By the law of his native South Africa, this son was legitimate, and after his father's death in 1890 he claimed the earldom. However, the House of Lords upheld the claim of the 8th Earl's nephew, William Grey, a teacher in Barbados, who after his succession as the 9th Earl supported so many charities that he became known affectionately as 'Good Will'. From 1905 he made his home at Dunham Massey, which he restored and redecorated, having not inherited the Staffordshire and Leicestershire estates. His bachelor son, the 10th and last Earl of Stamford, devoted his life to preserving the house, bringing back furniture and pictures which had gone to the other family seats and been dispersed. During his later years, he lived in only a very few rooms, the rest being shut up, their curtains and hangings carefully labelled and put away. By the time of his death in 1976 he had become something of a recluse, and Dunham Massey, though separated only by its park from the outskirts of Manchester, was one of the least known of England's great country houses.

Architecture and Contents

A moated medieval manor house rebuilt in the late sixteenth and early seventeenth centuries by Sir George Booth, whose grandson added a fourth side to enclose a courtyard. In the 1730s the 2nd Earl of Warrington remodelled the house; he did not change its Tudor and Jacobean plan, so that it kept its courtyard and its great hall, but he gave it an early Georgian character, plain red brick outside and fielded panelling within. He also gave the house its splendid collection of furniture and silver – the latter mostly by Huguenot smiths, whom he may have patronized on account of the extreme Protestantism of his family – and he was responsible for elaborate formal planting in the park. The 9th Earl of Stamford, who came to live at Dunham Massey in 1905, gave the south front an elaborate centre-piece of stone and dormer windows, his architect being Compton Hall. At the same time he commissioned Percy Macquoid to redecorate and rearrange the interior of the house. Of the rooms thus transformed in the Edwardian period, the most important are the great hall and the Green Saloon, where Macquoid's use of colour is particularly successful. Dunham Massey was bequeathed to the National Trust by the 10th and last Earl of Stamford.

The 2nd Lord Somers – afterwards 1st Earl Somers – in his robes, by John Harrison, Jr., 1816.

I N 1784 Charles Cocks, whose family had been Herefordshire landowners since about 1600, was raised to the peerage as Lord Somers, his title commemorating his descent from a sister of the great lawyer Somers, Lord Chancellor under William III. Despite his elevation, he made do with his old and rambling ancestral home in the Malvern Hills; but his son, whose splendidly theatrical full-length portrait in robes shows him to have been everyone's idea of a lord of the Regency period, wanted something very much

Eastnor Castle, built by Robert Smirke in the early nineteenth century for the 2nd Lord Somers.

grander, and so in 1811 he commissioned Robert Smirke to design him a castle. The result was Eastnor, one of the most spectacular castles of the Norman Revival: a building on a cyclopean scale which even before its walls had reached full height became one of the sights of Herefordshire, which people flocked to see from miles around. In 1813 the Irish novelist Maria Edgeworth paid it a visit and was greatly impressed; she also enjoyed the 'fine strawberries' with which she was regaled by Lord and Lady Somers at the old house, where they were still living. The 11th Duke of Norfolk, himself an experienced castle builder since he had just about completed his remodelling of ARUNDEL, was more critical. He declared that the timber bracing which Smirke had introduced into the walls would rot, not realizing that this was only temporary and would be removed after the mortar had set; it was made necessary by Somers' haste, enabling the walls to go up more quickly than would otherwise have been possible.

Soon afterwards, the work suffered a set-back when Lady Somers suddenly decided that the kitchen would be too far from the dining-room, which meant that the plan had to be altered. Then it was decided to concentrate on finishing the west wing so as to enable the family to move in here by the end of 1813. This was done and the old house demolished, but from now on progress on the main part of the building slowed down. It seems that Lord Somers, having what was in effect a spacious house by normal standards in the wing (which is where his collateral descendants live today) lost interest in the rest of his great project. There was also the inevitable shortage of money, though in the event the cost did not exceed Smirke's original estimate of £82,000 exclusive of the interior decoration. The castle was eventually finished in time for Somers' promotion to an earldom in 1821, but the vast rooms in the main part of the building were left rather bare.

The young Elizabeth Barrett, afterwards Elizabeth Barrett Browning, who came over to Eastnor in 1831 from her home, Hope End, a couple of miles away, to stay with the 1st Earl Somers and his daughter, Lady Margaret Cocks, did not enjoy herself. 'I won't stay a day longer than Monday morning', she wrote, 'and late enough – by the presiding Goddess of Ennui.' Lady Margaret, who had literary ambitions, was rather stiff: 'I dread her like a thunderstorm', Elizabeth wrote on another occasion, when expecting a visit from her in Wimpole Street. Lord Somers, now a widower, was very deaf: a fellow guest prophesied that he would marry again, to which Elizabeth observed, 'If he does, he should marry some great great great great ditto ditto ditto ditto granddaughter of Stentor.' She was, however, quite pleased when he admired the way her hair was done.

If Elizabeth Barrett Browning had lived to see Eastnor after its interior had been enriched by the 2nd and 3rd Earls she might have been more enthusiastic. The 2nd Earl commissioned Pugin to decorate the drawing-room in his most gorgeous House of Lords Gothic. The 3rd Earl adorned the great hall with a stupendous collection of armour and Moorish–Gothic frescoes by George E. Fox, who when he was working in the castle lived in one of the corner towers which the servants nicknamed 'the fox's den'. Fox was also responsible for the rich Renaissance-Revival decoration in the libraries. This was probably carried out under the influence of G. F. Watts, who became a close friend of the 3rd Earl and his wife, one of the five

The Gothic drawing-room with plasterwork by Francis Bernasconi and painted decorations designed by Pugin.

beautiful daughters of the wealthy Bengal civilian James Pattle, whose corpse made a macabre shipboard appearance when the spirit-filled barrel in which it was being conveyed back to England from India broke open during a storm.

With the death of the 3rd Earl in 1883 the earldom became extinct. Eastnor was inherited by his elder daughter, Lady Henry Somerset (*see* BADMINTON), while the Somers barony passed to a cousin. Lady Henry was as beautiful as her mother, whose portrait by Watts hangs near hers in the staircase hall. Like her younger sister (*see* WOBURN ABBEY) she had an unhappy marriage: she left her husband on the grounds that he was a homosexual, which condemned him to a life of exile abroad and caused her also to be ostracized by society, for Victorian ladies were not supposed to know about 'unnatural' behaviour, let alone accuse their husbands of it. Having thus been obliged to retire from the world in which she had grown up, she devoted her life to good works, particularly to campaigning for temperance, which she did all over England and in America. She took the pledge publicly in the hall at Eastnor among her assembled tenants and dependants, having enjoyed two last glasses of port in the refreshment room at Worcester station on her way down from London. She did not regard drink as evil in itself, astonishing the novelist E.F.Benson, when he was about to go and stay with her, by sending him a telegram which said: 'Please bring a bottle of whisky.' As she afterwards explained to him, her principles forbade her from providing her guests with alcohol, but her sense of hospitality revolted at the idea of forcing abstinence on them.

Lady Henry Somerset also did much to help the poor of Somers Town, St Pancras, the family's London estate. To raise money for her charities, she opened Eastnor to the public, producing a guide-book to the castle in which she wrote: 'My greatest desire is that a day spent at Eastnor may be a happy memory to tired and hard working men and women, and that they may retain some recollections of its peace and beauty in the midst of their toiling lives.' On her death in 1921, Eastnor passed to the present owner's father, the 6th Lord Somers, who was Governor of Victoria and Acting Governor-General of Australia and succeeded Baden-Powell as Chief Scout of the Commonwealth.

Architecture and Contents

A tremendous Norman-Revival castle by Robert Smirke, consisting of a symmetrical main block with corner towers, approached through a battlemented gateway and entered under a *porte-cochère*, with a wing containing the family rooms to the west. The great hall, sixty feet high, its walls closely hung with arms and armour and with an equestrian figure in full panoply as its centre-piece, constitutes a breathtaking prelude to the other great rooms: the drawing-room designed by Pugin and carried out by Francis Bernasconi and the firm of John Crace, with its painted and gilded vaulting, its vast metal chandelier and its Gobelin tapestries; the sumptuous Renaissance-Revival library by George E.Fox, with its inlaid walnut bookcases and its Flemish tapestries woven by order of Catherine de' Medici; the dining-room, one of the few interiors by Smirke, with its array of family portraits. The portraits at Eastnor include works by Romney and G.F.Watts, who is also represented by a series of allegorical paintings. A *Last Supper* by Bassano hangs in the state bedroom. Some of the furniture at Eastnor came from Italian palaces.

ELTON HALL
CAMBRIDGESHIRE

The drawing room at Elton.

THE highly picturesque assortment of nineteenth-century castellated architecture combined with staid mid-Victorian Charles II Revival which is Elton today also incorporates the early Tudor gatehouse and chapel of the Sapcotes, whose house was acquired in the seventeenth century by the Probys. Sir Peter Proby, a successful civil servant under Secretary Walsingham and the Cecils (*see* BURGHLEY HOUSE; HATFIELD HOUSE) founded the family fortunes towards the end of Elizabeth I's reign; he subsequently became Lord Mayor of London. Sir Thomas Proby was made a baronet in 1662, but the title died with him. In the following century, however, John Proby of Elton was raised to the peerage of Ireland as Lord Carysfort. The Irish place-name commemorated his marriage to the heiress of large Irish estates; subsequent Probys were to spend much of their time in Ireland, though Elton continued to be their principal seat. The 1st Lord Carysfort was a Lord of the Admiralty for two periods between 1757 and 1762, which was probably when Cape Carysfort, near Port Stanley in the Falkland Islands, received its name. In 1767 he retired from politics, being in dire financial straits. A letter written in that year by the wife of the MP for Huntingdon tells of his plight. 'The furniture at Elton was sold yesterday, it was first seized by a butcher at London for a debt of only £219, but his credit has been so bad for a long time that the butcher in the country would not trust him for a joint of meat, nor bakers for a loaf of bread. All this has been brought upon him by an enormous expense in kept women.'

The family fortunes recovered in the time of his son, who became Earl of Carysfort in 1789 and between 1780 and 1815 enlarged and castellated the house. A man of wide culture, he built up a splendid collection of pictures and added to the series of family portraits by Reynolds which his father had started, Sir Joshua being a friend of his. Another of his friends was the Younger Pitt, who in 1800 sent him on an embassy to the King of Prussia. A year later he went on a mission to the Russian Court, where he had many contacts. Pitt was a cousin to his second wife, Elizabeth Grenville, whose father and brother were also Prime Ministers. She appears to have been a lady of resource. The local parson once arrived at an impossibly early hour when invited to dinner by her husband, who in order to show that it was not dinner time asked him if he would like some refreshment. 'A glass of bitters' was the answer. Lord Carysfort ordered the drink, not knowing what it was; the footman was equally puzzled and asked Lady Carysfort, who also had no idea what bitters were. However, she went to her medicine chest and mixed a potion which she gave to the footman to take to the parson, who, swallowing it, told his host that it was excellent bitters.

The castellated exterior of Elton Hall.

The 1st Earl was followed in succession by two of his sons, one of them a General and the other an Admiral. Both served with distinction throughout the Napoleonic Wars: the Admiral, as a midshipman, was in Nelson's flagship at the Battle of the Nile and was sent in an unsuccessful bid to rescue 'the boy . . . on the burning deck' of the French ship *L'Orient* immortalized in the poem. The General, who when young was involved in an amorous escapade in which he lost his 'small clothes' – as recorded by the notorious demi-mondaine Harriet Wilson – suffered a severe head wound in 1813 as a result of which he was unable to manage his own business affairs after he succeeded as 2nd Earl in 1828. His properties were therefore administered by trustees and his reign was a period of financial stringency. Much of his father's picture collection was sold and Elton was allowed to get into a very poor state. Lady Charlotte Guest, who came here in 1840, described the great drawing-room which had been formed in the previous century in the upper part of the old chapel as 'one of the most desolate places I have ever seen'. The Admiral, who became 3rd Earl in 1855, restored the house, carrying out various additions and alterations.

Of the Admiral's sons, the eldest did not survive him and the second, who became Earl of Carysfort in 1868, died four years later as the result of a coaching accident in Hyde Park, driving four-in-hand having been his ruling passion. In his day there was, opposite the main entrance of Elton, a foundry belonging to a Mr Hayes, who had invented and manufactured the first hay elevator. A spark from the foundry once landed on one of Lord Carysfort's horses as he was driving up to his gate, whereupon he angrily demanded that Hayes should sell him the foundry. When Hayes refused to do so, Carysfort had the present entrance made a quarter of a mile away.

During the long reign of the Admiral's youngest son, the 5th and last Earl of Carysfort, many improvements were carried out both at Elton and on the family's Irish estates, for the 5th Earl, as well as having a great sense of duty, was shrewd and successful in business. Like many of his forebears he was a bibliophile, and as well as collecting books he added greatly to what remained of his grandfather's picture collection, though most of his acquisitions, which are now at Elton, were hung in his day at his Irish seat. The 5th Earl was the opposite of the proverbial Anglo-Irish landlord, and was really more interested in his Irish estates than in his East Anglian property. When Lord and Lady Carysfort migrated to Ireland, they would depart from Elton in state, driving to the station at Oundle with their servants in a procession of anything up to eleven carriages, each with matching horses and a coachman in dark and light blue livery. At Oundle there was a special coach on the train which was attached to the Irish Mail at Rugby.

When the 5th Earl died in 1909, the Carysfort title became extinct and Elton and the Irish estates passed to his sister's son, who took the name of Proby. Colonel Proby was a religious and benevolent Irishman, who subscribed to the old-fashioned Irish belief that nobody must be sent away hungry from one's house. Consequently, during the Depression, as many as forty tramps would come in one day to Elton to be fed, an enormous pot of stew being kept permanently on the kitchen fire for this purpose. But while this form of charity may have been stepped up at Elton with the advent of the Colonel and his wife, it was certainly nothing new here, any more than in other English country houses. A member of the family in the nineteenth century, writing of the Elton household as it was some years previously, recalled that the cook 'made very good soup for the poor'.

The Colonel's eldest son, Granville Proby, who for many years was Clerk in the House of Lords, followed in the family tradition by being a scholar and a patron of the arts. A bachelor, he is alleged to have taken a bachelor's point of view when, at the beginning of the Second World War, there was the question as to whether Elton should be lent to a girls' school or used to store works of art, saying: 'I think we ought to have the Old Masters. After all we do know that girls can be produced at any time by processes of nature; but Old Masters are quite irreplaceable.' In the event, the house was used as a hospital, as it had been during the previous conflict. In 1947 it passed to the Colonel's second son, the late Sir Richard Proby, a prominent figure in the political and agricultural worlds who in 1952 followed in the footsteps of the seventeenth-century Sir Thomas Proby by being made a baronet. The prospects were hardly encouraging, but Sir Richard was determined to keep the house, collections and estate together and succeeded in doing so. He expressed his philosophy in a speech which he once made as Chairman of the Country Landowners Association. 'People say to me, what are we to do with our country houses?' he told his audience. 'My answer to that is, live in them.'

Architecture and Contents

Elton incorporates an early Tudor gatehouse and chapel, to which in the 1660s Sir Thomas Proby added a typical Charles II block with a high hipped roof. The house was enlarged and remodelled between 1780 and 1815, when it was given most of its turrets and battlements. The 3rd Earl of Carysfort carried out a further remodelling after he succeeded in 1855, removing the castellations from Sir Thomas Proby's seventeenth-century building, which he enlarged and reconstructed in a mid-Victorian rendering of its original style. He also redecorated the great drawing-room, putting up the panels of gold brocade which survive to this day as a perfect background to the pictures. Elton has a splendid picture collection and a notable library.

ERDDIG

CLWYD

With its long façade, its formal garden and its canal, Erddig is more like the *schloss* of a European princeling than the home of Welsh squires of moderate means, and it must always have seemed a little too grand for the descendants of Simon Yorke, whose self-made lawyer uncle John Meller, Master in Chancery, bought it early in the eighteenth century after the original owner and builder of the house had gone bankrupt. The Yorkes, originally from Dover in Kent, were also connected with the law, Simon being a cousin of the Lord Chancellor, Philip Yorke, Earl of Hardwicke. But the Yorkes of Erddig had little of the ambition which carried not one but two members of the other branch of the family to the Woolsack; they just lived quietly in North Wales, a line of Simons and Philips of whom the Simons tended to be rather dim and the Philips somewhat brighter. Leading their uneventful lives, they left their house and its spendid early eighteenth-century furnishings remarkably unchanged.

'A large house in Wales is the worst thing in the world to manage', the wife of the first Simon Yorke of Erddig complained in 1765. She survived her husband by many years and became increasingly dependent on her maid, a clockmaker's daughter with an inherited talent for intricate work whose models of a pagoda and of the ruins of Palmyra are still in the house. Subsequent generations of the family were on no less friendly terms with their servants and tradesmen. There was a tradition at Erddig – which existed at certain other great houses, notably at KNOLE – of having portraits painted of the principal retainers. These are inscribed with verses about the sitters, composed by the Yorke of the day. For the portrait of the elderly Jane Ebbrell, who joined the Erddig household in the time of Meller and was still here in 1793, the first Philip Yorke wrote the following:

> To dignifie our Servants' Hall,
> Here comes the Mother of us all;
> For seventy years, or near have passed her;
> Since spider-brusher to the *Master*.

The first Philip Yorke, who married Elizabeth Cust (*see* BELTON HOUSE), was one of the more talented members of the family, a scholar and a wit, a Fellow of the Society of Antiquaries and the author of an illustrated history, *The Royal Tribes of Wales*. He carried out some alterations to the house, but his historical sense prevented him from changing too much. Charles Apperley, better known as the sporting writer 'Nimrod', who grew up close to Erddig, regarded him as a fine example of 'the accomplished English private gentleman, not of this school or of that, but of all schools'. And of Erddig in his day, he writes: 'When I say that its owner had a good seven thousand

Ruth Jones, a nanny at mid-Victorian Erddig, photographed in her old age in about 1912.

pounds per annum to spend, every shilling of which he did spend, it may be supposed to be a house of no small pretensions.'

Apperley also writes of Philip Yorke's hospitality. As well as entertaining friends and distinguished acquaintances, he suffered what he called 'visitations' by hangers-on, who would stay anything up to twelve months. He gave an annual 'juvenile ball' at Christmas which was the occasion for various pranks, such as when the young Nimrod and his friends put a calves' foot jelly into each of the coat-pockets of a clergyman and made him stand with his back to the fire. There was a tremendous celebration for the coming-of-age of Philip Yorke's son Simon; a marble cistern in the hall holding at least twenty gallons was filled with 'an exquisite punch' of which Apperley and other youngsters drank so deep that they had to be put to bed.

Philip Yorke was not much of a sportsman. On horseback, as Nimrod tells us, he was 'a figure of fun', clad in an immense blue military cloak, a relic of far-off days with the Denbighshire Militia. When asked if he had ever been fox-hunting, he replied, 'I have not. In fact, I could never reach the hare.' Subsequent Yorkes were no more sporting than he. The Victorian Simon – whose younger brother was a General and as such the only member of the family to achieve distinction – barely set foot outside the house in his later years, but spent his time filling notebooks with sermons and verse. His son Philip also wrote verse and was artistic.

The family blamed the failure of this Philip's marriage on his insistence that the honeymoon should be spent painting watercolours; whatever the reason, his wife left him after a few months without a word. They met again by accident, outside the Army and Navy Stores in Westminster, by which time she would have been willing to go back to him. 'Is it peace, Philip?' she asked. 'Madam, let me show you to your carriage', he replied, and they never met again. Philip spent some years travelling in Europe and the East, photographing and painting; he afterwards worked among the London poor. At Erddig, where he succeeded his father in 1894, he conducted services in the chapel, invited children from the local workhouse to tea parties and gave magic-lantern shows about his travels.

In 1899 his wife died and he looked around for a successor. Suitable ladies were invited to house parties at Erddig and when leaving were presented with a small packet tied with ribbon containing a proposal of marriage. As a rather elderly fifty-year-old, whose family fortunes had very much declined since the days of his prosperous Georgian namesake, he was not all that great a catch; however, a clergyman's daugher fell in love with him and accepted him when he proposed to her on St Valentine's Day under the Gainsborough portrait of the earlier Philip. They were married in 1902 and she presented him with two sons, of whom the elder, yet another Simon, succeeded him in 1922.

By then Erddig was getting short of staff, and during the long reign of this last Simon Yorke it became so run down as to qualify for the title of the most dilapidated major country house in Britain still occupied by a member of its family. For most people, Erddig was no more than a legend, its bachelor owner being such a recluse that, apart from the locals who were allowed to walk in the park, few ever managed to penetrate within the gates. If Mr Yorke met a car on one of the drives, he would order it to leave immediately, without turning round, advancing as the vehicle backed out ahead of him. When, in 1953, Lord Anglesey (*see* PLAS NEWYDD) and another member of the Historic Buildings Council for Wales somehow succeeded in inviting themselves to lunch, they found that saplings growing from the base of the house had all but shut out the view of the overgrown garden from the first-floor windows, while on the state bed were three basins and a chamber-pot to catch the rainwater dripping through the canopy from the crumbling ceiling. Not only was the roof neglected, but it leaked all the more on account of damage caused to the house by mining subsidence.

Simon's brother and successor Philip, the last of the line, was also unmarried and highly eccentric, but he was a gregarious character who had been an actor in the Northampton Repertory Company. He carried out various immediate repairs to the house and cleared the vista along the canal.

The last Simon Yorke and his brother, the last Philip, at Erddig in about 1907.

The east front of Erddig. The roof of the original house, built in 1684–7 can be seen in the centre. Wings were added on either side in the 1720s.

He also attempted to tidy up the formal garden by grazing it with sheep, which sometimes came in through the windows and grazed in the saloon. Eventually he gave Erddig to the National Trust, by which it has been completely restored.

Architecture and Contents

As enlarged by John Meller, who bought it in 1715, Erddig is predominantly of early eighteenth-century character, with a long façade of red brick and fielded panelling of oak in the principal rooms. While keeping his rooms plain, Meller filled them with furniture of great richness and quality, some of it gilded and silvered, also with tapestry and fine porcelain. His collection survives in the house intact, many of the chairs and the splendid state bed keeping their original upholstery. The entrance front of the house was refaced in about 1770 by the first Philip Yorke, who employed a local architect while consulting James Wyatt, and in 1826 his son Simon made a neo-classical dining-room to the design of Thomas Hopper. Apart from the treasures of its state rooms, Erddig is famous for its domestic offices and estate buildings, virtually unchanged from the days of plentiful labour before 1914 and complete with their original equipment, all of which (including the Edwardian motor car to be seen in one of the outbuildings) has been painstakingly restored by the National Trust.

GLYNDE PLACE

EAST SUSSEX

ALTHOUGH the Glynde estate has never in its history changed hands by purchase, it has passed more than once to cousins of a different name, who contrary to the more usual practice of British landowning families, did not assume the surname of the relations from whom they inherited it. William Morley, who was of Lancashire stock but whose family had inherited Glynde from a family named Waleys, built the present house towards the end of the 1560s. His seventeenth-century descendant, Colonel Harbert Morley, was prominent in the Civil War as a Parliamentarian of republican views, though he wisely avoided signing the King's death warrant and so at the Restoration was able to buy a pardon for £1,000.

From the Morleys, Glynde passed to cousins from the Welsh Marches, the Trevors, who also had a Parliamentarian connection, Sir John Trevor having married the daughter of John Hampden (*see* BLICKLING HALL). A younger John Trevor, the son of this marriage, and his wife carried out various alterations to Glynde which was further improved in the eighteenth century by Richard Trevor, Bishop of Durham, a prelate as pious and tolerant as he was handsome, so that George II referred to him as the 'Beauty of Holiness'. The Bishop's brother, Lord Trevor, inherited Glynde and was made Viscount Hampden, a title which died with his son (whose first wife was described as 'languid and insipid and addicted to musical parties and card playing'). On the death of the 2nd Viscount in 1824, Glynde passed yet again to a cousin, General Henry Otway Brand, whose roots were in Hertfordshire.

Henry Brand, the General's son, was married in 1838 to Eliza Ellice, whose mother was the illegitimate child of Georgiana, Duchess of Devonshire by Earl Grey of the Reform Bill. In 1843 he was engaged in redecorating Glynde, and his father, who was then in the south of France, wrote him a letter of advice. 'It's very likely that Buff would do better than stone colour, exercise your own taste in this respect, you may be sure of my approval. I rather incline to having the woodwork as oak, but this I leave also to you. You are right about the bedrooms, they (or such as have not been done lately) had better be done at the same time. ... I rather calculate that £100 may do the job, but may be wide of the mark. Verrall at Lewes had better do the papering.' Henry proposed moving the billiard table from the gallery to the hall, but his father was not so sure. 'I calculate roughly that the moving of this said table wd. cause an outlay of at least £200, you must reckon upon something in the Gallery to fill vacuum, lights for the night over the table in the Hall, repair or renewal of table, curtains in the Hall wd be called for, in short it so frightens me that I must suspend my assent to the proposal.'

In 1846 Henry embarked on a political career as private secretary to Eliza's

Golden Wedding group of Henry Brand, 1st Viscount Hampden, former Speaker of the House of Commons, and his wife Eliza, 1888. Henry, wearing a check suit, stands in the middle of the back row, with Eliza in front of him. Second from the right in the front row is Henry's and Eliza's grandson Freeman Thomas, a future Governor-General of Canada and Viceroy of India who rose to be Marquess of Willingdon.

cousin Sir George Grey, Home Secretary in the Whig administration of Lord John Russell (*see* WOBURN ABBEY). This kept him in London when Eliza was at Glynde seeing in the New Year: '*Do* come tomorrow if you can', she begged him in a letter written on 30 December. 'The house is turned out of windows in preparation for the hop, carpet up in the Hall.' And on the 31st, she wrote: 'The Hall looks grand, candles at the two ends, I expect it will be stunning in point of lights and company.' That same day, however, Henry was writing to her from London: 'I have been more than half tempted to run down by the Express tonight and up again by the Express tomorrow morning. But I shd be ashamed at having spent near two pounds so very extravagantly. I must positively have an Annual Ticket when they come down to £30 – and I shall then have a mind more at ease.' As well as her disappointment at Henry's absence, Eliza suffered the misfortune of having one of her dancing shoes accidentally put on the grate by a servant 'in the dark of the morning' to light the fire with, doubtless because the culprit was still suffering from the effects of a servants' ball at the neighbouring big house, Glyndebourne, a couple of nights earlier, to which the Glynde servants went. For those days, the domestic staff at Glynde was surprisingly small: according to a census return of 1851 it consisted of a housekeeper, butler, footman, valet and two lady's maids, a housemaid, under-housemaid, kitchen-maid, under-kitchen-maid and laundry-maid, together with a governess, nurse and wet-nurse for the children, who ranged in age from eleven years to two months. The fact that there is no mention of a cook must mean that the Brands were between cooks at the time of the census and making do with the kitchen-maid's cooking.

That same year, 1851, saw the conversion to Catholicism of Henry Brand's sister Fredericka and also of the local Archdeacon, the future Cardinal Manning. As a result, the custom of family prayers and a daily Bible reading was instituted at Glynde. 'While it is at all times our duty – rather our

privilege – so to worship God,' Henry told his family and servants on the first
occasion that they assembled for this purpose, 'it is, at a time like the present
when the faith of many appears to be unsettled, especially incumbent upon us
to seek His blessing.' The quiet determination which he showed in thus
attempting to strengthen the Anglican faith of his household was to show
itself during his thirty-two years as an MP, and especially during the twelve
years from 1872 onwards when he held the high office of Speaker. In 1881 he
made history by closing a debate which had dragged on for forty-one hours
owing to the Irish Party's campaign of obstruction: it was the first time since
Cromwell's famous coup that anyone had closed a debate in the Commons.
On his retirement from the Speakership in 1884, Henry Brand became the
1st Viscount Hampden of the present creation.

Glynde Place.

Architecture and Contents

A gabled Elizabethan house of stone and flint, little changed outside but
altered internally in the late seventeenth and mid-eighteenth centuries. The
present treatment of the hall, which has screens of marbled columns at either
end, dates from the latter period, while the long gallery above it is
predominantly of the late seventeenth century, with fielded panelling,
Corinthian pilasters, pedimented doorcases and overmantel carving in the
manner of Grinling Gibbons. There is a notable collection of seventeenth-
and eighteenth-century family portraits, including works by Cornelius
Johnson, Lely, Kneller, Gainsborough, Hoppner and Zoffany. Chief among
the other treasures of Glynde is Rubens' original sketch for his ceiling in the
Whitehall Banqueting House.

GOODWOOD HOUSE
WEST SUSSEX

Goodwood, which Charles Lennox, Duke of Richmond, Charles II's natural son by Louise de Keroualle, acquired in 1695, was originally no more than a hunting lodge. The 2nd Duke was even more devoted to hunting than his father, and maintained another house across the Downs at Charlton, which was then a fashionable hunting centre rather like Melton Mowbray at a later period. His other great interest was cricket, which greatly increased in popularity thanks to his patronage and the success of the Goodwood team. Like most great noblemen of his time, the 2nd Duke of Richmond improved his park, embellishing it not only with follies but also with a menagerie that boasted of tigers, leopards, wolves, bears and vultures, as well as a lion to which he became so attached that when it died he put up a life-sized statue of it over its grave. He did not, however, do much to the house, which remained small by ducal standards. His wife, writing to him one summer in anticipation of a house party, reckoned that she could provide a total of eleven

The lawn at Goodwood, overlooking the racecourse, painted towards the end of the last century by T. Wilson and F. Walton.

beds, one of them in the 'haunted room' and one in the gardener's house. 'The new bedchamber is finished and the bed made up,' she told him, 'but it smells of paint a good deal.'

It was his son, the 3rd Duke, who transformed Goodwood into a full-blown ducal seat, greatly enlarging the estate, commissioning Sir William Chambers to build the monumental stables, and employing James Wyatt to transform the house into the present three-sided mansion. And in 1801, towards the end of his life, he gave Goodwood the amenity for which it has since been most famous, the picturesque racecourse on the hill above the house.

As well as being a sportsman, a builder and an improving landlord, the 3rd Duke was a man of considerable brilliance who in 1765 at the age of only thirty was sent as Ambassador to France. There was, however, something erratic and unreliable about him, which blighted his political career and made him unpopular with his colleagues: 'If there were two Dukes of Richmond in this country, I would not live in it', one of them remarked. He also at the age of twenty-five made the fatal error of throwing up his appointment as Gentleman of the King's Bedchamber in a fit of pique, thereby offending George III who never forgave him. Had things gone differently, Richmond might have basked in the royal favour as the King's brother-in-law, for George III wanted to marry his sister, Lady Sarah Lennox; according to legend she was the Lass of Richmond Hill and the song 'I'd crowns resign to call thee mine' was written by the lovelorn young monarch himself. So stifling did Richmond find the royal displeasure in the days of Lord North that he contemplated leaving England altogether and settling in France, where he held the French dukedom of Aubigny and estates which had been conferred on his great-grandmother, Louise de Keroualle, by Louis XIV. That he should have thought of turning himself into a French nobleman on the eve of the Revolution certainly does not speak much for his judgement.

The 3rd Duke died heavily in debt, so that his nephew and successor spent long periods in official posts abroad. He was, however, at Goodwood in 1814 when he entertained Tsar Alexander and his sister to luncheon in the dining-room, which was decorated and furnished in the Egyptian taste. He was serving as envoy in Brussels at the time of Waterloo when his wife gave her famous ball. Later he went to govern Canada, where, during the course of a lengthy official tour, he contracted hydrophobia, but continued on his journey until a few hours before his death.

The 5th Duke who, like his father-in-law, Lord Anglesey (*see* PLAS NEWYDD), was severely wounded fighting against Napoleon, brought the Goodwood racecourse to its ultimate perfection. In this he was helped by Lord George Bentinck, probably the greatest figure of his time on the turf. The two of them were partners in an extremely successful racing stable at Goodwood, with as their trainers the two celebrated John Kents, father and son. 'I never come here without fresh admiration of the beauty and delightfulness of the place, combining everything that is enjoyable in life'. Charles Greville, a cousin of Bentinck, noted in his diary while staying at Goodwood for the races in 1831. 'Large and comfortable house, spacious and beautiful park, extensive views, dry soil, sea air, woods and rides over downs,

King Edward VII and George, Prince of Wales, sitting in a car outside Goodwood in July 1909 with the Austrian Ambassador, Count Albert Mensdorff, and their host, the 7th Duke of Richmond (white moustache).

Goodwood from the air.

and all the facilities of occupation and amusement. The Duke, who has so strangely become a Cabinet Minister in a Whig Government, and who is a very good sort of man and my excellent friend, appears here to advantage, exercising a magnificent hospitality, and as a sportsman, a farmer, a magistrate, and good, simple, unaffected country gentleman, with great personal influence.' That other diarist of the period, Thomas Creevey, came to Goodwood in 1828 and described it as 'perfection'. 'There were quantities of visitors in the house, many of whom one knows as *brother dandies* and Turf Men, and many I did not.' They were scattered about the libraries, the billiard-room, the hall and the drawing-room. It was all very gay, Creevey recorded: '"What a contrast", we all said, "to ARUNDEL."'

Later in the 5th Duke's reign, a journalist gave his readers an outsider's glimpse of Goodwood *en fête*.

Three miles of twisting, dusty lanes brings us to the gate of Goodwood Park, which being open we drive through the grounds directly past the house, in front of which is placed a marquee, under whose friendly awning the Duke of Argyll and

Colonel Udney may be seen taking shelter from the burning sun, while His Grace's bay and grey are stamping their feet under the neighbouring trees. At the door is a green landau with four bays, the postilions in red and white striped jackets, and the footmen in rich white and red liveries turned up with silver and turned down with yellow, while two other carriages and pair, with the coachmen and footmen in similar liveries, are waiting to convey the noble party to the stand.

It was at Goodwood during the meeting of 1846 that Bentinck startled the sporting world by announcing that he was giving up racing. Politics had prevented him from staying for the whole week; having been present on the first day and then gone up to London by train, he returned on the third day to stay with the Duke. That evening, 'he appeared to be half asleep, when he suddenly roused himself, rose, looked at the men in the room and said: "Will anyone give me £10,000 for all my lot?"' With the departure of Bentinck, which was followed in 1854 by the Duke's retirement from racing and the dispersal of his stable, some of the glory went from 'Glorious Goodwood'. The interests of the Victorian 6th Duke were divided between Sussex and Banffshire, where since the death in 1836 of his great-uncle, the last Duke of Gordon, the Richmond family had owned vast estates, in recognition of which the dukedom of Gordon was revived in his favour in 1876. Nevertheless, Goodwood Week kept its place in the social calendar and the 6th Duke carried out improvements to the Goodwood estate, enlarging the house and lighting it with gas. He and his son, the future 7th Duke – who in 1904, soon after succeeding, was to do away with the Egyptian decoration in the dining-room, reputedly at the behest of Edward VII – also brought back hunting to Goodwood, the original pack of hounds having been given up by the 4th Duke. The revived pack had in turn to be given up in 1895 owing to the late nineteenth-century agricultural depression, and as a sign of the changing times, the golf course of what afterwards became the Goodwood Golf Club was laid out in the park in 1900. After the Second World War, racing and golf were joined by motor racing, when the present Duke, a well-known racing driver in his younger days, started the Goodwood motor circuit at which meetings were held until 1966.

Architecture and Contents

A hunting lodge enlarged in several phases from the 1770s until about 1800 by James Wyatt. It was to become a classical mansion of unusual plan, three sides of what was intended to be a vast octagon, with domed corner turrets and a two-tiered colonnade as the central feature. The interior, which is austerely elegant, was redecorated in 1970 as a background to the magnificent French furniture, tapestries and porcelain acquired by the 3rd Duke of Richmond during his Embassy to the Court of Louis XV, and to display the pictures, among which Canaletto's famous views of London have pride of place. There are also portraits by Van Dyck, Lely, Kneller, Reynolds, Hoppner and Lawrence.

HADDON HALL
DERBYSHIRE

Rex Whistler's overmantel painting of Haddon in the long gallery. The 9th Duke of Rutland and his son, the present Duke, are depicted in the foreground.

HADDON is one of the best surviving examples of a great medieval house which was never a castle. That it did not need to be fortified was due to the peaceable nature of the Vernons – or, to use the older and more correct plural of their name, the Vernon – who acquired it in the twelfth century after the downfall of its original owner, Peveril of the Peak. From then on, as they increased in prosperity and importance, the house grew in size. Sir Henry Vernon of Haddon enjoyed the confidence of both Edward IV and Henry VII; the latter made him Treasurer to Arthur, Prince of Wales, who according to tradition came to Haddon on several visits. Sir Henry's grandson, Sir George, lived in such style at Haddon that he was known as the 'King of the

Peak'. He had no son, so that when he died, in 1567, Haddon passed to his daughter Dorothy, who had married Sir John Manners, second son of the 1st Earl of Rutland (*see* BELVOIR CASTLE). The well-known story of how Dorothy eloped with Sir John by slipping away from the ball which was being held to celebrate her sister's wedding appears to be an early nineteenth-century fabrication. There is no obvious reason why Sir George Vernon should not have approved of the second son of the Earl of Rutland as a son-in-law; moreover, if the effigy of her on her tomb is anything to go by, Dorothy's looks were not such as would have made her elopement – if it ever happened – much of a romance.

Dorothy's grandson, who succeeded his cousin as 8th Earl of Rutland in 1641, sided with Parliament in the Civil War and followed in the tradition of his Vernon ancestors by taking no active part in the conflict, during which he lived peacefully at Haddon and went on making the terrace garden. After the Restoration he rebuilt Belvoir, the castle in Leicestershire which had come to him with the earldom, but he and his family continued to spend so much time at Haddon that 'between 30 and 40 beefs and between 4 and 500 sheep, and 8 or 10 swine' were killed here every year during the 1660s. Belvoir, however, was favoured more than Haddon by his son, who after 1702, the year before he was made Duke of Rutland, ceased to come into residence here altogether. According to Horace Walpole, Haddon was abandoned by the family because the 1st Duke's son, Lord Roos – the future 2nd Duke – lost a

Above left Henry, Marquess of Granby, afterwards 8th Duke of Rutland, and his wife Violet (left) at Haddon in the early 1900s. The photograph was taken by Lady Granby's brother, Charles Lindsay.

Above Violet, Marchioness of Granby, afterwards Duchess of Rutland, and her son Lord John Manners, who became the 9th Duke of Rutland, photographed at Haddon in the 1890s by Charles Lindsay.

The 9th Duke of Rutland at work on the restoration of Haddon in about 1912. It was to be his life's work.

Parliamentary election in Derbyshire through the treachery of his agents. The 3rd Duke is said to have stayed here occasionally between 1721 and 1729, but when Walpole came here in 1760 he found the house 'totally stript'. This to him was not a cause for much regret. 'It is very low', he observed, 'and can never have been a tolerable house, the gallery is the only good room.'

A generation later, the house in its romantic decay began to cast its spell on tourists. The diarist John Byng, who visited Haddon in 1789 and found it deserted except for a fishing party of ladies from Bakewell for whom the Duke's steward had provided a collation of cold ham in the long gallery, was very much taken by 'this poor abandon'd place'. If he were the Duke of Rutland, he wrote, he would restore it. He reckoned that the cost of doing up the house and improving the grounds, including making the river into 'a lake of the utmost magnificence', would come to no more than £16,000 – 'one night's losses at play of the late Duke'.

The farmer who acted as his guide told him that many gentlemen thought Haddon more worth seeing than the nearby CHATSWORTH, an opinion with which the diarist heartily concurred. 'And some, Sir,' the farmer went on, 'will desire to take away pieces of armour.' 'That I should like to do too' said Byng hopefully. 'Why then, Sir,' said the obliging farmer, 'as you seem fond of these things, there is a sword hilt, with part of the blade, said to be worn by the Vernons in the wars of France.' And the diarist carried off his prize.

Haddon's long sleep continued until the eve of the First World War, by which time it had become 'obscured by the overgrowth of vegetation and legend', though it had at any rate escaped the heavy hand of nineteenth-century restorers. The family of the 8th Duke took to spending three months every summer in a house nearby. It was small and uncomfortable, but such was the Duchess's charm that all manner of important and fashionable people came to stay, including a recent Viceroy of India, Lord Curzon. These guests, most of them normally spoilt and sybaritic, cheerfully made do with the one and only bathroom in the house, which the Manners girls used for developing photographs, so that there was liable to be hypo in the wash-basin and a string of dripping negatives hanging over the bath. 'We would go to empty Haddon Hall most afternoons for water-colour sketching and gardening and, best of all, at full moon for an after-dinner drive in brother John's open screenless racing-car packed with young men and girls – fears and excitements, cries and claspings,' one of those girls, now the legendary Lady Diana Cooper, recalls. 'My mother was strongly against these expeditions, perhaps more from fear of cold and the fast car than from disapproval of escapade, but my brother invariably had his way.' The young future Duke was in love, not with one of the girls in his car but with a beauty who had slumbered for two hundred years and whom he was determined, one day, to awaken. He began his great work in 1912, bringing to it a knowledge of history and ancient crafts as well as sensibility and discrimination, so that everything possible was done to preserve the atmosphere of the past that pervaded the old house. He even built a modern kitchen at the foot of the hill – from which the food was conveyed in electrically heated trolleys by way of a tunnel – to avoid interfering with the medieval cooking arrangements. By 1927, his life's ambition had been realized: Haddon was restored, without the loss of any of its magic, and once again lived in by the heirs of the Vernon.

The great hall at Haddon.

Architecture and Contents

A great medieval house which grew gradually, extending round two courtyards; additions were made to it until the early seventeenth century, though it remained predominantly medieval. Abandoned in the eighteenth century, it was sympathetically restored from 1912 onwards. The hall has a fifteenth-century oak screen; its roof was entirely restored in the present century with oak from the estate. The kitchens retain their medieval and Tudor furniture and fittings. The dining-room has a ceiling decorated with medieval heraldic painting. In the long gallery there is Renaissance panelling of about 1603 painted to resemble walnut, and a romantic view of Haddon in the overmantel painted in 1933 by Rex Whistler. There is a fine collection of tapestries, including a French one dating from about 1460.

HAGLEY HALL
WEST MIDLANDS

THE Lytteltons, who held land in Worcestershire as far back as the beginning of the thirteenth century, have been at Hagley since 1565. The present mid-eighteenth-century house – Palladian outside, rococo within – and its idyllic landscape are the creation of George, 1st Lord Lyttelton, whose mother was Christian Temple from Stowe, so landscape gardening was in his blood. He certainly inherited a greater talent for planting and building than for politics, though he was, through his mother, a member of the powerful political cousinhood of Temples, Grenvilles and Pitts known as 'Cobham's Cubs' after his uncle, Lord Cobham. As Chancellor of the Exchequer he proved a failure – 'They turned an absent poet to the management of the revenue', Horace Walpole remarked of him – but as a poet and an historian he was esteemed by many of the literary giants of his time, including Pope, Shenstone and Fielding, who honoured him with the dedication of *Tom Jones*. Smollett, while satirizing him as Sir Gosling Scrag – 'a long, lean, lank misshapen Spectre, with an awkward, shambling, Goose-like Gait' – declared that the age was embellished by 'the delicate taste, the polished muse and tender feelings of a Lyttelton'. The beauties of his park at Hagley were sung by Thomson in *The Seasons* and recorded in prose by Dr Johnson who was less praising of Lyttelton's verses: 'They have nothing to be despised,' he wrote, 'and little to be admired'.

In building his new house just as in laying out his park, Lyttelton did without professional advice, preferring to consult his friends, which may explain why, having started planning his new house soon after his father's death in 1751, he did not have it finished until 1760. He celebrated its completion with a three-day housewarming which, according to Charles Townshend, was not a great success; the beds were not aired and 'before the dinner was ended, everybody was talking of their private affairs and pedigrees; Bacchus's hall was turned into the Herald's office and the whole company became jealous and sulky.' It was another ten years before Lyttelton had paid all the bills for the house and its contents, which cost four times what he originally intended to spend. 'This House ... is said to have cost £30,000 with the furniture and does infinitely more credit to the Taste than the prudence of its owner', observed a somewhat precocious girl of twelve after visiting Hagley in 1768, which was true enough, since Lyttelton, by the standards of the peerage, was by no means rich.

The family finances were not improved by the profligacy of the 2nd or 'Bad' Lord Lyttelton – who is said to have been visited by the ghost of a former mistress warning him of his impending demise – or by the mental derangement of his cousin, the 2nd Lord Lyttelton of the second creation, a pathetic, solitary figure 'tottering along on his melancholy evening walk ... talking loud to himself', as his sister-in-law Sarah Lyttelton, a daughter of the 2nd Earl Spencer (*see* ALTHORP), described him. For a period in 1826 Sarah and her husband William lived with him at Hagley, occupying two rooms on the top floor near the book-room, their children having been left in a house in the village. 'The said book-room', Sarah wrote, 'is a favourite snuggery of mine; for to own the truth the lofty awful rooms below with all their crimson damask, old china, japan cabinets, tapestry and carving, are not fit for a poor lone body to sit in of evenings, when her chicks are far away with all their merry noises and her husband gone to dine out, and she left in a strange disunited tête-à-tête with another poor, *poor* lone being!' Two years later the 'poor lone' Lord Lyttelton died and William and Sarah came into Hagley, which having been so empty was now filled with children, at times not only their own five but also the seven of William's sister, Mrs Pole-Carew (*see* ANTONY HOUSE). The new Lord and Lady Lyttelton found the house in very bad repair, particularly the drains. 'The bad smell broke out in the library and rooms beyond, sometimes in one, sometimes in the other, with great violence', William noted in his diary soon after they took up residence. New plumbing was put in, but the results were not always satisfactory. The 'great pipe' of the new water-closet was 'found to be defective'; the new and surprisingly advanced hot water system failed to work so that when William wanted a bath 'the servants were obliged to bring the hot water in buckets and the cold ... came in dirty.'

The year 1839 saw the start of another new regime at Hagley, when William's son and successor George, a brilliant classical scholar with a high sense of duty, brought home his bride, the former Mary Glynne, whose sister was married to William Ewart Gladstone. It was a regime of strict economy. George's income, which at the time of his marriage amounted to no more than £3,000 a year, was hardly enough to maintain Hagley and meet the other commitments of his rank. Mary kept a close watch on the household bills and was pleased when the year's groceries came to £70 as compared with £79 in the previous year; relations who came to stay each contributed £1 a week and 15s for each of their servants. Nevertheless, the food was plentiful, with a daily allowance of no less than a pound and a half of meat per head in the servants' hall.

Despite the lack of money, George's fits of melancholia and Mary's too numerous pregnancies – she was to die after giving birth to her twelfth child – Hagley in the early and middle years of Victoria's reign was an extremely happy house. The young Lytteltons grew up in an atmosphere of scholarship and philistinism, of good works, high principles, High Church piety and boisterous high spirits; there were napkin fights in the dining-room between George and his sons, and games of wet-weather cricket in the gallery, heedless of the plasterwork and the Venetian mirrors. Much as they loved Hagley, the Lytteltons of those days were blind to its rococo glories. There is a story of how the boys were only just prevented from sawing off the pie-crust edges of the Chippendale tables in order to make them more practical. Cricket was the ruling passion; there was a ground immediately outside the drawing-room windows where eleven Lytteltons played an annual match against Bromsgrove school. One of the elder girls, Lucy, who married Lord

Mr Gladstone, towards the end of his life, in a carriage outside Hagley. Sitting to the right of him is his hostess and niece by marriage, Viscountess Cobham, whose daughter, Maud Lyttelton, is perched on the box-seat. Lord Cobham, 5th Lord Lyttelton, stands to the right of the carriage; his younger brother Spencer Lyttelton, formerly Mr Gladstone's private secretary, leans over the balustrade of the perron. To the right of Spencer Lyttelton is his niece, May Talbot. The rather formidable lady next to her is Mr Gladstone's daughter Helen, who never married but became Vice-Principal of Newnham College, Cambridge.

Two of the daughters of the 5th Lord Lyttelton in the schoolroom at Hagley Hall.

Frederick Cavendish – who was afterwards Irish Secretary and was murdered in Dublin's Phoenix Park (*see* CHATSWORTH) – gives us an account of a match in 1867. 'Papa in flannels taking immense pains, fielding (I think) at short slip. Uncle Spencer, in magenta flannels, sitting on a bench as a distant long-stop, did two balls the honour of fielding them. Uncle B. running about rather vaguely. All the boys fielding capitally (except Bob who was no great shakes); little Edward really admirable . . . Alfred's batting was truly excellent; his defence being wonderful. They began sending him slow balls out of kindness, but soon found he was up to anything. Arthur made two or three very fine slashing hits.' All but one of the Lyttelton boys were legendary cricketers at Eton, of which Edward would one day be headmaster. Arthur, who became a bishop, admitted in later life that he could never walk up a church aisle without bowling an imaginary off-break. Alfred, the youngest, a future Colonial Secretary, was to rank in his cricketing heyday second only to W. G. Grace.

If Alfred was the most brilliant of the boys, the youngest daughter, May, was the most attractive of the girls. In 1875 she died of typhoid, and during her funeral Arthur Balfour (*see* HATFIELD HOUSE), who had hoped to marry her, sat under a tree in the park and wept. Her death was followed a year later by the suicide of her father, whose melancholia had grown steadily worse, despite a happy second marriage. The eldest son Charles, who became the

next Lord Lyttelton and inherited the Viscountcy of Cobham from a distant kinsman in 1889, had the business ability which his predecessors had lacked and improved the family fortunes. However little regard he may have had in his youth for the furniture at Hagley, in later life he appreciated it enough to say to a portly sister-in-law after a chair in the gallery had broken under her weight, causing her to protest that she might have broken her back, 'A great many backs like yours, very few chairs like mine.'

Hagley Hall, built in the Palladian style by Sanderson Miller for George, 1st Lord Lyttelton.

Architecture and Contents

A Palladian house of the 1750s designed by Sanderson Miller, with a pediment and corner towers. The principal rooms have wonderful rococo plasterwork by Francesco Vassalli: on the walls of the saloon, now the dining-room, there are festoons and emblems of the arts, music and the chase; in the Tapestry room, which takes its name from a splendid set of Soho arabesque tapestries, the ceiling incorporates mythological paintings by 'Athenian' Stuart. There are exuberantly rococo pier glasses and side tables in this room and also in the gallery, which contains other magnificent furniture. Among the pictures at Hagley are portraits by Van Dyck, Lely, Reynolds, Allan Ramsay and Pompeo Batoni. The house was formerly even richer in works of art, but much was lost in the fire of 1925 which badly damaged the side of the building containing the private rooms. The subsequent work of restoration was so well done that it is hard to tell what has been restored and what is original.

HAM HOUSE
GREATER LONDON

THE manor of Ham was granted early in the seventeenth century to William Murray, a Scottish royal favourite who started life as Charles I's whipping-boy and ended as Earl of Dysart. His daughter and heiress, who inherited his title – which like many Scottish peerages can pass in the female line – was the celebrated Elizabeth, Countess of Dysart, fascinating in her younger days, disagreeable when old. A staunch Royalist, she nonetheless managed to be in favour with Cromwell during the Commonwealth and Protectorate, and was therefore widely believed to have been his mistress. Though this is certainly untrue, she was for a time the mistress of a man almost as powerful and if anything more unattractive – John Maitland, Duke of Lauderdale, the 'L' of Charles II's Cabal. She married him as her second husband in 1672 and during the years that followed she and Lauderdale gave Ham its sumptuous Caroline interior, which survives wonderfully unchanged. This is to some extent due to the fact that for more than a century after her death the Tollemaches, descendants of her first marriage who inherited Ham and the Dysart earldom, spent much of their time at Helmingham, their ancestral seat in Suffolk. They also tended to be eccentric and parsimonious, so were inclined to leave the house as it was.

The stinginess of the 4th Earl of Dysart, who had an income of £13,000 a year in the 1760s, was commented on by several of his contemporaries. He kept an account in his own hand of everything he spent, down to the halfpenny which he gave a boy for opening a gate. When his son and heir wanted to marry a niece of Horace Walpole – whose home, Strawberry Hill, was across the river from Ham – he told him that he could not afford to make a settlement, but offered to lend him money at a low rate of interest. The marriage took place, but was not a happy one, for the next Lord Dysart turned out to be even more miserly than his father, as well as being a recluse and a jealous husband. He allowed nothing at Ham to be altered. 'In this state of pomp and tatters my nephew intends it shall remain', Walpole wrote:

> Because the gates were never opened by his father but once for the late Lord Granville, you are locked out and locked in; and after journeying all round the house, as you do round an old French fortified town, you are at last admitted through the stable-yard to creep along a dark passage by the housekeeper's room and so by a back door into the great hall. He seems as much afraid of water as a cat, for though you might enjoy the Thames from every window of three sides of the house, you may tumble into it before you would guess it is there.

The 6th Earl, a brother of Walpole's nephew by marriage, was also inclined to make no changes at Ham, where he seldom went after his wife's death in 1804. He did, however, carry out repairs to the house, and had the parquetry floors carefully taken up, cleaned and relaid, carpets being afterwards put over them to protect them. By now, people were beginning to appreciate the interior of Ham as the precious survival that it was: 'The place remaining in its old style is beautiful and magnificent both within and without, but truly melancholy,' wrote Queen Charlotte in 1809, after being taken there by Lady Caroline Dawson who lived nearby and was 'favoured with a key'.

With the death of the 6th Earl in 1821, the original male line of the Tollemaches came to an end. The descendants of two of his sisters took the name of Tollemache; from the elder of the two sisters were descended the subsequent Earls of Dysart and owners of Ham, while Helmingham in Suffolk passed to descendants of the younger sister. The 8th Earl, who succeeded in 1840, inherited his eighteenth-century forebears' dislike of spending money: he once ordered a single boot, telling his bootmaker that the other one was all right. Like Horace Walpole's nephew by marriage, he ended his days as a recluse. His son, Lord Huntingtower, who died before him, was eccentric in other ways. He devoted his time to horse-dealing. He had an aversion to ringing bells so kept a heavy weight in each room which he used to drop on the floor when he wished to summon a servant. He supported two mistresses, each of whom bore him a large family, and for a time he and his wife lived apart. When she announced her intention of returning to Ham he had a black crêpe bow tied round the leg of every animal on the estate, and sent a funeral cortège with black plumes on the horses to meet her.

In 1879 Augustus Hare paid a visit to Ham, which by then belonged to Lord Huntingtower's son, the twenty-year-old 9th Earl. 'No half-inhabited château of a ruined family in Normandy was ever half so dilapidated as this home of the enormously rich Tollemaches', Hare wrote, going on to describe the house as being 'like a caravansary', with different members of the family occupying various corners of it. The young Lord Dysart lived in one apartment, his mother and two sisters in another, a great-aunt in a third, a great-uncle in a fourth. In a fifth apartment lived another great-uncle, Algernon Tollemache, to whom Hare sent in his card. As the door at the head of the entrance stair opened, its handle went through a priceless portrait by Reynolds – which, according to Hare, it always did. The room in which Algernon Tollemache sat contained a glorious Lely of the Duchess of Lauderdale and a velvet bed in a recess backed with exquisite Chinese embroidery. A splendid and massive silver mirror stood on 'a hideous rough deal scullery table', the floor was of bare boards and ranged round the walls 'by way of ornament' were 'all Mr Tollemache's most extraordinary huge boots and shoes'. Hare was taken round the house and saw 'lovely delicate silk hangings of exquisitely beautiful tints mouldering in rags; old Persian carpets of priceless designs worn to shreds; priceless Japanese screens perishing'. The inhabitants of this Sleeping Beauty palace, as he recorded, kept scarcely any servants and no carriage, ate only bread and cheese for luncheon and never repaired or restored anything.

Not long afterwards, the 9th Earl did carry out a thorough restoration. His neighbours at OSTERLEY, the Jerseys, heard an obviously exaggerated report that it had been necessary to burn every bed in the house in order to get rid of the bugs. The 9th Earl entertained lavishly at Ham, though there were stories

The great staircase.

of his meanness and he was, like most of his family, a little eccentric. Some of his apparent eccentricities were, however, due to the fact that he was nearly blind. James Lees-Milne remembers seeing him towards the end of his life in the lavatory of a London club, scrubbing his false teeth with one of the hairbrushes.

When he died in 1935 his peerage passed to his niece, but Ham went to his octogenarian cousin Sir Lyonel Tollemache. Sir Lyonel's brothers were notable for their multiplicity of names; one of them was called Lyulph Ydwallo Odin Nestor Egbert Lyonel Toedmag Hugh Erchenwyne Saxon Esa Cromwell Orma Nevill Dysart Plantagenet Tollemache-Tollemache – their father having duplicated his patronymic on account of having married a cousin of the same name as his own who happened to be an heiress. Someone who went to luncheon at Ham shortly before the Second World War remembers how Sir Lyonel showed his guests a carpet so precious that it was roped off; nobody, he said, not even he, was allowed to walk on it. As he spoke these words his dog slipped under the rope, made its way to the middle of the carpet and started relieving itself. Since nobody dared venture on to the carpet Sir Lyonel and his guests could only stand by helpless, watching the dog do its worst.

Ham House.

Architecture and Contents

Basically a red-brick Jacobean house of 1610, enlarged and remodelled after the Restoration by the Duke and Duchess of Lauderdale, who are responsible for the sumptuous interior: the painted ceilings and ceilings of ornate plasterwork, the tapestries, the hangings of damask and gilt leather, the graining and the marbling. They filled the rooms with furniture of the utmost splendour, most of which is still in the house. In fact Ham has changed hardly at all since the Lauderdales' time, except that in about 1730 the 4th Earl of Dysart rebuilt the bays on the south front, giving them Venetian windows, and introduced more fine furniture. As well as furniture, the house is rich in pictures, notably portraits by Lely, Kneller and Reynolds, sea pieces by the younger Van de Velde and early miniatures by Hilliard. Since the end of the Second World War, Ham has belonged to the National Trust; it is leased to the Department of the Environment and managed by the Victoria and Albert Museum.

HAREWOOD HOUSE
WEST YORKSHIRE

Henry Lascelles, a member of an ancient Yorkshire family who had made a large fortune in the West Indies, bought the Harewood estate on his return to England in 1739. Twenty years later, his son Edwin began building a palatial mansion here to the design of John Carr of York and Robert Adam. Edwin Lascelles supervised the work himself. He wrote to his friend and fellow-Yorkshireman, Richard Sykes, who was then about to rebuild his own house, Sledmere: 'I ... shall stand much in need of the experience and assistance of such Adepts as you. The first step, I am told, is to provide the main materials; and wood and Iron being of the number, I flatter myself I shall learn from you the lowest price of the latter.' Sykes advised him to lay in stocks of these materials in case they became scarce owing to war with France.

Harewood House in a painting by John Piper.

Wedding of HRH Princess Mary, afterwards Princess Royal, and Viscount Lascelles, afterwards 6th Earl of Harewood, 28 February 1922.

The house was habitable by 1771, when that inveterate country house visitor, Elizabeth, Duchess of Northumberland (*see* ALNWICK CASTLE) came to see it. She remarked on how the portico was 'quite full of pots of Mignonette, Balm of Gilead and all kinds of green House Plants' – Edwin Lascelles may have had pleasant memories of plant-filled verandas in Barbados – while complaining of 'a water closet wch stinks all over the House.' When the Duchess came here, the splendid interior was still in its early stages; it was not completed until 1780. By that time, Harewood had become one of the sights of England – it was even depicted on an ice-pail made by Josiah Wedgwood for Catherine the Great, whose grandson, the future Tsar Nicholas I, saw its glories for himself in 1816. The Russian Prince and his entourage of eighteen, who had been looking at factories in and around Leeds, were received in great state by Edward Lascelles, 1st Earl of Harewood, the cousin and heir of Edwin. Servants in livery lined the hall where there was a great gathering of county neighbours waiting to be presented. Dinner was served on gold plate, fifty musicians and the Harewood church choir gave a concert, mainly of Handel. In the previous year, Harewood was visited by Queen Charlotte and the Prince Regent, who in his younger days had been irritated by the fact that Lord Harewood's son, known as 'Beau' Lascelles, looked very like him: somebody once tapped the Prince on the shoulder with the cheery greeting 'Ha, Lascelles, how is it?' The Prince consequently nicknamed him the 'Pretender', but by the time he visited Harewood, Beau Lascelles was dead. To keep his memory alive, there was his collection of pictures and Sèvres porcelain, for he was a connoisseur, an amateur artist and a patron of the arts. His connoisseurship was inherited by several of his father's descendants, notably the 6th Earl, and also by the 1st Earl's grandson, the 1st Lord Penrhyn (*see* PENRHYN CASTLE).

The diarist Thomas Creevey saw Harewood from the outside in 1822 and criticized its siting. 'The monsters who built the modern house have turned their backs upon the valley', he wrote. 'They have pitched their tent on the other side of the hill, with nothing to see from it but a mere common park place with an ordinary duck pond in the centre as a substitute for the Wharfe … the house is a great modern handsome structure and full, I am told, of gold and silver.' The famous Lascelles plate was brought out once again in 1835 for the young Princess Victoria, who came with her mother, the Duchess of Kent; sightseers were allowed into the gallery to admire the tables, at which

130 people sat down to dinner. The Princess's host was Beau Lascelles' brother, the 2nd Earl of Harewood, whose son, the 3rd Earl, employed Sir Charles Barry in the 1840s to enlarge the house and give it an Italianate face-lift. At the same time the interior was partly remodelled and equipped with such modern comforts as piped hot water and hot-air central heating; batteries of water closets were also installed – doubtless of a more advanced design than their eighteenth-century precursor which had so offended the Duchess of Northumberland's nostrils – with mahogany seats for the quality and oak for the servants.

The 3rd Earl died in a hunting accident in 1857. Hunting was even more of a passion with the next two Earls of Harewood. From his two marriages the taciturn 4th Earl had no fewer than fourteen children, but he only ventured into the nursery regions of Harewood twice in the entire recollection of one of his daughters.

The 4th Earl's first wife was a sister of the eccentric and miserly Marquess of Clanricarde, the last of his line, who was to be seen shuffling along the streets of St James's in London in the early years of this century, a white-bearded down-at-heel figure frequently mistaken for a tramp. His relations usually avoided him, but one day in 1916 his great-nephew Harry, Viscount Lascelles, who was then a charming young Grenadier on leave from the front, happened to meet him and made himself pleasant to him for an hour or so. This piece of politeness had its reward a couple of months later when Clanricarde died and left Harry Lascelles his vast fortune. The inheritance included some fine pictures, for Clanricarde, despite his meanness in other directions, had spent money on buying works of art. Harry Lascelles, who was himself a connoisseur, added to the collection which he brought to Harewood after succeeding his father as 6th Earl in 1929. As well as adding so greatly to its art treasures, the 6th Earl carried out many improvements to the house itself, making it a worthy residence for his wife, the Princess Royal, daughter of George V and Queen Mary.

Architecture and Contents

A house in the Palladian style begun in 1759 to the design of John Carr of York assisted by Robert Adam, consisting of a central block joined to wings by single-storey links. The entrance front has a pediment carried on six engaged Corinthian columns, with pilasters of the same order on either side. The magnificent interior, by Robert Adam and his stuccoist Joseph Rose, with decorative paintings by Biagio Rebecca and Angelica Kauffmann, was not completed until 1780. In the 1840s additional bedroom storeys were built to the design of Sir Charles Barry, who modified the exterior by giving it a heavy Italianate balustrade. The furniture in the principal rooms comprises some of the finest work of Thomas Chippendale and is in complete harmony with Adam's overall design. To enhance these decorative splendours, there is Sèvres and Chinese porcelain. And there are pictures by Titian, Tintoretto, Veronese, Giovanni Bellini and El Greco, as well as family portraits by Gainsborough, Reynolds, Romney, Hoppner and Lawrence.

HATFIELD HOUSE
HERTFORDSHIRE

Robert Cecil, Earl of Salisbury, the brilliant little hunchback who succeeded his father (*see* BURGHLEY HOUSE) as Elizabeth I's chief minister and continued in that office under James I, was granted Hatfield and other properties by James in exchange for his splendid mansion of Theobalds, which the King wanted for himself. Hatfield had been a royal residence where Elizabeth had lived before her accession, but the old palace here was not good enough for Cecil, who spent the remaining years of his life building a palace on a much grander scale nearby, in a style that marks the full flowering of the English Renaissance. At the same time he laid out magnificent gardens, helped by the botanist John Tradescant the Elder. One of the reasons why Cecil built himself so palatial a house was that he expected to have the King and Queen to stay here often; in fact the first floor was designed primarily for royal entertainment, with apartments for the King and Queen at either end of the long gallery. In the event, Cecil did not live to receive his sovereign at Hatfield, for he died in 1612, the year in which his

A ball given for Queen Victoria in the long gallery at Hatfield on 23 October 1846. The gallery runs the full length of the first floor between the wings, and apart from the gilding of the ceiling has remained unaltered since the house was built.

new house was finished, but James stayed here several times as the guest of his son, the 2nd Earl of Salisbury. It is a reflection on the ways of the Jacobean Court that after one of these royal visits, some valuable plate was found to be missing.

The 2nd Earl of Salisbury was an unsatisfactory character, who wavered at the start of the Civil War before throwing in his lot with Parliament, was Royalist enough to show great deference to Charles I when he stayed at Hatfield as a prisoner in 1647 yet afterwards supported the Commonwealth to the extent of sitting on the Council of State, which was largely composed of regicides. At the Restoration he made his peace with Charles II and entertained him at Hatfield, and as in King James's time he found, after the royal party had left, that he was short of a few pieces of plate. Hatfield was once again visited by royalty in 1679 when James, Duke of York, the future James II, proposed himself for a night on his way north, together with his family and entourage. It was at the time when the more extreme Protestants were seeking to exclude James from the succession to the throne on account of his Catholicism. Hatfield's then owner, the 3rd Earl of Salisbury, was himself strongly in favour of exclusion, and while he could hardly refuse to have the King's brother to stay, he went as far as he could to make him feel unwelcome. He found an excuse to be away from home, and when James and his party arrived at Hatfield they found the house deserted, dark and cold, with no fires and not a candle or a candlestick to be seen, no fuel except for a small bundle of faggots in the hall, and nothing in the way of sustenance but a barrel of small beer and the carcases of two does thought to have been surreptitiously left by Salisbury's son. By sending down to the town of Hatfield for supplies, the travellers eventually managed to make themselves tolerably comfortable, and James put his host to shame by leaving eight shillings on the hall table as payment for the faggots and beer.

If the 2nd and 3rd Earls were not of the stamp of the great Robert Cecil and his father, still less so were the three who came after them. None of these seventeenth- and eighteenth-century Salisburys really lived up to Hatfield – the house was too large not only for their personalities but also for their purses. Robert Cecil did not leave his heirs rich enough to maintain it in suitable style; the fact that the 2nd Earl did so without counting the cost merely reduced the family fortunes. By the time of the 4th Earl – who went the opposite way to his ultra-Protestant father and became a Catholic – Hatfield was sadly dilapidated, with not enough servants to keep it clean. There was some improvement in the time of the 5th Earl, thanks to his energetic if domineering wife, but his son, known as the Wicked Earl – though he was not so much wicked as reckless and dissipated, with a liking for low company – abandoned the house altogether in favour of a more modest abode soon after he succeeded in 1728. Though he lived in reduced circumstances, he nevertheless managed to be extravagant, and Hatfield became even more run down than in his grandfather's time. Many of its treasures were sold, including all the good silver except for a set of Charles II candle sconces which, according to tradition, his mother had painted to resemble wood so that he might not think them valuable enough to be worth selling.

The accession of the Wicked Earl's son, a politician who became the 1st Marquess of Salisbury in 1789, marked the turning of the tide. His wife, the beautiful and flamboyant daughter of an Irish peer, brought Hatfield back to life. When she was here, the house was always full of guests. On Sundays in summer her private band played on the terrace and the public was allowed into the grounds to listen to the music. The band would also serenade her from the banks of the river while she was rowed in a state barge by twelve men in livery. When she drove around the estate, she scattered largesse in the form of golden guineas from a bag carried by one of her postilions. In 1800 George III and Queen Charlotte came to Hatfield to review the local militia in the park. This was the most famous of Lady Salisbury's entertainments and also one of the most respectable; there were others of which people disapproved, such as her Sunday gambling parties when it was said that the long gallery became ankle-deep in cards thrown on to the floor. People were also shocked by her outspokenness and her love of hunting, which was then thought to be not a suitable occupation for a lady. When Lady Salisbury was old and a dowager, she became something of a figure of fun, tireless in the pursuit of pleasure, dressed like a girl and bedecked with family jewels which afterwards turned out to be fakes, for she had been obliged, on account of her extravagance, to sell the originals. She was known as Old Sal or Old Sarum:

Emily, wife of the 1st Marquess of Salisbury, painted by Reynolds.

once, during a ball at Hatfield, she was thrown by a couple treading too violent a measure in the long gallery, which prompted Bulwer-Lytton, who was present (*see* KNEBWORTH HOUSE), to produce the following epigram:

> At Hatfield House Conservatives
> Become quite harum scarum,
> For Radical could do no more
> Than overturn Old Sarum.

Old Sarum's end was spectacular. While staying at Hatfield with her son and daughter-in-law, she set fire to her elaborate coiffure and was burned to a cinder, nearly burning the house down in the process. The tragedy caused a great sensation at the time – there is a reference to it in *Oliver Twist*, when Bill Sykes sees the blaze as he escapes from London. The entire west wing of Hatfield was destroyed and had to be rebuilt by the 2nd Marquess, who also carried out an extensive restoration of the rest of the house, which was in poor repair. He introduced a great deal of panelling and carved woodwork, glazed the arcade beneath the long gallery to make the armoury, and gilded the gallery ceiling for the ball given in honour of the young Queen Victoria and Prince Albert, who came to stay in 1846.

The 2nd Marquess could afford to do all this because he had married Frances Mary Gascoyne, a rich heiress descended from a Lord Mayor of London. Frances Mary was not only rich but good-looking, cultured and highly intelligent. She became the friend and confidante of the Great Duke of Wellington (*see* STRATFIELD SAYE) who was twice her age. If it was thanks to her money that Hatfield was henceforth kept up as Robert Cecil would have wished, it was thanks to her brains that, from her son's time onwards, the house was inhabited by statesmen of the calibre of its builder. During the long reign of her son, the Prime Minister Marquess of Salisbury – who married another clever woman, though unlike his mother she was not rich – life at Hatfield had a unique quality. It was a mixture of grandeur and simplicity, of High Church piety, with daily services in the chapel, of intellectual brilliance and aesthetic philistinism: Lord Salisbury did not hesitate to cut a hole in a fine old tapestry to make a door, and he insisted that the railway should be brought as near to the house as possible so that he could walk to and from the station. Important guests came and went, ranging from Disraeli (*see* HUGHENDEN MANOR) to the Chinese statesman Li Hung-Chang, but their presence did not much affect the easy-going family life of the Salisburys and their children, who from an early age used to talk to their parents on equal terms about politics and religion. The youngest son Hugh once came into the room as a child and announced: 'I am afraid Nanny is a Semiarian heretic.'

Among the less important visitors to Hatfield in the Prime Minister's time was the writer Augustus Hare, who was much gratified when, as he arrived at the station, a groom touched his hat and asked: 'Please Sir, are you the Lord Chancellor?' But when, on the Sunday evening, Lady Salisbury made him entertain the house party with some of his celebrated stories, it unnerved him to see the Lord Chancellor sitting in the front row, flanked by the Attorney General and the previous Lord Chancellor. Hare wrote of Hatfield: 'There is something medieval in the band playing all dinner-time, yet without the sound being overwhelming, from the great size of the room; in the way that the host and hostess sit in the middle like Royalty and in the little lovely baskets of hot-house flowers given to each lady as she goes down the staircase to dinner.' The room to which Hare alludes is the Marble Hall, which was used in summer as a dining-room right up to the Second World War, even when the young grandson of the house was having breakfast by himself. In winter the family retreated upstairs to the winter dining-room off the long gallery, which, despite its great length, was the principal winter living-room.

Hare also remarked on how the bedrooms were named after different kinds of trees – as they are to this day – and he thought it incongruous for the panelled walls of the long gallery to be 'brilliantly lighted with gas'. On his later visits, he did not comment on what must have seemed to him the even greater incongruity of the electric light, which Hatfield possessed as far back as the mid-1880s, one of the very first country houses to have it. Exposed wires ran along the ceiling of the long gallery and would suddenly burst into flames; Lord Salisbury or his sons would nonchalantly toss up a cushion to put out the fire and then go on with their conversation. Lord Salisbury, who was of scientific bent and had a private laboratory, was also in advance of his time in installing an internal telephone system at Hatfield, down which he used to recite nursery rhymes to make sure it was working.

Hatfield continued to be at the centre of affairs after the Prime Minister's death, for the next Prime Minister, Arthur Balfour, was his sister's son and stayed here a great deal, while three of his own sons – the 4th Marquess, Lord Robert and Lord Hugh Cecil, who became, respectively, Viscount Cecil of Chelwood and Lord Quickswood – were also statesmen. Lord Hugh, who never married, lived at Hatfield with his brother and sister-in-law. He had a sitting-room of his own and occupied what is perhaps the best bedroom in the house. The 4th Marquess preferred to remain in the room on the top floor which had been his since boyhood and which he now shared with his wife. Lord Hugh's life at Hatfield is graphically recalled by his nephew Lord David Cecil – one of the two eminent writers produced by the family this century, the other being Algernon Cecil, nephew of Salisbury the Prime Minister.

He was never seen till lunchtime, when he appeared about twenty minutes late. After lunch he went for a walk. . . . Between tea and dinner he retired to his sitting room, an apartment on the ground floor, which he insisted on keeping bleakly and tastelessly furnished in heavy mid-Victorian style, as in his parents' days. He could be found there reclining awkwardly on a hard sofa, upholstered in dingy-coloured rep and reading, it might be, a newspaper or a sermon of Cardinal Newman's or a detective story he had chanced to pick up in the Drawing Ròom. At dinner he appeared, again twenty minutes late, to pass the evening in talk.

Lord David's brother, the late Lord Salisbury – who, like their younger sister, married a Cavendish (*see* CHATSWORTH) – was yet another statesman in the family. Today, the political tradition of Hatfield is as strong as ever, and so is the religious tradition: services are still held regularly in the chapel. But while in these two most important respects the house is the same as it has been for more than a century, its beauty is now greatly enhanced, largely thanks to the taste of the present Lady Salisbury, who as well as improving the decoration of some of the rooms and rearranging the furniture and objects

A garden party given at Hatfield in July 1889 for the Shah of Persia, Nasr-ed-Din, who stands at the front of the group between the Prince and Princess of Wales. His host, the 3rd Marquess of Salisbury, who was then Foreign Secretary as well as Prime Minister, stands beside Lady Salisbury on the next step up. This was the Shah's second visit to England, the first having been in 1873. He is said to have expressed surprise on this second visit that someone in Lord Salisbury's position should still have the same wife.

to show them to their best advantage, has made a new garden below the east front. This is now the private side of the house, the Marble Hall and the grand rooms on the first floor being for most of the time on view to the public, though they are still used by the family on special occasions, such as a few years ago when there was a dance. The guests passed through the dramatic emptiness of the Marble Hall lit only, as it seemed, by a blazing fire, so that the carvings and paintings on the screen and ceiling looked mysterious in the shadows; up the grand staircase into the colourful splendour of the King James drawing-room, with its full-length portraits by Reynolds and Romney and Lawrence, its gilt and rose-pink Chippendale furniture and its towering Renaissance chimney-piece of inlaid marble surmounted by King James's statue; then on into the long gallery, a vista of brown and gold, crowded for all its vast length just as it is in a picture of the ball given for Queen Victoria. The dancing took place in the winter dining-room, for the gallery itself has not been danced in since Queen Victoria was here, when the waltzes and polkas did havoc to the armoury ceiling. 'Don't hold a dance in the gallery', is the first thing told to every prospective bride of the son and heir; the second injunction being not to light fires in the two fireplaces at either end of the gallery, which are dummies.

Architecture and Contents

A Jacobean palace of red brick with facings of stone, designed by Robert Lyminge (who was also the architect of BLICKLING) and completed in 1612. The north front is massive and somewhat austere, but the south front has great movement and variety, with its turrets and cupolas, its deeply projecting wings and its arcade, which was glazed to form the armoury by the 2nd Marquess of Salisbury. As well as rebuilding the west wing after it was gutted by fire in 1835, he also carried out an extensive restoration of the rest of the house, making the interior more consciously Jacobean in character. In 1878 the Marble Hall was given its ceiling paintings, adding to the richness of what must already have been a sumptuous room with its Jacobean woodcarving and plasterwork and its Brussels tapestries. Next to the Marble Hall is the grand staircase of carved oak, leading up to the King James drawing-room which has an elaborate Renaissance chimney-piece of marble, as does the library at the other end of the long gallery. The chapel keeps its original Flemish stained glass and some of its original decorations, with painted panels of early saints. Among the royal and family portraits at Hatfield – which also include works by Dahl, Mytens, Wissing, Reynolds, Romney and Lawrence – Nicholas Hilliard's 'Ermine' portrait of Elizabeth I and the no less famous 'Rainbow' portrait of the same Queen have pride of place. A hat, a pair of gloves and a pair of stockings which actually belonged to Elizabeth can be seen in the long gallery, where other treasures include a crystal posset set given to Mary Tudor and Philip of Spain on their betrothal.

HOGHTON TOWER
LANCASHIRE

Hoghton Tower: a bird's-eye view drawn in 1884.

THERE have been Hoghtons at Hoghton since the twelfth century, but the spectacular hill-top mansion of Hoghton Tower, which looks from a distance more like a fortified village than a country house, dates mostly from the reign of Elizabeth I. In style and plan it is more medieval than Elizabethan, bearing witness to the conservatism of sixteenth-century Lancashire and of its builder Thomas Hoghton, who, as might be expected, was an adherent of the Old Faith. William Allen, the future Cardinal, himself a Lancashireman, is said to have been a guest at the festivities following the completion of the house in 1565, the year in which he left England for good. Four years later Thomas Hoghton was obliged to follow Allen into exile, for 'blessed conscience sake'; he settled in the Low Countries, where he died in 1580.

Thomas's nephew, Sir Richard Hoghton, enjoyed the favour of James I who made him a baronet at the institution of the Order in 1611 and came to stay with him at Hoghton in August 1617 on his way back from Scotland. It was in the nature of a business visit: the Hoghtons had a lease from the Crown of some alum mines which were losing money, Sir Richard hoped that the King would take them off his hands for a consideration, and the canny Scottish monarch wanted to see what they were worth. To put him in a good frame of mind, Sir Richard entertained him in the grandest possible style, at vast expense. Red velvet cloth is said to have been laid along the entire length of the half-mile avenue up to the house, where Sir Richard's tenants were assembled, together with those of the neighbouring gentry, all wearing the Hoghton livery. Not only had Sir Richard's neighbours agreed to dress their tenants in his livery for the occasion, but to oblige him had donned it themselves and were attending on him 'rather for the grace and reputation than any exacting of mean service', as one of them, Nicholas Assheton of Downham, has recorded.

Assheton tells of how the King was welcomed on his arrival by a speech in verse, delivered by two retainers dressed up as 'Household Gods', one of them in 'a purple taffata mantle', the other in huntsman's attire. The King went hunting immediately after the speech and fortunately a stag was quickly found and killed. Next day there was more hunting. Then came the main business of the visit, the inspection of the alum mines, where the King spent an hour 'and viewed them preciselie', after which he 'went and shot att a stagge, and missed'.

For dinner next day, at the top table – where the grandees were waited on by Assheton and other local gentlemen – no fewer than forty-four dishes were served, including roast beef, roast and boiled mutton, roast pork and roast

A visit to Hoghton by James I in 1617, painted by George Cattermole.

venison, salmon, goose and turkey, pullets, ducks, rabbits, plovers and pigeons, hot herons and cold curlew pie. The feast was not quite as gargantuan as it may seem, because not all the dishes were meant to go round the whole table; one of them, a dish of six quails, was for the King only. The fact that there was roast beef on the bill of fare is the only contemporary evidence to support the legend of James knighting the sirloin while he was here.

The dishes were just as numerous at supper that night, which was followed by 'a maske of noblemen, knights, gentlemen and courtiers, afore the King, in the middle round in the garden'. Next day, after a breakfast of thirty dishes, the royal party left, and Sir Richard was able to relax with Assheton and other neighbours over a drink in his cellar. It must have been a relief that the visit was over and had gone off well, but although the King agreed to treat for the mines, this did not save Sir Richard from being imprisoned in the Fleet for debt some years later.

Sir Richard's son, Sir Gilbert, fought as a Cavalier during the Civil War though he was no longer young. Early in 1643, after the Royalist garrison of Hoghton had surrendered the house to the Parliamentary forces, more than a hundred Roundheads lost their lives when the tower between the two courtyards, which was used as the magazine, suddenly blew up. This inevitably led to accusations of treachery, though it seems more likely to have been an accident. Had it been intentional, the Roundheads would surely have avenged themselves on the house, whereas the destruction of the tower, which was not rebuilt, was the only damage suffered by it throughout the

conflict. It is possible that the Roundheads respected Hoghton because the Cavalier Sir Gilbert's son Richard was a Roundhead himself. He had gone a long way from the Catholicism of Thomas Hoghton and had thrown in his lot with the Presbyterian party. After the Restoration he made Hoghton a refuge for persecuted Dissenters, who used to hold their prayer-meetings in the banqueting hall where King James had feasted.

The Hoghtons continued to be Presbyterians until the nineteenth century, and in the time of Sir Henry Hoghton, who succeeded as 5th Baronet in 1710, the banqueting hall was in regular use as a Dissenting chapel. Sir Henry, one of seven successive Hoghton baronets to sit in Parliament, was so much involved in the affairs of the borough of Preston that he gave up living at Hoghton, which he found too isolated. His two immediate successors also preferred being nearer to Preston, so that by the end of the century their ancestral home was abandoned and 'fast falling into decay', uninhabited except for the later buildings flanking the entrance which were tenanted by a few families of weavers. Charles Dickens visited Hoghton in 1854, and his short story 'George Silverman's Explanation', in which the house features under its real name (except that he calls it Hoghton Towers, in the plural) gives us some idea of the state in which he found it: 'the ancient rooms, many of them with their floors and ceilings falling, the beams and rafters hanging dangerously down, the plaster dropping, the oak panels stripped away, the windows half walled up, half broken.'

Some twenty years before Dickens' visit, there had been a plan for Hoghton's restoration which had come to nothing. It was not until the latter part of the century that the house was restored, by Sir Henry de Hoghton, 9th Baronet – whose interest in the past caused him to resume the 'de', which his sixteenth-century ancestors had dropped – and then by his brother and half-brother, who succeeded him in turn. Considering the extent of the buildings, it was a remarkable undertaking, particularly as the 9th Baronet had lost the then enormous sum of £200,000 by investing it in Confederate bonds during the American Civil War. As a further discouragement the family portraits and other heirlooms were destroyed by fire when they were being stored in London. Sir Henry and his two successors persevered, and the work, which was sympathetically done, was completed in 1901, the year in which the 11th Baronet's son Cuthbert came of age. The late Sir Cuthbert de Hoghton, in whose time the religious allegiance of the family went full-circle back to Catholicism, was a much-loved figure who combined an aristocratic presence with an engaging simplicity.

King George V and Queen Mary leaving Hoghton after their visit in 1913.

Architecture and Contents

A dramatic hill-top mansion of stone, extending round two courtyards, and completed in 1565. Having been neglected for more than a century, the house was restored from the 1870s onwards under the supervision of E.G.Paley and H.J.Austin. Some of the rooms contain fielded panelling of about 1700. There is a good Jacobean table in the banqueting hall, furniture by Gillow and a collection of dolls' houses.

126

HOLKHAM HALL
NORFOLK

The top of the staircase in the marble hall, which is modelled on a Roman basilica and rises to almost the full height of the house.

THE building of Holkham, that wide-spreading Palladian palace set in a great flat landscape near the Norfolk coast, was the life's work of Thomas Coke, Earl of Leicester, an eighteenth-century descendant of the famous Lord Chief Justice Coke of James I's reign. As well as studying buildings and collecting works of art during a protracted Grand Tour, Leicester took lessons in architecture, so that he was himself able to contribute to the design, along with two professionals, William Kent and Matthew Brettingham, and another distinguished amateur, Lord Burlington. This wealth of talent was not, however, matched by the wealth necessary for so ambitious an undertaking, since a large part of Leicester's fortune had been lost in the South Sea Bubble. The result was slow progress. Work began in 1734 on one of the four flanking pavilions, the one destined to be the family wing, which was completed in 1741; only after that was a start made on the main block. By 1747 there was enough to attract sightseers: Horace Walpole (*see* HOUGHTON HALL) wrote in that year of how Lord and Lady Bath and their son, having forgotten to tip the servant who showed them over the half-built house, 'upon recollection and deliberation . . . sent back a man and horse six miles with half-a-crown.'

The house was still unfinished when Mrs Lybbe Powys came here in 1756. The family was away, but the housekeeper thoughtfully provided 'a breakfast . . . in the genteelest taste, with all kinds of cakes and fruit, placed undesired in an apartment we were to go through.' It was not only the grander rooms which won Mrs Lybbe Powys's admiration. 'Such an amazing large and good kitchen I never saw,' she wrote, 'everything in it so nice and clever.' One of her companions told her that Lady Leicester never missed going round the kitchen wing every morning, and that once, when he was staying here, 'he was walking by the windows and saw her Ladyship in her kitchen at six o'clock (AM).' The industrious Lady Leicester also kept the building accounts and after her husband's death in 1759 she dedicated herself to finishing the house, which she succeeded in doing by 1764. It was she who completed many of the principal rooms, including the stupendous marble hall with its Ionic colonnades and high coffered ceiling.

When Lord Leicester died his title became extinct, his unsatisfactory only son, the husband of the diarist Lady Mary Coke, having died before him. Holkham passed to his nephew Wenman Roberts, who assumed the surname of Coke, and whose son Thomas was the celebrated Coke of Norfolk. During a reign of sixty-six years, from 1776 to 1842, Coke of Norfolk greatly improved the Holkham estate, which became famous for its advanced methods of husbandry. People interested in farming flocked here from all

Coke of Norfolk inspecting his Southdown sheep at Holkham.

over Britain and also from further afield, the more distinguished being lavishly entertained in 'Coke's rustic palace', with an abundance of partridges, pheasants and woodcock to divert those of them whose tastes were sporting as well as agricultural. The annual Holkham sheep-shearings, known as 'Coke's Clippings', rivalled the Derby as a national event. For most of his long life, the princely owner of Holkham was content to be plain Mr Coke, though he could easily have obtained a peerage. 'I had rather remain the first of the ducks than be the last of the geese', he used to say. There is a story of how when the Prince Regent was displeased with him, he threatened to knight him. When told of this threat, Coke is reputed to have said: 'If he tries to knight me, by God, I'll break his sword.' In 1837, however, Coke accepted a new earldom of Leicester, a reason for his change of heart being that his second wife, whom he married in 1822 when he was approaching seventy, had presented him with four sons.

By his first marriage, Coke of Norfolk only had daughters. One of them married the 1st Viscount Anson (*see* SHUGBOROUGH). Another married Admiral Sir Henry Digby and was the mother of the beautiful but wayward Jane Digby, known as 'Aurora, the Light of Day', who after leaving her first husband, Lord Ellenborough – a future Governor-General of India – had a succession of husbands and lovers, including King Ludwig I of Bavaria, and ended up happily and respectably married to a Bedouin Sheikh. In 1827, when she was still married to Ellenborough, the blue-eyed and golden-haired Jane went to stay with her grandfather at Holkham, where a young man from the British Museum who was cataloguing the library fell madly in love with her. 'Lady Ellenborough is such a charm that I find the library become a bore', he confided to his diary on 16 March. Next day he mentioned having been with her in the saloon: 'she sings to me the most bewitching airs, the words of which are enough to inflame one.' On 19 March he was 'with Lady E. till past 5 hearing her play the guitar and sing.' And then, as he recounted

The south front of Holkham Hall, 344 feet long from wing to wing and designed in a careful adaptation of the Palladian style. To the right is the large Victorian orangery.

128

on 24 March, the inevitable happened. 'In the evening drew pictures for Lady Anne Coke and Miss Anson. Also played whist and won. Lady E. lingered behind the rest of the party and at midnight I escorted her to her room – Fool that I was! I will not add what passed. Gracious God! Was there ever such good fortune!'

Coke of Norfolk's eldest son, the 2nd Earl of Leicester, lived to be eighty-six so his reign, which lasted from 1842 to 1909, was even longer than his father's. Like his father, he married a second wife very much younger than himself. She lived until 1937 and would surprise people by opening a conversation with 'As my father-in-law said to Marie Antoinette', for Coke of Norfolk had been received at the French Court before the Revolution. Though they inhabited a palace filled with works of art, the 2nd Earl and his family were more sporting than artistic – one of his daughters used even to go ratting. But if the beauties of Holkham were less appreciated in the Victorian and Edwardian era than they had been by previous generations, the great house continued to be run in its old style: at Christmas, eighteen large turkeys were roasted on a spit in the kitchen; even after 1900 it was a duty of the housemaids to sleep in all the beds throughout the house in order to air them.

Not long before the 2nd Earl died, the sixteen-year-old Lady Diana Manners (*see* BELVOIR CASTLE; HADDON HALL) was staying in the neigh-bourhood and she and her friends came to see Holkham as tourists rather than as guests, the house being for some reason open, possibly for a charity. In the vast basilica of a hall their guide pointed, as though at a portrait, and said, 'That is his present Lordship.' It was not, however, a portrait but Lord Leicester himself who was on view, lying, apparently unconscious, on a

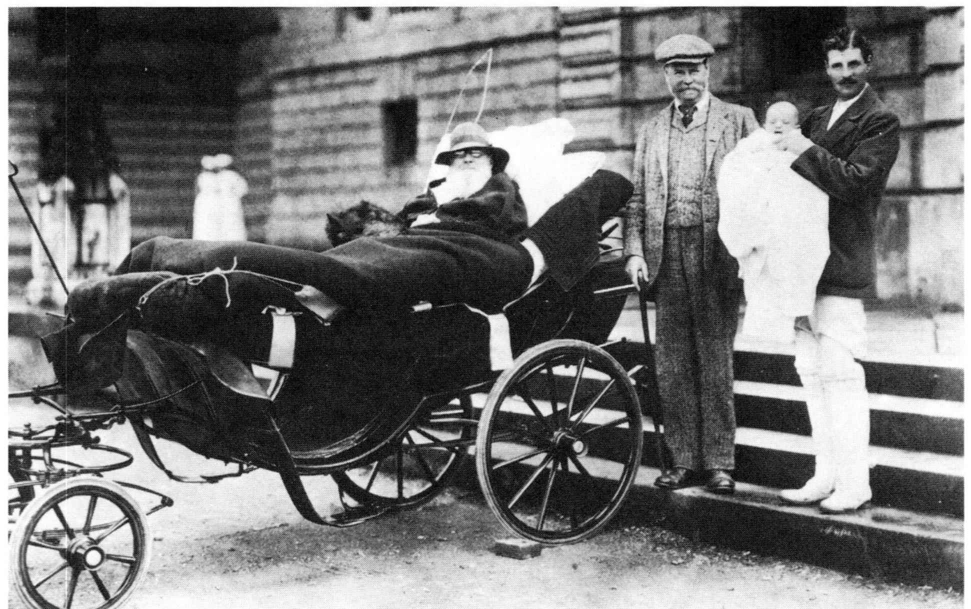

The octogenarian Thomas, 2nd Earl of Leicester – Coke of Norfolk's son – at Holkham in 1908, with his son Thomas, Viscount Coke, his grandson Thomas Coke and his great-grandson 'Little Tom' – afterwards 3rd, 4th and 5th Earls of Leicester in succession. The 2nd Earl died in 1909, soon after his eighty-sixth birthday. His even longer-lived son, the 3rd Earl, died in 1941 at the age of ninety-three.

hospital-like bed with one or two nurses standing beside him. Why he was there Lady Diana never managed to find out: perhaps he was anticipating and upstaging Evelyn Waugh's Lord Marchmain by wishing to die in what is arguably the most monumental country-house interior in all England.

Architecture and Contents

Holkham, started in 1734 and completed thirty years later, is one of the grandest of the great Palladian mansions, consisting of a central block on a palatial scale flanked by four pavilions (instead of the usual two), each of which would, on its own, constitute a sizeable country house. The hall is of stupendous height, surrounded by fluted Ionic columns and with a richly coffered and ornamented ceiling. A broad staircase in the apse at the inner end leads up to the state rooms, which are hung with Genoa velvet and Brussels and Mortlake tapestries and contain a magnificent collection of pictures: there is a Rubens and an array of Claudes and Poussins as well as works by Guido Reni, Carlo Maratta, Annibale Carracci, Luca Giordano, Van Dyck and Gainsborough. The furniture in the state rooms is no less splendid, while the sculpture gallery contains a collection of antique statues. In one of the pavilions, which was designed as a self-contained wing for the family, is a great library; in another is a monumental chapel.

The house stands in an immense park, which was improved in the late eighteenth century by Coke of Norfolk, who turned many square miles of the surrounding country into one of the most important agricultural estates in England, spending something like £500,000 on the estate buildings, more than fifty of which were designed for him by Samuel Wyatt.

HOUGHTON HALL
NORFOLK

S IR Robert Walpole, the first Prime Minister, who came of a line of
Norfolk squires long seated at Houghton, built the present splendid
Palladian Houghton Hall from about 1720 onwards. While he was in office,
Walpole was only able to come to Houghton for ten days in the summer and
three weeks in the autumn, when he held those convivial gatherings of
political colleagues and county neighbours known as his 'Norfolk Congresses'. Lord Hervey of the *Memoirs*, who attended one in the summer of
1731, reported to the Prince of Wales that everybody could do as they
pleased, so that 'one's next room neighbour' was 'no more trouble to one here
than one's next door neighbour in London . . . we used to sit down to dinner a
little snug party of about thirty odd, up to the chin in beef, venison, geese,
turkeys, etc.; and generally over the chin in claret, strong beer and punch.
We had Lords spiritual and temporal, besides commoners, parsons and
freeholders innumerable.' The governess to Walpole's daughter once
counted thirty-six young turkeys that had been served at one of these dinners

*Houghton Hall, a splendid classical
exterior crowned with cupolas and faced
with stone, which was brought here at
vast expense.*

and never touched, it being customary for such delicacies to appear towards the end of the meal, by which time most people were already replete.

During the so-called Congresses, Walpole and his guests mainly frequented the ground floor or 'rustic storey' of the house, which, as Hervey put it, was 'dedicated to fox-hunters, hospitality, noise, dirt and business'. There was, on this floor, 'a room for breakfast, another for supper, another for dinner, another for afternooning'. One of the colonnades joining the central block to the wings, which had fireplaces to keep it warm, was used 'for walking and quid-nuncing'. The grand rooms on the first floor or *piano nobile*, what Hervey called 'the floor of taste, expense, state and parade', were reserved for more formal occasions such as when, a few months after Hervey's visit, Walpole entertained the Duke of Lorraine, the future husband of the Empress Maria Theresa. The party dined in the lofty stone hall, which was lit by fifty wax candles; as many wax candles again lit the richly gilded saloon.

The profusion of gilding at Houghton impressed Mrs Lybbe Powys when she came here in 1756. 'The cornishes and mouldings of all the appartments being gilt, it makes the whole what I call magnificently glaring, especially as the rooms are, instead of white, painted dark green olive,' she wrote. By then, Houghton was owned by the Prime Minister's grandson, the mentally unstable 3rd Earl of Orford, who during the course of his life was to dissipate the family fortunes, which were never really enough to support so large a house. His uncle, the writer, antiquary and wit Horace Walpole, wrote sadly in 1773 about the state into which Houghton had fallen. 'The glorious house dilapidated, and open in many parts to the weather; the garden destroyed by horses, the park half unpaled and overgrown with nettles and brambles, a crew of plunderers quartered on all parts.'

When Mrs Lybbe Powys paid a second visit to Houghton in 1781, the Prime Minister's picture collection had been sold to Catherine the Great of Russia. ''Tis really melancholy to see the hangings disrob'd of those beautiful ornaments', she lamented. 'And only one picture now there, a portrait of the Empress herself, which she made my Lord a present of . . . it rather gives one pain to see the person who must deprive every one who now visits Houghton of the entertainment given to them by these pictures.' Writing in that same year to his old friend Sir Horace Mann, Horace Walpole compared the decay of Houghton with the loss of the North American colonies. 'You and I have lived long enough to see Houghton and England emerge, the one from a country gentleman's house to a palace, the other from an island to an empire, and to behold both stripped of their acquisitions and lamentable in their ruins.'

Ten years later, at the age of seventy-four, Horace Walpole succeeded his unsatisfactory nephew in the earldom, which became extinct on his death in 1797. A new earldom of Orford was afterwards conferred on the Prime Minister's nephew, Lord Walpole, who did not, however, inherit Houghton, which went to the Marquess of Cholmondeley, a grandson of Horace Walpole's sister. A few years later there was a rumour that Houghton was to be bought by the nation and given to Nelson, but Lord Cholmondeley said that he had heard of no such proposal and that in any case he had no intention of parting with it. After Waterloo he appears to have changed his mind, for he

The Green Velvet Bedchamber, with its magnificent bed.

Sybil, Countess of Rocksavage, afterwards Marchioness of Cholmondeley, who enriched Houghton with works of art inherited from her brother, Sir Philip Sassoon.

was prepared to sell Houghton to the nation as a country seat for the Duke of Wellington, who in the event chose STRATFIELD SAYE. The Cholmondeleys have continued to own Houghton down to the present time, though their principal seat is in Cheshire, and the house has long been restored to its original splendour.

Architecture and Contents

This magnificent Palladian mansion was begun in 1722 and completed in 1735. The original design of Houghton was by Colen Campbell, altered by James Gibbs and carried out by Thomas Ripley. Unusual for Norfolk in being faced entirely with stone – brought at vast expense from outside the county – it consists of a central block with corner towers crowned with domes and cupolas and with a pediment and engaged portico on the principal front, joined by curving colonnades to service wings. The finest rooms on the *piano nobile* are the stone hall and the saloon. The hall is a cube of forty feet with a monumental chimney-piece by Rysbrack and a ceiling of bold plasterwork by the 'gentleman' stuccoist Giuseppe Artari; the saloon has a coved ceiling with painted decoration incorporating *Phaeton* by William Kent, who was responsible for the decorative painting on the ceilings of some of the other rooms and for the *chiaroscuro* murals on the great staircase. Kent also designed most of the furniture, which in the present century has been augmented by even more magnificent furniture of French provenance from the collection of the present Lord Cholmondeley's uncle, Sir Philip Sassoon.

133

HUGHENDEN MANOR
BUCKINGHAMSHIRE

'IT IS all done, and you are the Lady of Hughenden', Disraeli wrote, with a characteristic flourish, to his beloved wife Mary Anne in September 1848, having with the help of a legacy from his father and a loan from Lord George Bentinck and the two other sons of the wealthy Duke of Portland bought the Buckinghamshire seat on which they had set their heart: a simple late-Georgian house in a park with beechwoods and a small estate. They proceeded to engage servants and move in furniture from Isaac D'Israeli's house at Bradenham. Mary Anne acquired carpets from Maple's, shields to make the hall look baronial and – an essential for an up-and-coming Conservative politician and his wife – a marquee for garden parties. In 1863, under Mary Anne's direction, the house was enlarged and transformed into a red-brick mansion with a skyline of finials. 'We have restored the house to what it was before the Civil Wars, and we have made a garden of terraces, in which cavaliers might roam, and saunter, with their ladye-loves', the incurably romantic Dizzy wrote when the work was nearing completion, though in fact the so-called 'restoration' produced a building unmistakably Victorian, with an interior of dark panelling, patterned wallpapers and flowered fabrics. It contained many books and family portraits, and, in the hall, portraits of his friends, living and dead, including D'Orsay, Bulwer Lytton (*see* KNEBWORTH HOUSE), George Smythe – the original of Coningsby in his novel of that name – and another member of the Young England party, Lord John Manners (*see* BELVOIR CASTLE).

Disraeli called the hall at Hughenden the Gallery of Friendship; there was also a room in the house called the Statesman's Room. In the words of G.W.E. Russell, a writer and politician who was a nephew of the 9th Duke of Bedford (*see* WOBURN ABBEY), he had a 'quaint trick of transferring the grandiose nomenclature of palaces to his own very modest domain. ... He called his simple drawing room the Saloon; he styled his pond the Lake; he expatiated on the beauties of the terrace walk, the "Golden Gate" and the "German Forest".' Much of the latter was planted by Mary Anne with her own hands. She would put on a short skirt, boots and gaiters and go out to plant trees or work in the garden with its parterres, its statues and its urns full of pink geraniums and blue African lilies. Both she and Disraeli loved Hughenden: they would say how much they would like to live here all the year round, free from the cares of politics, but both of them knew perfectly well that they did not really mean it. 'No dear, I will never give you the chance', she would say, when Disraeli dreamt of a rustic retirement. 'It is quite dull in the country when we are alone together', she wrote in a letter, 'for Dizzy takes his book (he does nothing but read books, old Greek and

Group at Hughenden, Whitsuntide 1874, some three months after Disraeli became Prime Minister for the second time. Disraeli sits on the right, with his friend and confidante Selina, Countess of Bradford, on the left in a striped dress. Behind her stands another of Dizzy's devoted friends, his private secretary Monty Lowry-Corry, afterwards Lord Rowton, who founded the Rowton Houses to provide accommodation for poor men in London.

Latin books) and I take my book, but I am so tired with planting that I am afraid it often falls out of my hand and I go asleep.'

For Disraeli, Hughenden was not only a delightful retreat but also a suitably squirearchical background for the leader of the Conservative Party. 'How he tried to act up to the character he had imposed upon himself, that of the country gentleman!' wrote Lady Battersea, formerly Constance Rothschild, whose home was a few miles away at Aston Clinton. 'Dressed in his velveteen coat, his leather leggings, his soft felt hat, and carrying his little hatchet, for relieving the bark of trees from the encroaching ivy, in one of those white hands which probably hitherto had never held anything heavier than a pen, Mr Disraeli was *the Squire*.' When Mary Anne died, according to G.W.E.Russell, 'he sent for his agent and said: "I desire that Her Ladyship's remains should be borne to the grave by the tenants of the estate." Presently the agent came back with a troubled countenance and said, "I regret to say there are not tenants enough to carry a coffin."'

In 1873, a few months after her death, Disraeli had a portrait of her painted from a miniature, for somehow she had never got round to sitting for her portrait. To help fill the void which her passing had left in his life, he had his friend and confidante Selina, Lady Bradford and her sister Anne, Lady

135

Chesterfield to stay with him at Hughenden for the Whitsun of 1874, at the beginning of his second and longer period as Prime Minister. When he returned in the following autumn, he wrote wistfully to Lady Bradford: 'I have not been to Hughenden since you were here. I have been into your rooms and could scarcely persuade myself that they had been inhabited by the Lady of the Lake.' There were times during those last years of his life when he was alone at Hughenden, though he naturally was not short of visitors, some more welcome than others. In September 1877 Lord Lyons, then Ambassador in Paris, telegraphed to announce that he was coming down the same day. 'We have not a servant in the house,' Disraeli wrote despairingly to Lady Bradford after hearing that the great diplomatist was about to descend on him, 'all being engaged in a grand cricket match in the park with a neighbouring parish. It is impossible to disturb them. We are at our wit's end.'

In the December of that same year, Disraeli was afforded the supreme honour of a visit by the Queen, who drove over to luncheon at Hughenden from Windsor, accompanied by her daughter Princess Beatrice. She planted a tree on the south side of the house to commemorate her visit and he gave her, as a souvenir, his statuette by Trentanova; to the Princess he gave 'the most beautiful *bonbonnière* you ever saw or fancied: just fresh from Paris.' His satisfaction at the Queen's visit was somewhat overshadowed by his anxiety about the Russo-Turkish war, but as he reported to Lady Bradford, it was 'a great success: fine day, and with some gleams of sunshine. The Faery seemed to admire, and be interested in, everything, and has written to me a very pretty letter to that effect.'

The Queen came again to Hughenden in 1881, soon after Disraeli's funeral. The vault in the little church in the park was reopened in order that she could lay a wreath of porcelain flowers on the coffin, above his heart. She then went into the house and had tea in the library, after which she sat for an hour in the little study which Disraeli used to call 'My Workshop', sometimes silent, sometimes weeping.

Hughenden was inherited by Disraeli's nephew, Major Coningsby Ralph Disraeli, who made various alterations to the house. James Lees-Milne came here as an undergraduate from Oxford and Major Disraeli received him in the former saloon, which had become the library, wearing 'a dusty velvet skull cap and, if I remember right, a blue velvet jacket and string bow tie'. After Major Disraeli's death in 1936, the property passed to his sister Mrs Calverly, who decided to sell it. Fortunately it was bought, together with the contents of the house, by a purchaser anxious to preserve it as a museum, and it was eventually handed over the National Trust.

Architecture and Contents

As transformed by the Disraelis to the design of Edward Buckton Lamb, Hughenden is a red-brick Victorian mansion of somewhat unusual aspect, with camber-headed windows, a skyline of battlements and finials and a cloister-like arcade joining shallow projecting wings on the entrance front.

The garden front of Hughenden. Disraeli used often to pace up and down in the sun on the sheltered terrace.

The decoration and furnishing of the interior is much as it was in Disraeli's time, with portraits, books and relics all strongly evocative of the great statesman and his contemporaries.

KNEBWORTH HOUSE
HERTFORDSHIRE

KNEBWORTH, the ancient home of the Lyttons, having passed by a somewhat indirect descent to the eighteenth-century scholar Richard Warburton, was inherited in 1810 by his daughter Elizabeth, the widow of General William Bulwer. The house, mainly Tudor and built round a courtyard, was in poor repair by the time Elizabeth Bulwer-Lytton (as she became) inherited it, and in 1811 she pulled down all but one side, which she refaced in a mild form of Gothic. She lived at Knebworth until her death in 1843. Five years earlier she gave bread, meat and ale to the poor of the neighbourhood to celebrate the emancipation of the Negro apprentices, a measure which had been carried through Parliament largely thanks to a brilliant speech by her son Edward. As well as being a politician and a reformer, Edward Bulwer-Lytton was a novelist, a journalist, a poet and a playwright, also remembered as a dandy and a romantic, a friend of Disraeli (*see* HUGHENDEN MANOR) and Dickens. As a lifelong lover of the stage, he brought in the Bill abolishing the monopoly in serious drama hitherto held by Covent Garden and Drury Lane, as well as introducing dramatic copyright which up till then had not existed. He also tried, without success, to end theatrical censorship. 'The true censor of the age', he told the House of Commons, 'is the spirit of the age.'

On succeeding his mother at Knebworth, Bulwer-Lytton turned the house into a Gothic fantasy in keeping with his romantic temperament. The outside was embellished with cupolas, pinnacles and gargoyles; the interior was redecorated by John Crace, with gorgeously coloured and gilded ornament, with stained glass and innumerable coats-of-arms of Bulwer-Lytton's ancestors, real or supposed. To complete the effect there were banners, suits of armour and portraits of English kings. The owner of all this baronial splendour lived here alone, having parted from his beautiful but neurotic wife Rosina, who nevertheless continued to persecute him for the rest of his life. Once, when he was fighting an election, she appeared on the hustings and declared that Parliament was not the proper place for him: 'His proper place', she shouted, pointing to the ground, 'is below.'

To console him in his matrimonial troubles, Bulwer-Lytton had his friends, many of them from the world of literature and the stage. The actor-manager William Charles Macready came to stay at Knebworth in the summer of 1850, and he and his host went for a walk together, 'discoursing on religion, the immortality of the soul, youth, marriage'. In the autumn of that same year, Dickens brought his amateur theatrical company to Knebworth and gave a performance of Ben Jonson's *Every Man in His Humour* in the banqueting hall on three consecutive nights, the first night being for the

Bulwer-Lytton in his study at Knebworth in 1854, smoking his chibouk: a painting by E.M.Ward.

Knebworth House, soon after it was enlarged and embellished by Bulwer-Lytton in 1844.

tenants and the other two for the county neighbours. The cast included Dickens himself, his wife, his brother Frederick and his friend and future biographer John Forster, as well as the playwright Douglas Jerrold, the painter Augustus Egg and the two *Punch* luminaries Mark Lemon and John Leech. On the first evening, the actors were given an early dinner before the performance, but nothing much to eat afterwards, with the result that they all went to bed hungry. Dickens did not feel equal to asking Bulwer-Lytton or his cook for food, so next day two of the cast bought supplies in the village and after that night's performance a 'surreptitious supper' was held in the bedroom of Douglas Jerrold, which being isolated in a tower seemed a safe enough venue. Nevertheless, Bulwer-Lytton somehow found out about the dormitory feast, and 'called his guests to account for not taking him into their confidence on so important a point . . . it was like the headmaster taking the big boys of the school to task for a breach of discipline.' Dickens promised they wouldn't do it again, and Bulwer-Lytton not only forgave them but took the hint and provided a splendid supper after the final performance. While Dickens was at Knebworth on this occasion, he and Bulwer-Lytton had the idea of holding further performances to raise money for a guild to help impoverished writers and artists; £4,000 was eventually raised, but the scheme proved a failure.

Dickens came again to Knebworth in 1861, bringing the proofs of *Great Expectations* for his friend's comments. Another time he brought Edward FitzGerald, the translator of Omar Khayyám, whose first impression of Bulwer-Lytton in his study was of 'an Eastern potentate sitting on luxurious cushions, with dreamy eyes and reposeful manner' smoking a long Turkish pipe, the bowl of which rested on the floor. To get from this sanctum to his bedroom, Bulwer-Lytton had to pass through the gallery, where his guests would congregate. Towards the end of his life, after he had been raised to the peerage as Lord Lytton, he did not feel up to greeting the newly arrived guests on his way to change for dinner, so his butler used to say to them: 'His Lordship is invisible', and they would pretend not to notice him.

Bulwer-Lytton's son, who succeeded him in 1873 and was promoted to being Earl of Lytton in 1880, was a poet and a romantic like his father as well as being a diplomat and one of the least conventional of Indian Viceroys. After his return from India he led a life of poetic retirement at Knebworth, where he was visited one summer by the novelist Ouida, who having fed him on expensive early strawberries when he was in Florence in the previous spring, came here convinced that he was passionately in love with her. 'Why don't you leave this bourgeois man-and-wife *milieu* behind you and prove in some Sicilian palace what life may really mean for people like you and I ?' she asked him; but he was not tempted. A week later, a less demanding writer, W. H. Mallock, was playing whist in the drawing-room at Knebworth with Lytton and two other men after the ladies had gone to bed, when somebody happened to express a doubt as to whether Coleridge's 'Kubla Khan' had really been composed in a dream. Whereupon Lytton's eyes began to wander and he presently threw down his cards. 'I dreamed a poem in India,' he said. 'It has never been written down but I still can remember every line of it. Listen.' As he recited the poem, which was 'full of vague Oriental imagery', his voice, as Mallock recalled, 'acquired new tones ... giving to it the qualities of an incantation; and round us, as though fashioned out of the shadows, was the large, dimly-lighted drawing room, which the old novelist had encrusted with impossible heraldries, culminating in scutcheons of pre-Christian Welsh Kings.'

Bulwer-Lytton's drawing-room, complete with the 'impossible heraldries', survives intact, but the other principal rooms at Knebworth were mostly given back their original sixteenth- or seventeenth-century character by the Viceroy's son, the 2nd Earl of Lytton, helped by the great architect Sir Edwin Lutyens who was his sister's husband. The 2nd Earl, who married the beautiful Pamela Plowden, an early flame of the young Winston Churchill (*see* BLENHEIM PALACE), himself went to India as Governor of Bengal. His elder son died in a flying accident in 1933 and his younger son was killed in the Second World War, so on his death in 1947 Knebworth passed to his daughter Hermione (the present owner's mother) whose husband, now Lord Cobbold, was subsequently Governor of the Bank of England. In 1968, as Lord Chamberlain, Lord Cobbold was instrumental in the ending of dramatic censorship, hitherto a duty of his office, thus achieving what Bulwer-Lytton had tried without success to achieve in the 1830s.

*A bazaar at Knebworth in April 1913,
with the beautiful Pamela Countess of
Lytton at her stall.*

*The state drawing-room, decorated by
John Crace.*

Architecture and Contents

Knebworth now consists of the surviving range of a quadrangular early
Tudor mansion, its brick walls largely concealed by a Gothic and baronial
cloak of stucco, partly dating from about 1811 and partly from 1843. The
house as it is includes the original hall, which has a Jacobean screen and
panelling of about 1660 in the style of Inigo Jones, but most of the interior
was sumptuously decorated and furnished in the mid-nineteenth century by
John Crace, some of the rooms being redesigned in the present century by Sir
Edwin Lutyens. The family portraits include works by Gheeraerts, Lely,
John Riley and G.F.Watts; the library contains the literary collection of
Bulwer-Lytton; and there is a fascinating Indian exhibition based on the
Viceroyalty of his son, the 1st Earl of Lytton.

KNOLE
KENT

MORE like a medieval town or a college than a country house, Knole was built towards the end of the fifteenth century as a palace of the Archbishops of Canterbury. Then, having been taken over by Henry VIII, it was granted by Elizabeth I to Thomas Sackville, Lord Buckhurst, her cousin through Anne Boleyn. The Sackvilles were descended from Herbrand de Sackville who came over with the Conqueror and had long been living at Buckhurst in Sussex, where they continued to spend much of their time even after they had acquired Knole. Thomas's father, Sir Richard, became so wealthy as to be known as 'Fillsack', while Thomas himself, who started life as a poet and wrote the earliest English tragedy in blank verse, consolidated the family fortunes by holding various important offices, notably that of Lord High Treasurer. It was not until 1603, the year before James I made him Earl of Dorset, that he was able to take possession of Knole. But from then until his death in 1608 he spent many thousands on enlarging the late medieval archiepiscopal palace and sumptuously decorating its apartments.

Thomas's son and heir survived him only by a few months so his real successor was his spendthrift and dissipated grandson, the 3rd Earl of Dorset, who having married Lady Anne Clifford, heiress of vast estates in the north of England, was constantly quarrelling with her over the question of her patrimony. 'This night my Lord should have lain with me, but he and I fell out about matters,' is a typical entry in Lady Anne's diary, which gives us a vivid picture of her life at Knole, where for much of the time she was left to her own devices while her husband was away in London or elsewhere. 'I made an end of reading *Exodus*. After supper I played at Glecko with the steward as I often do after dinner and supper . . . The time grew tedious, so as I used to go to bed about 8 o'clock I did lie a-bed till 8 the next morning. . . . I made an end of my Irish stitch cushion. . . . This night I went into a bath. . . . We made Rosemary cakes. . . . Couch puppied in the morning. . . . After supper, because my Lord was sullen and not willing to go into the nursery, I had Mary bring the Child to him in my chamber.' Occasionally her husband was in a better humour, such as when he and she 'supped privately . . . in the Drawing Chamber, and had much discourse of the manners of the folks at court', or when she spent a peaceful evening in 'my Lord's closet', where she 'sat and read much in the Turkish history, and Chaucer'. And while during one of Dorset's many absences she complains of 'the time being very tedious with me, as having neither comfort nor company, only the Child,' her diary records a few sublime moments such as: 'After supper I walked in the garden and gathered cherries, and talked with Josiah who told me he thought all the men in the house loved me.'

Tea party at Knole, 26 August 1899, during the visit of the Duchess of York – the future Queen Mary – and her brother, Prince Alexander of Teck, afterwards Earl of Athlone. The white-bearded man in front of the table is the 2nd Lord Sackville. His granddaughter, Victoria Sackville-West, was to depict the young Duke, Sebastian, looking down from the roof of the house on to a scene such as this in her novel The Edwardians.

Josiah was the French page, one of twenty or so members of the Knole household who counted as gentry and had their meals at the parlour table. Others included the Steward, the Gentleman of the Horse, the Chaplain and Mr Matthew Caldicott, 'my Lord's favourite'. The main body of servants, some seventy in number and all male, ate at two tables in the hall: about twenty – including the cooks, brewers and clerks of the kitchen – at the smaller clerks' table, the rest at the long table where the hierarchy ranged from senior functionaries like Thomas Poor, Yeoman of the Wardrobe, down by way of the footmen and grooms to the 'men to carry wood'. The women were greatly outnumbered by the men. About twelve of them, including Grace Robinson, 'a Blackamoor', ate at the laundry-maids' table, with a single male, the porter, to keep them company; the remaining four, who constituted the nursery staff, ate separately. Also at a separate table were six lesser servants employed in the kitchen and scullery, including the 'Black-amoor' boy, John Morockoe. The Dorsets themselves did not eat with their household, in the medieval manner, but followed the more modern custom of restricting their company at meals to their family and a few favoured guests.

The worthless Lord Dorset died in 1624 at the age of thirty-five; Lady Anne, after a second and equally disastrous marriage to the 4th Earl of Pembroke (*see* WILTON HOUSE), retired to her ancestral kingdom in the north where she reigned contentedly and autocratically for the remainder of her long life. Since her two surviving children by Dorset were both girls, the Sackvilles obtained no long-term benefit from her wealth. Her brother-in-law, who became the 4th Earl of Dorset, started his reign very short of money, though in 1636 he repaired the family fortunes by marrying his son to a daughter of James I's 'financial wizard', Lionel Cranfield, Earl of Middlesex. He celebrated this occasion in such style that he spent £40,000. The bill of fare for a banquet which he gave at Knole runs to nearly seventy dishes, including crabs, lobster pie, 'salmon soused', sturgeon, larks, plovers, 'roast venison in blood', 'chine of veal roast' and 'hash of mutton with anchovies'. At the top of the bill of fare the following instructions are written: 'To perfume the room often in the meal with orange flower water upon a hot pan. To have fresh bowls in every corner and flowers tied upon them, and sweet briar, stock, gilly-flowers, pinks, wallflowers and any other sweet flowers in glasses and pots in every window and chimney.'

During the Civil War, when the 4th Earl sided with the King, Knole was seized by the Parliamentarians who held their Court of Sequestration for Kent in the room now known as the Poets' Parlour. This room is so called on account of the poets whose portraits hang on its walls – many of them, such as Dryden, Waller and Prior, were friends of the 6th Earl who was a poet himself and wrote the words of the song 'To all you ladies now at land'. The 6th Earl is also remembered as a genial Restoration rake, the lover, for a brief period, of Nell Gwyn. His extravagances once again depleted the family fortunes, though he left Knole the richer for its incomparable collection of Charles II furniture, much of which came out of the royal palace of Whitehall, a perquisite of his office as Lord Chamberlain.

In the eighteenth century the Sackvilles became Dukes of Dorset. A younger son of the 1st Duke was the unfortunate Lord George Sackville who as a soldier was accused of disobeying orders at the Battle of Minden and as a statesman has been held responsible for the loss of the North American colonies – perhaps in both cases unfairly. The 3rd Duke, who succeeded in 1769 at the age of twenty-four, was handsome and brilliant, a patron of the opera and the ballet. As Ambassador in Paris on the eve of the Revolution he was extremely popular and enjoyed the friendship of Marie Antoinette. He was irresistible to women and in the years when he was single had a succession of mistresses, the most celebrated being the Italian dancer Giannetta Baccelli, whom he installed at Knole in what was known ever afterwards as Shelley's Tower, the English servants having garbled her name. He had her sculpted in the nude and painted by Reynolds and by Gainsborough, who also sketched her in the ballroom attended by a Chinese page. The Chinese, educated at Sevenoaks Grammar School at the Duke's expense, had succeeded the long line of black boys – invariably called John Morocco – who had been exotic figures in the Knole household from the time of the 3rd Earl until the 1st Duke's house steward killed the last John Morocco in a fight in what was known as Black Boy's Passage.

In 1789 the 3rd Duke ended his affair with 'the Baccelli' and a year later married a suitable wife, but marriage made him parsimonious and autocratic and he suffered from the melancholia which afflicted so many of the Sackvilles. His only son, the 4th Duke, Byron's schoolfriend, was killed by a fall from his horse at the age of twenty-one, and on the death of the cousin who succeeded him the dukedom and other titles became extinct. Knole eventually passed to a son of the 4th Duke's sister, who in 1876 became the 1st Lord Sackville.

The diplomatist 2nd Lord Sackville never married, but had children by a Spanish dancer known as Pepita, including a son who afterwards tried unsuccessfully to prove that he was legitimate, and a daughter who married her father's nephew and eventual heir. She was the mother of the poet and novelist Victoria Sackville-West, known as Vita, who lived with her grandfather at Knole when she was a child, and has left an unforgettable picture of him, a silent, unsociable but not unamiable old man.

He knew nothing whatever about the works of art in the house; he spent hours gazing at the flowers, followed about the garden by two grave demoiselle cranes; he turned his back on all visitors, but sized them up after they had gone in one shrewd and sarcastic phrase; he bore a really remarkable resemblance to the portraits of the old Lord Treasurer, and he seemed to me, with his taciturnity and the never-mentioned background of his own not unromantic past, to stand conformably at the end of the long line of his ancestors. He and I, who so often shared the house between us, were companions in a shy and undemonstrative way ... When I was at home he would put after dinner a plate of fruit for my breakfast into a drawer of his writing-table labelled with my name, and this he never once failed to do, even though there might have been thirty people to dinner in the Great Hall, who watched, no doubt with great surprise, the old man who had been so rude to his neighbours at dinner going unconcernedly round with a plate, picking out the reddest cherries, the bluest grapes, and the ripest peach.

Under the name of Chevron, Knole is the background to Victoria Sackville-West's novel *The Edwardians*. One summer's afternoon the young Duke, Sebastian, escapes from having to play host for his mother by going on the roof. 'Acres of red-brown roof surrounded him, heraldic beasts carved in

Lord and Lady Sackville and their daughter Victoria Sackville-West (left) on 16 February 1910, after the Sackville succession case had ended with a verdict in their favour.

stone sitting at each corner of the gables. Across the great courtyard the flag floated red and blue and languid from a tower. Down in the garden, on a lawn of brilliant green, he could see the sprinkled figures of his mother's guests, some sitting under the trees, some strolling about; he could hear their laughter and the tap of the croquet mallets.' As well as being the author of one novel about Knole, Victoria Sackville-West is the hero-cum-heroine of another, *Orlando*, by her friend Virginia Woolf, in which she transmigrates down the line of her Sackville ancestors, ending as herself. 'Indeed, when Orlando came to reckon up the matter of furnishing with rose-wood chairs and cedar-wood cabinets, with silver basins, china bowls and Persian carpets, every one of the three hundred and sixty-five bedrooms which the house contained, he saw that it would be no light one.' Three centuries later, the modern female Orlando returns home in her sports car. 'She drew up in the courtyard where, for so many hundred years she had come, on horseback or in coach and six, with men riding before or coming after . . . She strode into the dining room where her old friends Dryden, Pope, Swift, Addison regarded her demurely.'

In the year that *Orlando* was published Knole ceased to be Victoria Sackville-West's home, for her father, the 3rd Lord Sackville, died and was succeeded by her uncle. Her cousin, the late Lord Sackville, better known as the writer and music critic Edward Sackville-West, inherited the literary talent with which Sackvilles had been blessed since the time of the Lord Treasurer, whom he came to resemble in his later years just as his great-uncle had resembled this same ancestor. He differed from many of his forebears in being sociable and gregarious – he is believed to have been the original of Davey in the novels of his friend Nancy Mitford – and he did not share his cousin Vita's passionate love of Knole, where he was never entirely happy; he used to say that the house, being confiscated Church property, brought the Sackvilles little happiness. On a more frivolous note, he would complain that if he went out to dinner he had to be back before the great doors at the entrance to the Green Court were shut for the night, or else he would be unable to get in. But while he spent much of his life away from Knole, he came here on visits, having his meals in the Poets' Parlour, playing the piano in the Colonnade, which, with its ravishing grisaille wall-paintings, was his favourite room. Those of his friends whom he entertained here were struck by his knowledge of the house and its history: when he showed them round he was the perfect guide, informed and appreciative yet not unduly reverent. He would point out his dislikes as well as his likes, one of his pet aversions being that popular piece of furniture, the so-called Knole sofa, of which the seventeenth-century prototype is in the Leicester Gallery. And when he spoke of his ancestors, there was generally an overtone of slightly sardonic humour. On one occasion a guest, admiring the recumbent nude statue of the Baccelli at the foot of the Painted Staircase, asked him if there was any statue or portrait of Pepita in the house. 'No', he replied, in a voice which conveyed a whole world of Victorian propriety. 'There is *not*.'

The Cartoon Gallery at Knole.

Architecture and Contents

Knole is one of the largest of English country houses, its buildings of grey-brown Kentish ragstone – mostly irregular with battlemented towers and gables of varying shapes and sizes – covering four acres, enclosing several courts. Though it was originally built in the late fifteenth century, it owes its present appearance, both outside and in, largely to the 1st Earl of Dorset, who decorated the incomparable succession of state rooms – including no fewer than three long galleries – with ornate Jacobean panelling and plasterwork ceilings. There is magnificent seventeenth-century furniture acquired by the 6th Earl of Dorset from Whitehall Palace and Hampton Court. Other treasures were inherited from Lionel Cranfield, Earl of Middlesex, including copies of Raphael's cartoons by Mytens, which give the Cartoon Gallery its name. The 3rd Duke of Dorset also added to the collection: through his friendship with Reynolds he brought to Knole the group of portraits by that artist which is yet another of its glories. Knole was given to the National Trust in 1946, but has continued to be the home of the Sackville family.

LAMPORT HALL
NORTHAMPTONSHIRE

Thomas Isham, the diarist, after he had succeeded his father as the 3rd Baronet, painted by Carlo Maratti.

THE Ishams were established at Lamport early in the reign of Elizabeth I by John Isham, a successful London mercer who married a mercer's widow. Though his family had been prominent in Northamptonshire since medieval times, he was himself a fourth son so had to make his way in the world. Having, in his son's words, 'gotten somm good store of substance with good credit and honest report', he was able to leave the City and settle down at Lamport as a country gentleman, applying himself 'to plantinge, buildinge, making of pooles, includeing of grounds and all other works of good husbandry, as though he had been brought up in them from his infansy'.

John Isham's son Thomas had the misfortune of being blind from boyhood, but this did not prevent him from riding and generally leading an active life. He also had that love of learning and literature which was notable in so many of his descendants, and his collection of early editions of Elizabethan authors was to make the Isham Library famous in the nineteenth century. The family continued to prosper in the early seventeenth century, a younger John Isham being made a baronet by Charles I, though his adherence to the Royalist cause in the Civil War was naturally a setback. His son, Sir Justinian, was imprisoned twice under the Commonwealth, yet he was rich enough during this period to enlarge the old manor house at Lamport by adding to it the splendid classical block by John Webb which now forms the centre of the principal front. Sir Justinian Isham followed in the family tradition by being a man of taste and learning, a scholar and a connoisseur; he was also interested in science and was to become one of the earliest Fellows of the Royal Society. He did not, however, impress the clever young Dorothy Osborne, then already in love with William Temple, when, as a widower of forty, he aspired to her hand. She nicknamed him 'the Emperor' and described him as a 'self-conceited learned coxcomb'. Nevertheless, she was not too pleased when her middle-aged suitor married someone else.

By this second marriage Sir Justinian had, together with other children, an eldest son, Thomas, to whom he gave a good classical education. In 1671, when Thomas was fourteen, his father promised to pay him £6 a year if he kept a diary in Latin, and for the next two years the boy assiduously did so, thereby leaving a fascinating record of life at Lamport in the reign of Charles II. We learn of how 'the carpenter made new shelves to put our public books on'; of how the cook 'lost his self-control' and played at dice with their guest Doctor Alexander Curtius, an eccentric Lithuanian physician; of how another servant, Grace Ibbs, went up to London to be touched by Charles II for the 'King's Evil'. Visitors to Lamport during those two years ranged, we are told, from the Earl and Countess of Devonshire (*see* CHATSWORTH) to Tom a' Bedlam, the local lunatic, who called to say 'that his only son had been eaten by a sow'.

Thomas Isham tells us that each Christmas two oxen were killed and the Ishams hired a company of minstrels from Daventry. They gave three feasts, the first for the poor of the locality, the second for the labourers and the third for 'the more substantial inhabitants'. The fact that the poor were entertained first shows that there was no question of giving them the left-overs from the other two dinners. During Christmas 1671 Thomas and his brothers challenged the boys from the nearby Maidwell Hall to a cock fight, but in the following April Sir Justinian forbade his sons from keeping fighting-cocks. They were allowed to indulge their taste for sport by attending race-meetings at Harleston, Rowell and elsewhere.

The Ishams were evidently much taken with the newly invented 'stentorophonic trumpet', a megaphone through which it was claimed that voices could be heard a mile away. Sir Justinian ordered one from London: it cost £4, was six or seven feet long and 'made on a new plan, to shut in or pull out as desired'. Another new invention which he purchased was 'a machine on a cart; it throws up a powerful jet of water and is very useful for putting out a fire. Father gave nine pounds for it.' A stir was caused at Lamport in November 1672 when 'a hundred redcoats' passed through the village on their way to York and 'stole a great many cocks and hens'; while in the following February there was a great deal of excitement over a case of witchcraft in the Leicestershire village of Great Bowden, the facts of which were reported to the Royal Society.

One is impressed by the breadth of young Thomas Isham's observation. Details of day-to-day life are interspersed in his diary with items of local interest such as the Great Bowden witch, county gossip such as the travels of Lord Sunderland (*see* ALTHORP) and Lord Roos's divorce (*see* BELVOIR CASTLE), and also with national and foreign news. His entry for 19 April 1672 begins with 'War being proclaimed and begun against Holland' and ends with 'Dell had three pups, one of which she carried one night to the bedroom after its tail had been docked.' Two consecutive entries in the following month concern the swarming of his sister Vere's bees and the capture of a Dutch vessel. The latest illness of the King of Spain is mentioned in the diary and so is the midsadventure suffered by a local small farmer who 'went to Northampton and on the way back got down from his horse to relieve himself, whereupon the horse slipped from his hand and returned home, leaving its master in gorse at Pitsford.'

Thomas grew into 'a young gentleman of a beautiful person and a sweet disposition'. Having succeeded his father at the age of eighteen, he left Oxford and went to enjoy himself in Italy, taking a villa at Frascati, collecting pictures and sitting for the painter Carlo Maratti. But his life was cut short in 1681 when he died of smallpox at the age of twenty-four on the eve of his wedding. He was succeeded by his brother, another Justinian, whose son, yet another Justinian, enlarged the house to form a grand front. The adjoining front was twice rebuilt in the nineteenth century, the second time by Sir Charles Isham, the 10th Baronet, in a style that harmonizes with the

Some nineteenth-century ancestors of today's ubiquitous garden gnomes, in Sir Charles Isham's rock garden at Lamport.

*The splendid classical façade of
Lamport Hall.*

Georgian additions. One is surprised that Sir Charles, who reigned at Lamport from 1846 to 1903, should have chosen so sensible a style, for he appears to have been whimsical and a little eccentric. He devoted much of his time to creating a vast rockery, peopled with some of the very first of the now ubiquitous garden gnomes. The antiquary Walter Rye who visited him at Lamport for the first time in 1874, described him as 'a most interesting and highly educated man, though a thorough mystic, and had a great globe in which he thought he saw spirits.' He left only daughters and was succeeded by a kinsman, whose son, the late Sir Gyles Isham, adopted the stage as his profession, appearing in plays in England, the United States and elsewhere, and also in films. After the Second World War, Sir Gyles devoted himself to Lamport, which had suffered through neglect and wartime military occupation. He died in 1976 and bequeathed the Hall, its contents and surrounding endowment land to a charitable trust which aims at promoting 'historic and aesthetic education'. To this end the Lamport Hall Trust is collaborating with the local education authority and the University of Leicester and puts on a programme of arts events each summer.

Architecture and Contents

A splendid classical block by John Webb was built on to the old manor house at Lamport under the Commonwealth. Wings of the same height were added to it in 1732 and 1741, to the design of Francis Smith of Warwick, forming a grand front. The adjoining front was rebuilt to the design of William Burn in 1861–2 in a style which harmonizes with the Georgian additions. The two-storey High Room or Music Hall in the Webb building has elaborate baroque stuccowork on the ceiling and the upper part of the walls which dates from 1738 and is by John Woolston of Northampton. In this room hangs a version of Van Dyck's equestrian portrait of Charles 1, and the house has another Van Dyck and a Guido Reni. Lamport has a fine library, in which the greatest treasure is Charles 1's 1638 Bible.

LANHYDROCK

CORNWALL

Rᴵᴄʜᴀʀᴅ, 1st Lord Robartes bought the manor of Lanhydrock in 1620, and started building the present house. He came of a family which settled in Truro in the sixteenth century and grew rich in business, particularly in the tin trade, and was given a peerage, allegedly in return for a payment of £10,000 to James ɪ's favourite, the Duke of Buckingham. Although his nineteenth- and twentieth-century descendants were to pronounce the name Robartes as it is spelt, there seems little doubt that it was originally

Above *Lanhydrock from the east, with its charming mid-seventeenth-century gatehouse in the foreground.*

Right *The long gallery.*

pronounced Roberts, being frequently spelt in this more usual way. Thus the Cavalier, Richard Symonds, who came to Lanhydrock in 1644 before the Battle of Lostwithiel, wrote in his journal of 'the seate of the Lord Roberts'. The 2nd Lord Robartes was at that time away fighting for Parliament, holding the rank of Field Marshal under the Earl of Essex who had made his headquarters at Lanhydrock earlier that year. With the advance of the Royalist army the house was captured by Sir Richard Grenville, grandson of Sir Richard Grenville of the *Revenge*. Robartes escaped by sea to Plymouth, leaving his children as prisoners. Lanhydrock was deemed forfeit and granted by the King to Grenville, one of the least attractive of the Cavaliers, who managed to extract more revenue out of the property and from other forfeited West Country estates which he was granted than their former owners had done in peacetime. The defeat of the King's army in the west saw Robartes once again in possession of Lanhydrock, where he remained in retirement during the Commonwealth and Protectorate, being opposed to Cromwell's policy of making the Church subordinate to the State. In 1651 he completed the gatehouse which is Lanhydrock's most charming feature, having started it at the same time as he completed the house itself, shortly before the outbreak of the war.

Robartes managed to get back into royal favour after the Restoration and held several important posts, including that of Lord Privy Seal, in which capacity he was described by Pepys as 'a destroyer of everybody's business'. He was created Earl of Radnor in 1679 and died in 1685, being succeeded by his grandson, who through marriage to an heiress acquired the magnificent Cambridgeshire seat of Wimpole, but sold it in 1710. With the death of the 4th Earl in 1764, the Robartes peerages became extinct. Lanhydrock passed to descendants of the 3rd Earl's sister, whose mother was a daughter of the 1st Earl of Warrington (*see* DUNHAM MASSEY), and was eventually inherited by Thomas James Agar, who in 1822 assumed the additional surname of Robartes and in 1869 became the 1st Lord Robartes of the second creation. He and his wife, who was Juliana Pole-Carew of ANTONY, devoted their life to the welfare of the people on their estate and of the workers in the mines from which came much of his wealth. They laid out the formal gardens at Lanhydrock and enlarged the house, which, however, suffered a disastrous fire in 1881, when all but the gallery wing was gutted. Lady Robartes, who was rescued out of an upstairs window, never recovered from the shock and died a few days later; her broken-hearted husband survived her by less than a year.

It was left to their son, known as the 'Little Lord' because of his small stature, to rebuild the house. A philanthropist like his parents, he is said to have been anxious to avoid any sort of ostentation in the rebuilding. The main aspect of the house remained unchanged, with the same low seventeenth-century ranges on three sides of an open court. The interior, however, apart from the gallery, became uncompromisingly Victorian Jacobean, and at the side and back of the original court a whole new complex of rooms was added, to provide accommodation for Lord and Lady Robartes' ever-increasing family as well as for the domestic offices required by a well-run if unostentatious aristocratic household in the 1880s. For its time, the resurrected Lanhydrock was unusually well equipped: it had electric light

Tom Agar-Robartes at the time of the Bodmin election in 1906.

and central heating, heated cabinets for keeping the food hot on its way to the dining-room, a cooling system and fire hydrants – though steel and concrete had been used in the rebuilding to make the house as far as possible fireproof.

In 1899 Lord Robartes inherited the Viscountcy of Clifden (though not the Clifdens' Irish estate) from a cousin. He already possessed an estate outside Cornwall, having in 1895 acquired Wimpole, largely for reasons of family piety since it had belonged to his forebears: a second estate was also likely to come in useful since he had five sons. The eldest, Tom Agar-Robartes, a young man of great promise, fought a memorable election in south-east Cornwall in 1906, winning what had been a Conservative seat for the Liberals with a substantial majority. There were scenes of wild rejoicing and a golden bangle was presented to the young Member's mother, who, seeing an unusually beautiful sunset on polling day, took it as a happy augury. Five months later Tom was unseated on petition for a technical breach of the election law. In the previous summer his parents had given a garden party at Lanhydrock for the local Liberal workers to which, through an unfortunate oversight, not only workers were invited but all party members in south-east Cornwall and the neighbouring divisions: Tom's political opponents were able to represent this as an attempt to influence the electorate by handing out free teas. Tom re-entered Parliament in 1908 as Member for another Cornish constituency; but in 1915 he died in Flanders after trying to rescue two of his men under enemy fire, an act for which he was recommended for a posthumous VC. He died unmarried, as did three out of his four younger brothers, so the Clifden and Robartes titles, the succession to which had seemed so secure before 1914, have now become extinct.

Architecture and Contents

An early seventeenth-century mansion of granite, rather low and old-fashioned for its time, originally built round four sides of a courtyard, one side being demolished in 1780 so there is now an open court facing towards the enchanting little detached gatehouse of 1651, with its skyline of obelisks. The northern range of the court contains the splendid seventeenth-century long gallery with its barrel-vaulted ceiling of vigorous plasterwork by local craftsmen. This is unfortunately the only original interior to survive the fire of 1881: the other rooms are all Victorian Jacobean. The outside of the house was rebuilt as it was, with additional accommodation added to the side and back of the original court. The family quarters and lavishly equipped domestic offices, which remain exactly as they were in the spacious days of late-Victorian and Edwardian country-house life, are now on view to visitors, together with the grander rooms where there is some fine furniture and a series of family portraits that includes works by Kneller, Romney, Arthur Devis and George Richmond. Lanhydrock was given to the National Trust by the 7th Viscount Clifden in 1953.

MOUNT EDGCUMBE
CORNWALL

'THE beacon blazed upon the roof of Edgcumbe's lofty hall', Macaulay sang in his ballad 'The Armada', and certainly the tower above the central hall of Mount Edgcumbe, on its promontory at the entrance to Plymouth Sound, would have been the place for a warning beacon when 'Castile's black fleet' was sighted. The Spanish commander, the Duke of Medina Sidonia, is said to have been so impressed with the view of Mount Edgcumbe from the sea that he resolved to have it for himself when England was conquered, though this story is likely to have originated in the peaceful visit of an earlier Spanish admiral in 1554. That was a year or so after the house built by Sir Richard Edgcumbe was completed, when it would have been something of an architectural prodigy, for unlike the usual rambling English courtyard house of the period, Mount Edgcumbe was compact and symmetrical, a mock castle with four corner towers (inspired by the same dream of chivalry as the contemporary *châteaux* of the Loire). It also had a broad rectangular tower in the centre, with clerestory windows lighting the lofty hall which took the place of the courtyard. 'The hall rising in the midst above the rest . . . yieldeth a stately sound as you enter it', wrote Sir Richard Edgcumbe's grandson, Richard Carew of ANTONY, in his *Survey of Cornwall* of 1602. Carew also enumerates the attractions of the Mount Edgcumbe domain.

It is supplied with a never failing spring of water, and stored with timber, wood, fruit, deer and conies . . . On the sea-cliff groweth great plenty of the best ore-weed, to satisfy the owner's want, and accommodate his neighbours. A little below the house, in the summer evenings, seine boats come and draw their nets for fish, whither the gentry of the house, walking down, take the pleasure of the sight, and sometimes, at all adventures, buy the profit of the draughts. Both sides of the narrow entrance to the harbour are fenced with block-houses, and that next to Mount Edgcumbe was wont to be planted with ordnance, which at coming and parting greeted such guests as visited the house.

During the Civil War the guns of Mount Edgcumbe thundered out a different sort of greeting, for its owner, Colonel Piers Edgcumbe, was a Royalist and Plymouth strongly Parliamentarian. Edgcumbe and his small garrison held out in the house for more than a year; they drove off an attack by three hundred Roundheads, killing eighty of them. Eventually, though still undefeated, they accepted terms of surrender. The house survived the siege but the dining-hall and outbuildings were destroyed. No doubt to make up for the accommodation thereby lost, Colonel Edgcumbe's son or grandson built a new wing, but even thus enlarged the house was regarded by most eighteenth-century visitors as unworthy of the grounds, which

The hall rebuilt.

Mount Edgcumbe, as rebuilt after being gutted in the Blitz.

successive generations of the family made into one of the most famous of England's great landscape gardens. Mount Edgcumbe became a 'must' for the cultured tourist, and distinguished people flocked to see it, ranging from George III and Queen Charlotte to Dr Johnson, who pronounced its situation the second noblest in Britain, while having reservations about the view across the Sound to Plymouth: 'Though there is the grandeur of a fleet,' he declared, 'there is also the impression of there being a dockyard, the circumstances of which are not agreeable.'

Among the buildings with which the grounds were adorned was a Doric temple built by the 1st Lord Edgcumbe who, when his favourite dog died, had its skeleton put here so that he could sit and gaze at it. The skeleton remained in the temple – which was subsequently enlarged to form what is now known as the Garden House – until about thirty years ago, when, since it was falling to pieces, the 6th Earl of Mount Edgcumbe had it buried nearby. Soon afterwards the Garden House was occupied by his cousin whose wife, though she did not know about the dog's skeleton, used to hear the sound of a ghostly dog panting at her heels when she returned from walks.

The 1st Lord Edgcumbe was painted with his beloved dog by Reynolds, who as a boy of twelve painted his first portrait on a piece of sailcloth in a boathouse at Cremyll, just outside the Mount Edgcumbe domain. The Edgcumbes were his first influential patrons, and he painted three generations of the family, including the 2nd Lord Edgcumbe who was a wit and a patron of the arts but also unfortunately a gambler: 'What parts, genius and agreeableness, thrown away at a hazard table', Horace Walpole lamented of him. He died in 1761, less than two years after his father, leaving no legitimate issue, and was succeeded by a brother in the Navy who became an admiral and Earl of Mount Edgcumbe.

The wife of the 1st Earl is said to have suffered a horrifying experience, though according to different versions of the story, the incident happened not to her but either to the mother of the 1st Lord Edgcumbe or to the wife of the 2nd Earl. She was thought to be dead and was duly laid to rest in the family vault, but that night the sexton, who knew that she had been put into her coffin with a valuable ring on her finger, returned in order to steal it. He removed the coffin lid and attempted to pull off the ring, and while he was doing so the body started to move. The sexton fled, fortunately leaving the door of the vault open, and the lady, who had by now completely revived, managed to get out of the coffin and walked barefoot the mile or so back to the house. Her grieving husband and family were in the dining-room with the windows shut. They heard tapping on the window and when they opened it and found her standing outside in her shroud they naturally thought at first that she was her own ghost. Then she walked in through the front door, fainted into her husband's arms, and when she eventually came to in her own bed, her family managed to convince her that it had all been a bad dream. She recovered completely and lived for many years afterwards.

Mount Edgcumbe was the only major English country house to fall a victim to the Blitz: it was gutted by incendiary bombs during a raid on Plymouth and its contents destroyed, including nearly all the splendid series of family portraits by Reynolds. The only one to survive was that of the gambling 2nd Lord Edgcumbe, which, on account of his bad reputation, had been put away. Between 1958 and 1964 the house was rebuilt within its original sixteenth-century walls. The later wing has disappeared and so has the central tower. The hall is now lit by a much lower clerestory; nevertheless, it is still a room of noble proportions, and still, as in Carew's time, 'yieldeth a stately sound as you enter it'.

Architecture and Contents

An unusual Tudor house of 1547, built in the form of a mock castle with round corner towers and a rectangular tower in the centre. The house was subsequently enlarged and in 1749 the shape of the corner towers was changed from circular to octagonal. Having been gutted in the Blitz it was restored in 1958–64 by the architect Adrian Gilbert Scott, without the later additions and the central tower. Although nearly all the original contents perished in the fire, the restored rooms contain some good furniture, some of it brought from Cotehele, the family's other house, also in Cornwall. The pictures include the one surviving Reynolds and three seascapes by Van der Velde. Mount Edgcumbe is famous for its gardens and park, extending along the western shore of Plymouth Sound, with forts and blockhouses to give added interest to a landscape adorned with temples and a ruined folly. After the death of the 6th Earl of Mount Edgcumbe in 1965, the house and six hundred acres of the park were acquired jointly by the City of Plymouth and the County of Cornwall, with the condition that the house should continue as the home of the present Lord Mount Edgcumbe.

MUNCASTER CASTLE
CUMBRIA

A fanciful picture of Henry VI with the Luck of Muncaster.

WHEN Henry VI, as a fugitive after the Battle of Towton, was wandering about the Border country, he is said to have been found by shepherds on Muncaster Fell and brought by them to Muncaster Castle, the ancestral stronghold of the Penningtons high above the Esk. Here, according to tradition, he lay hidden for several days, and on his departure left behind a small glass bowl, praying that the family should prosper so long as it remained unbroken. Whatever the truth of the story, there is no doubt that the bowl, still unbroken and known as the Luck of Muncaster, has been in the family for a very long time, and although the Penningtons died out in the male line early this century, their descendants in the female line still own the castle where the saintly Henry is reputed to have found shelter. According to another legend, the Luck was once very nearly broken when it was thrown from an upper window. The family never had the courage to look for it and it lay buried in the earth for some years, but was then dug up intact.

Apart from the medieval pele tower at one corner, the castle as it is today is mostly a restrained nineteenth-century rebuilding by Antony Salvin. 'The castle appears, infinitely picturesque in outline and in its red and grey colouring, on the edge of a gorge, wooded on both sides,' Augustus Hare wrote when staying here in 1887, some twenty years after Salvin's work was completed. He was also impressed by 'the thick velvet pile carpets of the long passages hung with portraits, the fine collection of books in the (too dark) octagonal library and the low hall, which has an organ, flowers and books, and is the common sitting room.' His bedroom was known as the 'ghost room' and believed to have been the room in which Henry VI slept.

Hare found his host, Josslyn Pennington, 5th and last Lord Muncaster, 'geniality itself and very amusing'. Others who knew the last Lord Muncaster attributed his habit of holding his head on one side to his grief over the tragedy which occurred when he and his wife and a party of friends were captured by brigands while on a tour of Greece in 1870. The brigands released the women of the party – Lady Muncaster having prudently hidden her rings in her mouth – and allowed one of the men to go with them to arrange the ransom. Lots were drawn as to which of the men should go and it fell to a young bachelor, Frederick Vyner, who, however, insisted that as Lord Muncaster was married, he should go in his place. Lord Muncaster and the women got back to safety, but the Greek government, instead of sending a ransom, sent troops. The brigands were duly wiped out, but not before they had murdered Vyner and his fellow prisoners.

Architecture and Contents

A fourteenth-century pele tower with later additions which were remodelled in restrained baronial style by Antony Salvin soon after the middle of the nineteenth century. The principal rooms all date from Salvin's remodelling: there is a barrel-vaulted drawing-room, a dining-room hung with gilded and embossed leather above panelling and a spectacular octagonal library with a ribbed ceiling, taking its shape from the eighteenth-century library which it replaced. The pictures at Muncaster include a Velazquez and some excellent Ferneleys; the remarkably complete series of family portraits includes works by Van Dyck, Lely, Reynolds, Hoppner, G. F. Watts and Philip de Laszlo. The castle is rich in seventeenth-century furniture and its numerous and varied treasures range from sixteenth-century Flemish tapestries to silver by Paul Storr, from an alabaster nude by Giovanni Bologna to a bronze by Benvenuto Cellini. Muncaster is splendidly situated, with magnificent views, and its grounds are famous for their rhododendrons.

Muncaster Castle.

The library.

159

ORMESBY HALL
CLEVELAND

THE Pennymans, who came originally from Stokesley, a little way to the south, acquired Ormesby in 1600. James Pennyman who, together with his son, was active on the Royalist side in the Civil War, was heavily fined for having 'with some others of the country assembled with such armes as they had to hinder and oppose the seamen from coming ashore at Marske from aboard the Rainbow and other shippes.' The son, another James, was knighted for bravery in the field and made a baronet after the Restoration. An eighteenth-century James Pennyman, who predeceased his father and so did not inherit the baronetcy, began building the present house shortly before his death in 1743. The work was completed by his widow, while some redecoration was done in the 1770s by his nephew the 6th Baronet. This Sir James Pennyman – for many years a Member of Parliament – though commended by his political chief as 'a Yorkshire gentleman of very good principles', was a spendthrift who ran through much of his fortune and fell so deeply into debt that Ormesby was seized by the bailiffs and had been shut up for thirty years by the time of his death in 1808.

His son, Sir William, who repaired and reopened the house, was the last of the original male line of the family. When he died in 1852 the baronetcy became extinct and Ormesby passed to a descendant of the 3rd Baronet's daughter, who had married one of the Worsleys of Hovingham – the family of which HRH The Duchess of Kent is a present-day member. The heir of Ormesby, James White Worsley, who took the name of Pennyman, inherited an empty house, the last Baronet's sister having left the contents to her in-laws. Nevertheless, he quickly established himself here and the house became the background to a life of public service, church-going and periodic entertaining typical of the Victorian country gentry.

We get a picture of this life from the diary which his son James Stovin Pennyman kept from 1855 to 1896. It is mainly a record of Petty Sessions and Quarter Sessions, meetings of the Board of Guardians, the Gas Company and the Lunatic Asylum Committee, laying foundation stones and lecturing to the Mechanics' Institute on geology, with, by way of recreation, croquet and charades, as well as the somewhat less decorous pastime of ratting. In 1857 magnesium lighting was tried at Ormesby; in 1858 photographs were taken of the house, church and stables, and in 1862 the diarist drove into Middlesbrough to see 'Blondin, the celebrated high tight rope dancer, etc, perform'. In 1877 his son Jem came of age. A dinner was given in the house at two o'clock for the tenant farmers, who presented him with a silver inkstand. This was followed by three separate teas, one for the Sunday School children which was held in the laundry, one for the cottagers who presented young

Jem with a writing-desk, and one for the farmers. It was all over by eight, 'when we got a cold dinner ourselves – to bed tired'. 22 December 1882 was a day of rejoicing to welcome Jem and his bride, Dora Beaumont. A dinner was given in the hall for all the tenantry and a few friends, and there was once again a tea for the Sunday School children in the laundry and a tea for the cottagers; at a quarter past seven a conjurer and ventriloquist performed in the kitchen.

The son of Jem and Dora, the late Colonel Pennyman, bequeathed Ormesby to the National Trust in 1962. The house continued to be the home of his widow, Ruth, until her death in 1983. Ruth Pennyman was one of those people blessed with eternal youth. When she died, in her ninetieth year, she had a host of friends fifty or sixty years her junior who thought of her as someone of their own generation, so that when she died they felt they had lost a contemporary. Her hospitality at Ormesby was legendary: she was constantly putting people up, in particular the artists and poets who took part in the concerts, theatrical performances and poetry readings which she so often held here – she was herself a poet and celebrated her eighty-ninth birthday by publishing her first book of poems, *The Intruder*. But while being so much at home in the world of 1983 and a keen supporter of the Labour Party – her husband, to whom she had been most happily married, had been a pillar of the local Conservatives, so that while he was alive there had been no need for either of them to vote – she was very much the *grande dame*, having

161

Ormesby : the garden front.

been chatelaine of Ormesby before the Second World War when there were still footmen in livery. She remembered how in those days the younger members of the house party were given rooms on the second floor and called in the morning by the second housemaid; the head housemaid only called the older people on the first floor. When she herself was staying in the house as a guest during her engagement, she did not yet qualify to be called by the head housemaid, whereas the second housemaid did not feel exalted enough to call the squire's fiancée. So she was late coming down and found the household at morning prayers in the hall, 'bottoms out'.

In those days it was the duty of one of the footmen to bring drinking water in two buckets from a spring in the park, while another footman baked bread in a brick oven. The footmen were allowed two eggs at breakfast whereas the maids only got one, which to Ruth Pennyman smacked of discrimination, and she recalled that even this sexist privilege did not prevent the footmen from always giving notice at the most inconvenient time, just before the start of the shooting and the high-pressure entertaining which it entailed.

Architecture and Contents

A square, pedimented, three-storey house of stone, built in the mid-eighteenth century but rather earlier in character, with a high-pitched roof on a sturdy cornice. At one side is a lower office quadrangle which appears to date from the early seventeenth century, having a Jacobean doorway. In the eighteenth-century block there is a hall with fluted Ionic columns, a handsome first-floor gallery with panelling and pedimented Corinthian doorcases of mid-eighteenth-century date, and 'Tower of the Winds' columns which were probably introduced in the 1770s at the same time as the drawing-room and dining-room were given ceilings of Adamesque plaster-work. In the dining-room there is a portrait of the spendthrift Sir James Pennyman by Reynolds and a copy of Romney's well-known group of the Beaumont family, of which the original is now in the National Gallery. Ormesby was bequeathed to the National Trust by the late Colonel J.B.W.Pennyman in 1962.

OSTERLEY PARK
GREATER LONDON

Robert Child, the wealthy banker who transformed Osterley : a portrait by Allan Ramsay.

W HEN Horace Walpole saw Osterley in 1773 after the Elizabethan house built by Sir Thomas Gresham had been transformed by Robert Adam for another City tycoon, the banker Robert Child, he could scarcely contain his enthusiasm. 'Oh, the palace of palaces! – and yet a palace *sans crown, sans coronet*, but such expense! such taste! such profusion!' And when he wrote these words the most sumptuous of the state rooms were not yet finished, though five years later, when they were, he was inclined to be critical. The Etruscan room he thought would be all right as a bathroom or a 'pretty waiting room in a garden', but that to pass into it from the other rooms in the sequence was like 'going out of a palace into a potter's field'. The bed in the state bedroom was 'too theatric and too like a modern head-dress ... What would Vitruvius think of a dome decorated by a milliner?'

Robert Child did not live long to enjoy all the magnificence which Adam had created for him; he died in 1782 aged forty-three. A few months before his death, his only child Sarah, who was good-looking as well as being a very great heiress, had caused a sensation by her elopement with the 10th Earl of Westmorland (*see* BRYMPTON D'EVERCY). Child did not want a son-in-law with a title and estates, but hoped his daughter would marry someone who

A view of Osterley by Anthony Devis (1729–1817) : a pastoral scene from the south-west.

would take his name and succeed him as head of the bank. Westmorland is said to have asked Child, as an apparently hypothetical question, what a man should do if he were in love with a girl whose father refused to let him marry her. 'Why, run away with her, to be sure,' Child replied, thus giving his implicit approval to what Westmorland was about to do with his daughter. Child went in hot pursuit of the 'amourous fugitives', but called off the chase after one of his servants' horses had been shot under him by Westmorland's people. Though he failed to prevent the marriage, he saw to it that future Earls of Westmorland should not have the benefit of his fortune, for under his will the Child inheritance passed eventually to the Westmorlands' daughter Sarah, who married the 5th Earl of Jersey, head of the family of Villiers which produced so many seventeenth-century royal favourites. Sarah Lady Jersey, who lived until 1867, was one of the great political hostesses of her day; she was also, in accordance with her grandfather's wishes, senior partner in Child's Bank. A friend of Byron, she remained loyal to him after he had been ostracized.

'Queen Sarah' survived her eldest son so that on her death Osterley passed to her grandson, whose wife Margaret was another remarkable Lady Jersey, a traveller and a writer, the friend of Henry James, Rudyard Kipling and Robert Louis Stevenson, whom she visited in Samoa. Having been a great lady in the middle of Queen Victoria's reign, she was to achieve the ambition of her extreme old age, which was to outlive Hitler and Mussolini.

When she was newly married, Osterley was let, the Jerseys' principal seat being Middleton Park in Oxfordshire. On the death of the tenant, the ninety-one-year-old Duchess of Cleveland (see RABY CASTLE), in 1883, there was a plan to let it again. Then, as Margaret later recalled, she and her husband became 'fascinated with the place and decided to keep it as a "suburban" home'. So from then on it was very much a family house. She slept in the state bedroom when her own room was needed for somebody else; her children – one of whom was to be the mother of the present Lord Longford – did their lessons in the Etruscan room, and 'whiled away the tedium by peeling the paint off the chairs painted to match the wall decorations'; the gallery was used as a sitting-room. For the next thirty years – apart from a brief interval when Lord Jersey was governing New South Wales – the Osterley garden parties were a feature of the London Season, and at most times during the Season the house and garden were full of guests.

Henry James was a frequent visitor, and his description of 'Summersoft' in 'The Lesson of the Master' is, as he himself admitted, a picture of Osterley: 'The large smooth house, the expanse of whose beautiful brickwork, which had been kept clear of messy creepers (as a woman with a rare complexion disdains a veil), was pink rather than red', the steps descended 'in two arms' from 'the door which, from the long, bright, gallery, overlooked the immense lawn'; in the gallery the young writer Paul Overt walked with Miss Fancourt – 'they strolled to the end of it, looking at the pictures, the cabinets, the charming vista, which harmonized with the prospect of the summer afternoon, resembling it in its long brightness, with great divans and old chairs like hours of rest. Such a place as that had the added merit of giving persons who came into it plenty to talk about.'

Although the Jerseys and their friends are not individually recognizable in

The splendid portico of Osterley Park.

164

Henry James's story, the party at Summersoft resembles the Osterley gatherings in its mixture of writers and men of affairs. Among the writers who came to Osterley was Henry James's fellow American J.R. Lowell. Lady Jersey recalled him 'sitting in the garden ... on peaceful summer evenings enjoying specially that blue haze peculiar to the valley of the Thames which softens without obscuring the gentle English landscape.' Among the men of action was Kitchener, who spent his time sorting out china, separating Chinese from Japanese, which he despised. He also wanted to pick strawberries in the garden when they were not yet ripe. Among the politicians was Joseph Chamberlain, whom the Jerseys befriended after his break with Gladstone, much to the disgust of their ultra-Tory butler. Many Conservatives had their first sight of the great Birmingham Radical at Osterley, rowing on the lake wearing a top hat and smoking a pipe.

Politics made a dramatic intrusion into the cedar-shaded peace of Osterley one summer's afternoon in 1895. A hot and dusty figure suddenly appeared and demanded of Lady Jersey: 'Give me an egg beaten up in brandy and find me Arthur Balfour.' The egg in brandy was duly fetched and he swallowed it; then, having conferred with Balfour, who was playing tennis, he left on his bicycle. The unexpected visitor was Schomberg McDonnell, Private Secretary to Lord Salisbury, and he had cycled from HATFIELD to London and on to Osterley in search of Balfour – a total of twenty-six miles – to tell him that Lord Rosebery's Liberal Government had just resigned.

The Etruscan room at Osterley.

Architecture and Contents

A red-brick Elizabethan house with corner towers built round a courtyard. It was transformed into an eighteenth-century palace by Robert Adam, who gave it a feature unique in English domestic architecture, the great double hexastyle portico, like an open classical temple, through which the courtyard is entered. But if Adam's treatment of the exterior of the house is masterly, it was in the interior that his genius found full scope, producing a series of state rooms of the utmost magnificence. They remain unchanged, complete with the furniture and carpets which Adam designed for them, and the ravishing rose-red tapestries in the tapestry room made at the Gobelin factory under the supervision of his acquaintance and fellow Scot, Jacques Neilson. Osterley was given to the National Trust by the 9th Earl of Jersey in 1949, and is now administered by the Victoria and Albert Museum.

PECKOVER HOUSE
CAMBRIDGESHIRE

THIS early Georgian house with its rococo interior, urban in its frontage on Wisbech's North Brink but very much a country house at the back where it faces over fifty acres of grounds, was bought during the last quarter of the eighteenth century by Jonathan Peckover, a descendant of one of Cromwell's Ironsides who had joined the Society of Friends. In 1782 Peckover founded a local bank with premises adjacent to the house, his partners being members of two other notable Quaker families, the Gurneys and the Birkbecks. The bank flourished, though there is said to have been an occasion when it was threatened with a run, which was averted by displaying a peck measure full of gold pieces in the window, with a notice that said: 'Enough to pay and a peck over.'

Unlike the other Quaker banking families of East Anglia, the Peckovers still professed Quakerism this century. Alexander Peckover, who inherited the house in 1877 and afterwards became Lord-Lieutenant of Cambridgeshire, was dispensed on religious grounds from wearing a Court sword. And when, in 1907, he was raised to the peerage as Lord Peckover, he told his butler not to call him 'My Lord' but to continue addressing him as 'Alexander Peckover', pure and simple, in accordance with Quaker custom. He did, however, allow himself, for reasons of health, to drink vintage port, thus scandalizing his even more orthodox Quaker daughters, who after his death in 1919 had his remaining bottles emptied into the gutter. His daughters lived on in the house, one of them surviving until after the Second World War. They loved jewels, but could not, as strict Quakers, wear them on their persons, so instead they collected exquisite jewelled objects such as golden birds with which to adorn their chimney-pieces.

Architecture and Contents

A handsome early Georgian house of brick with a richly decorated interior partly contemporary with the house and partly dating from the middle of the eighteenth century. The rooms are panelled and have elegant plasterwork. There are carved overmantles, the one in the drawing-room being delightfully exuberant and rococo. The house has belonged to the National Trust since 1948.

The library.

The garden front.

PENRHYN CASTLE

GWYNEDD

THE vast Norman-Revival castle of Penrhyn, with its stupendous keep which looms up among trees against the waters of the Menai Strait, is almost entirely the creation of George Hay Dawkins Pennant and his architect, Thomas Hopper. Dawkins Pennant was a landowner who was immensely rich through being the proprietor of the nearby Bethesda slate quarries, which supplied roofs for the new industrial Britain. It is thus fitting that slate should be so much in evidence in his castle, even some of the furniture, including the canopied state bed, being of elaborately carved and moulded slate. The castle was begun in 1827 and finished ten years later. The work was in progress when Prince Pückler-Muskau came here and was shown the plan, in which he thought he recognized 'the nice perception of the useful and commodious, the exquisite adaptation and means to ends, which distinguishes the English'. But the practical good sense which these words convey was hardly evident in the Slate King's castle when it was completed, not even in the early years of Victoria's reign when coal was cheap and servants unlimited.

The Prince also commented on the fact that the butler's pantry was fireproof and remarked on the tremendous park wall topped with points of slate. 'At every entrance a fortress-like gate with a portcullis frowns on the intruder – no inapt symbol, by-the-bye, of the illiberality of the present race of Englishmen who shut their parks and gardens more closely than we do our sitting rooms.' It was doubtless the 'illiberality' of the Slate King in shutting his park gates against the wandering German Prince – who nevertheless succeeded in forcing an entry – which prompted Pückler-Muskau to disparage Dawkins Pennant's origins. Having mentioned how Penrhyn was modelled on William I's castle at Rochester, he goes on to say: 'What could then be accomplished only by a mighty monarch, is now executed, as a plaything – only with increased size, magnificence and expense – by a simple country gentlemen, whose father very likely sold cheeses. So do times change!'

In fact Dawkins Pennant's forebears made their fortune in the West Indies, owning large plantations in Jamaica. He had inherited the Penrhyn estate from his cousin, Richard Pennant, first and last Lord Penrhyn, who had in turn acquired it through marrying an heiress to whom it had passed by descent from the great Welsh family of Tudor. The present castle incorporates fragments of the Tudors' medieval house as well as of the short-lived Georgian castle which took its place. Dawkins Pennant had no son and was succeeded at Penrhyn by his son-in-law, Edward Gordon Douglas, whose roots were primarily in Scotland (he was a brother of the 17th Earl of

The 1st Lord Penrhyn of the present creation with his house party outside the main entrance to the castle.

Morton) but who also had West Indian connections, being a grandson of the 1st Earl of Harewood (*see* HAREWOOD HOUSE).

Edward Gordon Douglas assumed the additional surname of Pennant and in 1866 the Penrhyn barony was revived in his favour. A few years earlier he and his second wife entertained Queen Victoria at Penrhyn, providing her with a royal suite in the keep; the bed in which she slept was not, however, of slate but of carved oak. As well as bringing a coronet to the Slate King's castle, the 1st Lord Penrhyn of the second creation also embellished it with a notable collection of pictures. At the same time he came near to losing that source of wealth which had paid for the building of the castle by handing over the management of the family slate quarries to a committee elected by the workmen. As a result of this misguided if enlightened gesture, by 1885 the concern was on the verge of bankruptcy. His son, the 2nd Lord Penrhyn, who succeeded him a year later, put an end to this arrangement and restored the prosperity of the quarries, which in a good year brought in an income of as much as £150,000. A section of the men, however, resented being excluded from the management, and in 1897 there was a great strike, to which Lord Penrhyn replied with a lock-out. The struggle between him and the trade unions continued until his death in 1907.

This background of industrial unrest did not affect Augustus Hare's enjoyment of a visit to Penrhyn in 1895. 'Penrhyn Castle has been delightful, and my room, with its exquisite views over sea and mountains, the most delightful thing in it', he wrote. 'Lady Penrhyn presides over the great place with the calm of perpetual moonlight: sunlight is left to her beautiful and impulsive step-daughter, Miss Alice, who orders out no end of carriages to take guests up into the hills or wherever they want to go.' He came again the following year, not long before the strike, and enjoyed it every bit as much, including 'the excursions, in spite of furious storms, into the Welsh hills'.

Architecture and Contents

An immense and spectacular Norman-Revival castle, built over a period of ten years from 1827 to the design of Thomas Hopper, incorporating fragments of two earlier houses. The interior of the castle maintains the drama of the exterior, combining spatial effects with restless, sinuous ornament. Much use is made of slate, even some of the furniture being of this material. As a relief from the Norman-Revival style, there are the pictures collected by the 1st Lord Penrhyn of the present creation. The castle also now contains a doll museum and in the stables is a museum of industrial locomotives, both established by the National Trust to which Penrhyn was made over in 1951.

172

PETWORTH HOUSE
WEST SUSSEX

T HE manor of Petworth, which had belonged to the Percys since the twelfth century, was part of the great inheritance of Elizabeth, only child and heiress of the last of the original Percy Earls of Northumberland who died in 1670. Having already been twice widowed, she was married in 1682 at the age of fifteen to the 6th Duke of Somerset, who from 1688 onwards transformed the medieval house at Petworth into a Sussex Versailles. There the 'Proud Duke', as he was known, kept up a state which his contemporaries found faintly ridiculous, particularly towards the end of his long life, when it was no longer customary for someone who was not royal to live in such a way.

Fête at Petworth *by*
W. F. Witherington, 1836.

He is said to have insisted on his children standing in his presence and to have disinherited one of his daughters because he found her seated when he woke up after having a nap. A gentleman who came to Petworth in 1743 (by which time the Proud Duke was over eighty and married to his second wife, the Percy heiress having died in 1722) wrote of how he lived –

in a grand retirement peculiar and agreeable only to himself. He comes down to breakfast at 8 of the clock in the morning in his full dress with his blue ribbon; after breakfast, he goes into his offices, scolds and bullys his servants and steward till dinner time; then very formally hands his Duchess downstairs. His table, tho' spread in a grand manner as if company was expected consists of his own family the Duchess and his 2 daughters; and when he has a mind to be gracious the chaplain is admitted. He treats all his country neighbours, and indeed everybody else, with such uncommon pride, and distance, that none of them visit Him.

The same writer also remarked on how, 'out of an unusual and ridiculous whimsy', the Duke 'studiously concealed' the artists of most of his pictures.

On the death of the 7th Duke of Somerset, the Proud Duke's son by Elizabeth Percy, the Percy inheritance was divided. ALNWICK and other properties went to his only surviving child, Elizabeth, whose husband became Earl of Northumberland of a new creation and afterwards Duke of Northumberland. Petworth and the Cumberland estates of the Percys' medieval ancestors, the Lords Lucy (*see* CHARLECOTE PARK), went to his sister's son, Sir Charles Wyndham, who came of the Somersetshire branch of an old Norfolk family. Wyndham also inherited the earldom of Egremont, which had been conferred on the 7th Duke of Somerset with a special remainder to him. In 1761 he succeeded Pitt the Elder as Secretary of State for the South, with, as his Under-Secretary, the traveller and antiquary Robert Wood, author of *The Ruins of Palmyra*. Like Wood and so many other eighteenth-century men of affairs, Egremont was himself a connoisseur as well as a politician, though as a patron of the arts he is overshadowed by his son, who succeeded in 1763 at the age of twelve and reigned until 1837.

This long-lived Earl became a close friend of Turner, who from 1809 was a frequent guest at Petworth, painting some of his most important pictures here in a room into which nobody was allowed but Egremont himself – and even he would not dare enter without first knocking. A man of great kindness and hospitality, Egremont numbered many other artists among his friends, and he gave open house at Petworth to painters wishing to copy his Old Masters. The diarist Joseph Faringdon mentions how when two gentlemen of his acquaintance came to Petworth in 1798, they found some of the Van Dycks standing in the hall being copied by a couple of professionals and a clergyman from Cambridge. When there was no company, these three self-invited copyists dined with Egremont and his mistress, who was known as Mrs Wyndham; when there was company they dined with Mrs Wyndham alone. Egremont eventually married Mrs Wyndham, after she had borne him six children, but as his lawful wife she proved a failure and they soon parted.

Egremont's interests and talents were not limited to the arts; he was also a keen and highly competent agricultural reformer. He so greatly improved his estates that someone observed that 'the very animals at Petworth seemed happier than in any other spot on earth'. If he liked to see his livestock happy, he was even more concerned about the happiness of his tenants and

The laundry at Petworth House in about 1900.

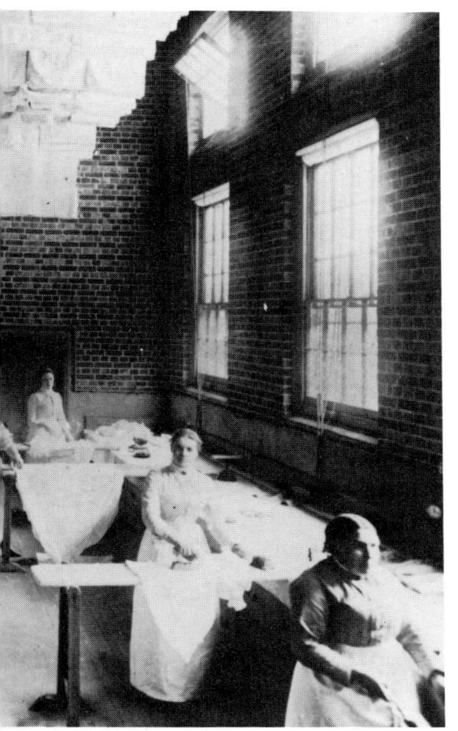

Silver Wedding presentation to the 3rd Lord Leconfield and his wife at the opening meet of the Leconfield Hunt, Petworth House, November 1936.

labourers: to celebrate his birthday he would entertain the women and children from miles around to a feast. Charles Greville has left an account of one of the last of these great occasions, in May 1835, when Egremont was eighty-three.

Fifty-four tables, each fifty feet long, were placed in a vast semicircle on the lawn before the house ... Plum puddings and loaves were piled like cannon-balls, and innumerable joints of boiled and roast beef were spread out, while hot joints were prepared in the kitchen, and sent forth as soon as the firing of guns announced the hour of the feast. Tickets were given to the inhabitants of a certain district, and the number was about 4000; but, as many more came, the Old Peer could not endure that there should be anybody hungering outside the gates, and he went out himself and ordered the barriers to be taken down and admittance given to all. They think 6000 were fed. Gentlemen from the neighbourhood carved for them, and waiters were provided from among the peasantry ... A band of musick paraded round, playing gay airs. The day was glorious – an unclouded sky and soft southern breeze. Nothing could exceed the pleasure of that fine old fellow; he was in and out of the windows of his room twenty times, enjoying the sight of these poor wretches, all attired in their best, cramming themselves and their brats with as much as they could devour, and snatching a day of relaxation and happiness.

When the 'Old Peer' died, he was succeeded at Petworth by his son, George Wyndham, who having been born out of wedlock could not inherit the Egremont earldom (which eventually became extinct), but who was himself raised to the peerage as Lord Leconfield. The 2nd Lord Leconfield, who succeeded in 1869, employed Anthony Salvin to make various alterations to Petworth. A less fortunate project was the special greenhouse which he had built in order to be able to grow his own bananas, having been assured by a friend that nobody really knew how delicious a banana could be who had not tasted one straight off the tree. Tended by his head gardener, Lord Leconfield's banana tree flourished, and the day came when it had a banana on it. 'I will have that banana for dinner tonight', Lord Leconfield said as soon as the banana was ripe; and in order to witness the great event the head gardener concealed himself behind a screen in the dining-room. What followed is recounted by the late Lord Egremont, Lord Leconfield's grandson. 'The banana was brought in on a lordly dish. My grandfather peeled it with a golden knife. He then cut a sliver off and, with a golden fork, put it in his mouth and carefully tasted it. Whereupon he flung dish, plate, knife, fork and banana on to the floor and shouted, "Oh God, it tastes just like any other damn banana!" Banana tree and all were ordered to be destroyed ... the banana cost my grandfather some £3,000.'

The 2nd Lord Leconfield's nephew was the handsome, brilliant and charming George Wyndham, the brightest star in that galaxy of beauty and wit known as the Souls, which also included his sister Lady Elcho and George Curzon. He died prematurely having, as a politician, failed to live up to his youthful promise. In contrast to the romantic and ill-fated George was his cousin Charles, the 3rd Lord Leconfield, who was taciturn and gruff, loved his food and lived to be eighty, reigning at Petworth from 1901 to 1952. Until the end of his life, he always dined in a white tie and tails. The late Lord Egremont, who was his nephew, gives us a picture of dinner with him in the Square Dining-Room at Petworth on the eve of the Second World War:

The golden candelabra are throwing a glittering light on the Paul Storr gold and silver plate, the Monteith bowls, the silver wine-coolers on the side-tables, the rococo pier-glasses – and Uncle Charles himself, at the head of the table, is silently pegging his way through a huge bill of fare . . . In the background were the footmen in their blue Wyndham livery with their silver-crested buttons agleam. Over all hovered the butler, like a god but often a bit unsteady. To me he seemed a god until one day I heard Uncle Charles remark that one can keep a cellar or a butler, but one cannot keep both.

James Lees-Milne tells of a visit to Petworth a few years later on behalf of the National Trust. Having shown him round, Lord Leconfield dismissed him at the street entrance at 5.45 p.m. 'Pointing to a tea house with an enormous notice CLOSED hanging in the window, he said: "You will get a very good tea in there. Put it down to me. Goodbye."' After the 3rd Lord Leconfield's death, Petworth became the home of the late Lord Egremont, best remembered as John Wyndham, the private secretary, friend and confidant of Harold Macmillan. In 1963 the title of Egremont was revived in his favour, since when he and his son, who succeeded him in 1972, have used it in preference to the nineteenth-century title of Leconfield.

Architecture and Contents

The present Petworth, with its long, French-influenced front, which now overlooks the incomparable eighteenth-century landscape created by Capability Brown for the 2nd Earl of Egremont, was built between 1688 and 1696 by the 'Proud' Duke of Somerset, replacing the old manor house of which little now remains except for the thirteenth-century chapel. The most notable interiors dating from the Proud Duke's time are the Marble Hall and the Painted Staircase, with its walls and ceiling painted by Laguerre. The more famous Carved Room, though it displays the magnificent work by Grinling Gibbons which the Proud Duke commissioned, was created after his time by the 3rd Earl of Egremont, who also enlarged the sculpture gallery formed by the 2nd Earl at the northern end of the house. As well as giving Petworth its collection of Turners, the 3rd Earl acquired works by most of the leading British artists of his time, among them Gainsborough, Reynolds, Romney and Richard Wilson. But for all their glories, the 3rd Earl's pictures constitute only part of the Petworth collection, which also includes the Van Dycks, the Lelys and the Titian acquired in the seventeenth century by the 10th Earl of Northumberland, the series of portraits of the 'Beauties' of Queen Anne's Court commissioned by the Proud Duke from Dahl and Kneller, and the seventeenth- and eighteenth-century Dutch, Italian and French paintings acquired by the 2nd Earl of Egremont, who also gave the house its collection of antique sculpture. Petworth was made over to the National Trust in 1947, but it is still the home of Lord and Lady Egremont.

PLAS NEWYDD

GWYNEDD

The Dancing Marquess.

HAVING been acquired in the sixteenth century by the Anglo-Irish family of Bagenal, through marriage to an heiress of the local dynasty of Griffith, Plas Newydd passed again through the female line at the beginning of the eighteenth century to another Anglo-Irish family, the Baylys. In 1737 Sir Nicholas Bayly of Plas Newydd married Caroline Paget, a descendant of Henry VIII's Secretary of State, William, Lord Paget, one of the most remarkable of the Tudor 'New Men', and as a result of this marriage his son inherited the Paget estates and barony, took Paget as his surname and was eventually created Earl of Uxbridge. Though Plas Newydd was now supplanted as the principal family seat by the Pagets' Elizabethan mansion of Beaudesert in Staffordshire, Lord Uxbridge took advantage of his greatly improved circumstances to rebuild his rambling ancestral home on the Menai Strait in fashionable Gothic. The work began in 1793 and was completed after Uxbridge's death by his son, the great Field Marshal who lost a leg and gained the Marquessate of Anglesey at the Battle of Waterloo. Although he completed the house, 'One-leg' did not spend much time here, as Prince Pückler-Muskau noted when he visited Plas Newydd in 1828. It may have been the Prince's disappointment at not finding the Field Marshal at home that made him dismiss the house and its beautiful grounds as being unremarkable, commenting only on the cromlechs and the 'Druidical Cottage' – equipped with a kaleidoscope and camera obscura – from which

Plas Newydd, its lawns sloping down to the Menai Strait. In the distance are the mountains of Snowdonia.

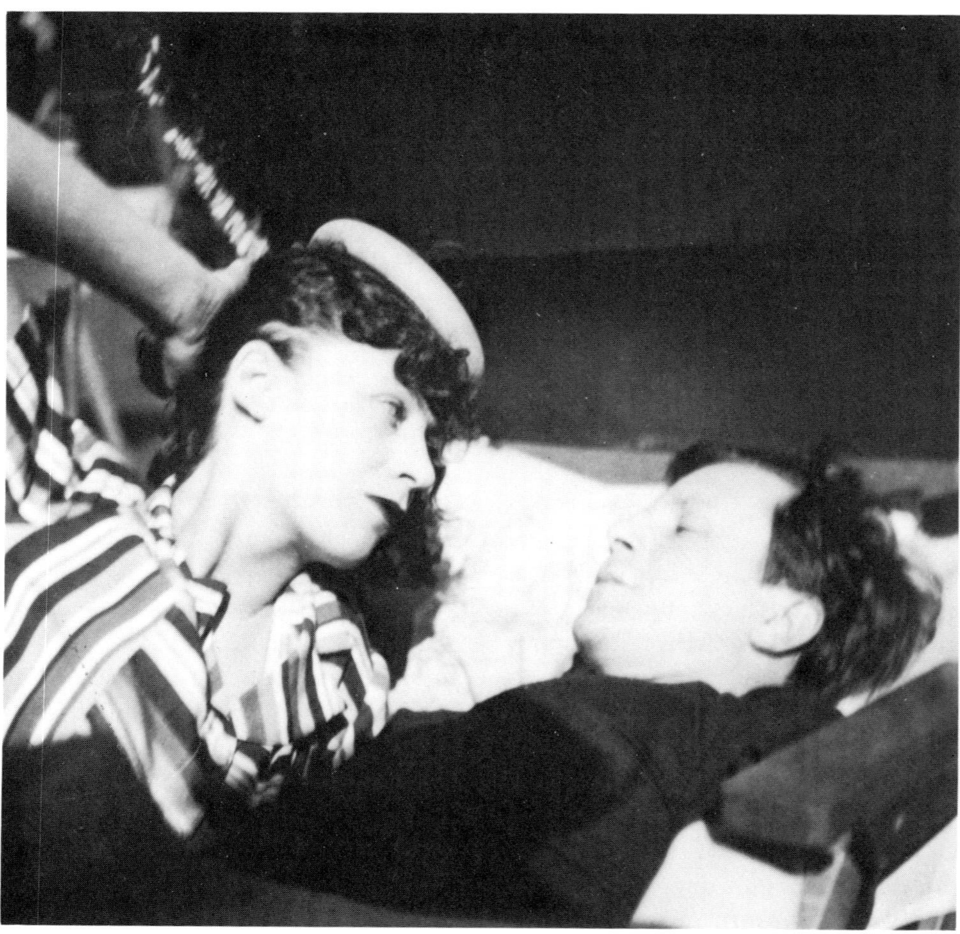

Lady Caroline Paget, daughter of the 6th Marquess of Anglesey, with Rex Whistler at Plas Newydd in the 1930s.

The dining-room made by the 6th Marquess of Anglesey, with the 58-foot mural which Rex Whistler painted in 1937.

there was a view of Snowdon. Towards the end of the 1st Marquess of Anglesey's life, when, largely owing to the excesses of his elder sons, he was feeling the pinch financially – though he had an income of something like £70,000 a year – Plas Newydd was let.

The 1st Marquess's children and other close relations of his made up a formidable clan at the Court of the young Queen Victoria, headed by his eldest son, Lord Uxbridge, who is alleged, perhaps falsely, to have obtained a place in the royal establishment for a mistress. The most faithful courtier among them was the Field Marshal's fifth son, Lord Alfred Paget, who served at Court for more than fifty years while rising to the rank of general in the army. At the beginning of Victoria's reign, when Lord Alfred was a dashing young equerry, he and the Queen were believed to be in love: he was said to wear her portrait over his heart and even to have hung her miniature round the neck of his dog. Forty years later, when he accompanied the Prince of Wales to India, he had ceased to be a figure of romance and was known to the Prince and his friends as 'Old Beetroot'.

In contrast to the multitude of nineteenth- and early twentieth-century Pagets who became courtiers and generals, admirals and ambassadors was the 5th Marquess of Anglesey, who succeeded at the age of twenty-three in 1898. In fact he was so different from the rest of his family that he is alleged not to have been a Paget at all, but a son of the French actor, Coquelin. His ruling passion was dressing up in bizarre and extravagant costumes. At Plas Newydd, which he grandly renamed Anglesey Castle, he ran a private theatre. This he made in what had formerly been the chapel in the northern wing of the house. He modelled it on Sarah Bernhardt's theatre in Paris, decorated it in white and blue and named it the Gaiety. It was opened in 1901 with a production of *Aladdin* by the London company of Mr Alex Keith. The young Lord Anglesey himself played the role of Pekoe 'the vizier's son, a bit mooney on Yummy-yum', wearing a series of costumes including one covered with something like £40,000 worth of jewels. The performance included a solo act by Anglesey called the 'Butterfly Dance' which was a favourite of his and caused him to be known as the 'Dancing Marquess'. Another of his favourite roles was that of Queen Eleanor, for which he put on gorgeous female attire, regardless of the fact that he had a moustache.

Admission to the Plas Newydd Gaiety was free, and the audiences, made up largely of tenants and local shopkeepers, gave the Dancing Marquess's productions an enthusiastic reception, which encouraged him to take his company on tour all over the Continent. His productions in various European capitals were well received by the critics, but these tours were ruinously expensive. He went bankrupt in 1904, a year before his death, owing a total of £255,969, mainly for jewels, of which he was a compulsive buyer. He was also a compulsive buyer of clothes: when his personal effects were auctioned, the sale of his wardrobe alone took a full three days.

Despite the Dancing Marquess's prodigality, the reign of his successor, the 6th Marquess, was a golden period for Plas Newydd, which gained the reputation, between the wars, of being Britain's most comfortable great country house, with a bathroom to every bedroom. He and his wife, a daughter of the 8th Duke of Rutland (*see* BELVOIR CASTLE), very much improved the interior of the house, bringing pictures and furniture here from Beaudesert which, after the First World War, was demolished, and commissioning Rex Whistler, a friend of the family, to decorate the new dining-room with the wall-paintings which are his masterpiece.

Architecture and Contents

A house rebuilt in Georgian Gothic to the design of James Wyatt assisted by Joseph Potter of Lichfield. The hall and music room have ceilings of plaster vaulting, while other rooms are neo-classical. Between the wars the 6th Marquess of Anglesey removed the battlements and other Gothic features from the exterior, and transformed the theatre into the long dining-room. This has magnificent *trompe l'oeil* wall-paintings by Rex Whistler of the Menai Straits and Snowdonia transported to eighteenth-century Italy. Another attraction is the Cavalry Museum in which can be seen the 1st Marquess's articulated wooden leg. Plas Newydd is now in the care of the National Trust, while still being the home of Lord and Lady Anglesey.

POWDERHAM CASTLE
DEVON

T HE crusading Courtenays, who from their ancestral castle of Courtenay near Paris went out in the twelfth century to rule a semi-independent principality in Syria, also established themselves as great magnates in the English West Country, being made Earls of Devon by Edward III. The 2nd Earl married Lady Margaret de Bohun, whose dowry was Powderham, which was inherited by his sixth son Sir Philip Courtenay, who built the nucleus of the present castle. During the fifteenth and sixteenth centuries the descendants of Sir Philip lived peacefully at Powderham as Devon gentry, while their grander cousins were being slaughtered in the Wars of the Roses or suffering at the hands of Henry VII and Henry VIII on account of their Plantagenet blood, which brought them dangerously close in the succession to the throne. When the handsome but pathetic Edward Courtenay – that unsuccessful suitor for the hand of both Mary Tudor and Elizabeth I – died in exile in Italy, allegedly by poison, his kinsman at Powderham became the head of the family. He did not, however, become Earl of Devon, the original earldom having been fortfeited and that conferred on Edward Courtenay by Queen Mary being presumed to have died with him. In the seventeenth century the Powderham Courtenays became baronets and in 1762 the 3rd Baronet was made Viscount Courtenay.

The eighteenth-century Courtenays had considerable taste, as is evident from the sumptuous rococo plasterwork with which they adorned the interior of Powderham, though one may regret their modernizing of the exterior of the castle. They were also musical: the accounts of the 2nd Viscount carry an annual payment for '5 musicians for their Attendance at Powderham Castle on Master Courtenay's birthday'. The said Master Courtenay succeeded as 3rd Viscount in 1788 while still a minor. There were tremendous festivities at Powderham when he came of age, a 'Large Marquee Tent with Furniture compleat' being supplied by the firm of John and Coutts Trotter of London at a cost of £769 1s 10d. The castle still did not possess a room large enough for grand entertainments, and to remedy this deficiency the 3rd Viscount created the music room, decorated by James Wyatt and furnished in the most elegant manner – too elegant for Lady Ailesbury, who came here in 1803. 'Powderham Castle is fine,' she wrote, 'but the furniture suits it as ill as its master does.'

She was clearly aware of the aura of scandal surrounding the 3rd Viscount, who was none other than the notorious 'Kitty' Courtenay, the object, as a boy, of William Beckford's infatuation. It was after having stayed at Powderham in 1784 that the millionaire Beckford was obliged to leave the country, though there is no real evidence of anything scandalous having

Powderham, a fourteenth-century castle adapted in the eighteenth century, was remodelled in baronial style in the 1840s.

A portrait of 'Kitty' Courtenay in his music room at Powderham.

occurred during that unfortunate house party which included Beckford's wife as well as himself.

Whatever the truth about Kitty Courtenay's relationship with Beckford, there was no doubt about his subsequent goings-on. 'Reports respecting Lord Courtenay ... are daily becoming more particular', the diarist Joseph Faringdon noted, while staying in the locality in 1810. 'Many of the neighbouring gentlemen refuse to hold intercourse with him; but several respectable families still continue to visit him.' Faringdon also tells of Kitty's extravagance: he kept a beautiful yacht anchored near Powderham, which he never used; he built himself a house at Torquay and then got bored with it and started another at Brixham. A few months later, the blow fell, as Faringdon relates. 'When he was informed that the Officers of Justice were ordered to pursue him, he lost all resolution; wept like a child, and was willingly taken on board a vessel, the first that could be found, an American ship, and passed there under a feigned name.' He spent the remaining twenty-five years of his life abroad, at first in a house outside New York, then in Paris, and during those years Powderham stood abandoned and desolate, much of its contents being sold. In 1831, a few years before his death, he established his claim to the sixteenth-century earldom of Devon, which was found to have been created with remainder to all Edward Courtenay's male heirs.

The earldom was in fact claimed on Kitty's behalf by the cousin who succeeded him as 10th Earl of Devon in 1835, and who carried out an extensive restoration of Powderham, giving it back its medieval character and adding a castellated gatehouse and a baronial hall. The latter was completed by his son, the 11th Earl, though according to Augustus Hare, who stayed here for the first time in 1874, he let the bedrooms of the castle fall into decay because the family estates were encumbered and he would not sell any land to raise money, though he spent freely on planting Wellingtonias in the park and making expensive fences round them. Whatever his faults as a man of business, he was in himself 'absolutely seraphic': his son-in-law told Hare that the 11th Earl knew 'only two perfect forms of happiness, reciting the Holy Office or attending the Board of Guardians'. At a dinner which he once gave to the people living on the estate, a man got up to propose his health, and expressed his admiration for him by saying: 'I don't know what Lord Devon du, but all I du know is that if more would du as Lord Devon du du, there wouldn't be so many as would du as they du du.'

The set-up at Powderham under the 11th Earl could not have been more different from what it was in Kitty Courtenay's time: to Hare it recalled 'the Little Gidding of John Inglesant in its intense, its real saintliness – in the constant chapel services, with the wonderful singing of the servants, in the commemorative hymns for such saints as Martin and Bricius, in the spirit of harmony and universal love.' Chapel services were interspersed with innocent amusements. Lord Devon's son, Lord Courtenay, once arrived during a house party disguised as Madame Bekker purporting to be looking for a chairman for a meeting in Exeter in favour of the Rights of Women, and made a most eloquent speech to the guests assembled for tea in the hall, who included the Bishop of Winchester, the American Minister and the former Secretary of State for India, Lord Halifax. Each of these distinguished men

Three of the thirteen daughters of the 2nd Viscount Courtenay : a painting by Cosway.

made a polite speech of refusal, whereupon Madame Bekker 'declared herself so indignant as to be led to unsex herself'.

Architecture and Contents

A fourteenth-century castle, modernized in the mid-eighteenth century, further improved by James Wyatt in the 1790s and enlarged and remodelled in baronial style in the 1840s by Charles Fowler, the result being a picturesque battlemented pile with a mixture of mullioned and sash windows. The imposing castellated gateway and the Gothic hall both date from the 1840s, the staircase and other interiors are of the mid-eighteenth century and have exuberant rococo plasterwork by John Jenkins of Exeter. The music room, by Wyatt, is in the more refined if less vigorous taste of the 1790s: it has scagliola pilasters, a domed ceiling and a chimney-piece of Carrara marble by Sir Richard Westmacott. The gilt and white seats, with dolphin arms – a dolphin being one of the two family crests – were made for the room, probably by the firm of Marsh and Tatham. Among the other furniture in the castle, a remarkable pair of rosewood bookcases with broken pediments and brass inlay, signed by John Channon and dated 1740, has pride of place. The family portraits at Powderham include works by Kneller, Reynolds, Thomas Hudson, Richard Cosway and John Opie.

POWIS CASTLE
POWYS

Robert, 1st Lord Clive, whose son became 1st Earl of Powis of the present creation : a version of the well-known portrait by Nathaniel Dance.

THE rose-red castle of Powis was bought in 1587 by Sir Edward Herbert, a younger son of the Earl of Pembroke (*see* WILTON HOUSE). His son, who in 1629 became Lord Powis, defended the castle against the Roundheads, who captured it in 1644 after the destruction of its western gateway. The castle was remodelled later in the seventeenth century by the 3rd Lord Powis, who was made Earl of Powis in 1674 and Marquess of Powis in 1687. As a Catholic, Powis was imprisoned in the Tower of London at the time of the Popish Plot. He was one of those Catholic peers who urged moderation on James II; however, when James was forced to leave the country in 1688, Powis out of loyalty went with him, and the infant Prince of Wales, the future Old Pretender, was entrusted to the care of Lady Powis, a Lady of the Bedchamber. Despite his Jacobitism, Powis, who was made a duke by the exiled monarch, did not suffer forfeiture of his estates, although after his death in 1696 they were granted to Lord Rochford, a cousin of William III who was reputed to be the Dutch King's natural son.

The 2nd Marquess of Powis, son of the Jacobite Duke – whose dukedom was not recognized by the House of Hanover – was restored to his ancestral estates in 1722. The castle, which had been stripped of its furniture, was embellished by him and he completed the splendid terraces. In 1748 the original line of the Herberts of Powis became extinct and a new earldom of Powis was conferred on the husband of the last Marquess's niece and heiress, who was himself a Herbert, a descendant of that Carolean all-rounder, Lord Herbert of Cherbury. This first Earl of Powis of the second creation preferred Oakly Park, his seat in Shropshire, to Powis, though in 1771, the year before his death, he sold Oakly to his rich friend Clive of India, who already owned more than one Shropshire estate. Clive had obliged Lord Powis by lending him money, and Powis in return gave Clive political patronage. He also gave him advice in his battle against ill-health. When Clive tried cold baths as a form of treatment, Powis counselled him: 'For God's sake be cautious in the use of this powerful remedy!' And he urged him to take an emetic by way of preparation for his plunge into cold water.

The next Earl of Powis, though he no longer had the rival attractions of Oakly to entice him away, preferred London to his ancestral castle in the Welsh Marches. In the words of the diarist John Byng, he spent his rents 'in driving high phaetons up St James's Street'; he was 'the bauble of his mistress, and of his steward consequently, who . . . comes here to sneak about for a day or two.' Byng, when he visited Powis, found the castle 'sadly neglected and hourly falling to decay'. Some of the windows had blown in and the curtains were 'waving in the air'. It was unsafe to walk on the terraces, for the balustrades were falling down – 'should you slip, you are lost'. Horses grazed on the parterres and there were no longer any deer in the park. The inside of the castle was 'all in dampness and uninhabited'. There were 'some pompous bedchambers', but not a bed fit to sleep in. Nor was there a single carpet or a hogshead of wine. Yet the floors were kept so well waxed that a local lawyer had recently slipped in one of the rooms and broken his leg. And for all his neglect of the castle, Lord Powis had in fact carried out some improvements to it: the ballroom in the detached wing in the courtyard had been redecorated for his coming-of-age celebrations and he had also 'trick'd up a frenchify'd drawing room'.

Lord Powis never married and when he died in 1801 the peerage once again became extinct and the castle and estates passed to his nephew Edward Clive, grandson of his father's friend Clive of India. It is said that the reason why he left them to his nephew rather than to his sister was because her husband, the 2nd Lord Clive, who was a lover of the picturesque, had remarked, when walking with him in the grounds of Powis, that the castle would make a beautiful ruin which could be admired from a new house built on a different site. Lord Powis may have neglected the castle, but he had no wish for it to be turned into a picturesque ruin by his brother-in-law. On the strength of his son's inheritance, the 2nd Lord Clive, who had himself served in India as Governor of Madras, was given a third creation of the Powis earldom, while his son changed the family name from Clive to Herbert. But while the descendants of Clive of India have thus been metamorphosed into Herberts of Powis, Clive's memory has been kept very much alive at the castle, where his pictures and his Indian collections form a notable addition to the earlier Herbert heirlooms. The family's link with India might have been renewed in the 1870s when Disraeli offered to send the 3rd Earl there as Viceroy, but Lord Powis preferred to stay in Britain.

If P.G. Wodehouse had a real castle in mind when he wrote of 'Blandings Castle', that castle was surely Powis. As well as being in the same part of the country, Blandings resembles Powis in several other respects: it has terraces, reception rooms upstairs and a wing detached from its main building.

Architecture and Contents

A thirteenth-century fortress of the Welsh Marches, remodelled in the Elizabethan period by Sir Edward Herbert who gave it its superb long gallery. It was again remodelled in the late seventeenth and early eighteenth centuries, when the ancient walls were enriched with classical detail and the rock on which the castle stands was transformed into a wonderful succession of terraces and hanging gardens, probably designed by William Winde, with balustrades, statues and an orangery. Inside the castle, Winde was probably responsible for the staircase, with its richly carved woodwork. It has a painted ceiling by Verrio and wall paintings dating from thirty years later by Lanscroon, who also painted the ceiling of the blue drawing-room. This room has early eighteenth-century panelling hung with Brussels tapestries; there are more Brussels tapestries in the elaborately moulded and gilded state

Powis Castle: the south front, with its early eighteenth-century yews, and the terraces which are the most famous feature of the garden.

bedroom, which has a rail in front of the bed reminiscent of the contemporary bedroom of Louis XIV at Versailles. The ballroom in the detached wing was redecorated in the 1770s by Thomas Farnolls Pritchard of Shrewsbury, whose other work in the castle mostly disappeared early this century when the dining-room and the oak drawing-room were given an Elizabethan character by G.F.Bodley, in accordance with surviving fragments of sixteenth-century plasterwork. The pictures at Powis include a notable Bellotto, as well as portraits by Dahl, Kneller, Gainsborough, Reynolds, Romney, Nathaniel Dance and Pompeo Batoni; there is also Isaac Oliver's celebrated miniature of the reclining Lord Herbert of Cherbury. The furniture ranges from a sixteenth-century Italian table inlaid with marble and semi-precious stones, and Queen Anne chairs and stools of silvered gesso and Spitalfields velvet, to a pair of black lacquer commodes attributed to Pierre Langlois. For full measure, there are the Indian works of art brought back by Clive of India and also by his son, whose treasures include a Sèvres coffee service that belonged to Tipu Sultan. Powis was vested in the National Trust by the 4th Earl of Powis before his death in 1952; it continues to be the home of his cousin, the 6th Earl.

185

RABY CASTLE
DURHAM

THE great medieval stronghold of the Nevills was bought early in the seventeenth century by Sir Henry Vane, whose roots were far away in Kent, where his family – of which the Fanes represent another branch (*see* BRYMPTON D'EVERCY) – had become rich through iron-smelting. Vane acquired Raby chiefly for its estate; to him, the historic castle was 'a mere hullock of stone'. Nevertheless, he repaired it and received Charles I here on his way to be crowned as King of Scotland, entertaining him again at the time of the First Scots War in 1639. By 1641 Vane had fallen from the royal favour and he supported Parliament throughout the Civil War, during which Raby was attacked on five separate occasions. His son, Sir Henry Vane the Younger, was even more strongly wedded to the Parliamentary cause, going so far as to hold Republican views, which cost him his head after the Restoration. The Republican Sir Henry's son, who was made Lord Barnard in 1698, ended by taking such a dislike to his own son Gilbert Vane that he attempted to demolish Raby in order to prevent him from enjoying it. Furniture was sold, lead stripped from the roof, floors were taken up. But before further damage could be done, Gilbert brought a successful Chancery action against his father, though this did not prevent Lord Barnard from cutting down the best trees in the park and slaughtering the deer.

Gilbert succeeded as the 2nd Lord Barnard in 1723 and set about repairing his father's ravages in the park, while his son Henry – afterwards Earl of Darlington – tackled the castle itself, forming a series of delightful Georgian rooms within its ancient walls. The castle was more drastically remodelled later in the eighteenth century by the 2nd Earl of Darlington, who made a spectacular Gothic entrance hall, through which a carriage could be driven, underneath the old Baron's Hall of the Nevills. This Caserta-like solution to the problem of turning a carriage and horses in the rather small inner courtyard seemed a wonderful idea to the dramatist George Colman, who wrote of a visit to Raby in the 2nd Earl's time:

As we passed through the outer gateway of the Castle, the vapour was dense upon the moat, and we were enveloped in night fog – we might have fancied ourselves victims to the darkest times of Gallic despotism, condemned by a *lettre de cachet* to linger out our lives in the deepest dungeons of the Bastille; but lo! on the opening of a massive door, a gleam of light flashed upon us: crack went the whips, we dashed forward at full trot, and in a moment drew up, not to a piazza, nor a vestibule, nor a flight of steps in a cold courtyard, but before a huge blazing fire in the spacious hall.

The diarist John Byng, who came here in 1792 shortly before Lord Darlington's death, thought the hall very cold. 'To make it a thoroughfare street is wretchedness indeed', he wrote. 'A contrivance of the smallest utility

The drawing-room at Raby Castle in August 1900.

Raby Castle in August 1900 during the visit of the Duchess of York – the future Queen Mary – who sits between her hostess, Lady Barnard (right), and Raby's former chatelaine, the last Duchess of Cleveland. Lord Barnard stands behind his wife, and their three sons, Henry, Christopher and Ralph Vane, sit on the ground in front. To the right of Lady Barnard is Lady Beatrice Pretyman; her husband, E.G.Pretyman MP, stands at the back, behind the Duchess of Cleveland and next to Lady Katharine Coke (see HOLKHAM).

and of the most devilish effect ... must chill the house with winds.' Byng, who came as a tourist, was obliged to send in his name to Lady Darlington before he was admitted. 'I am told that many are refused! Why not a fix'd day, or fix'd hours?' He asked the 'fat housekeeper' to show him 'anything ancient' and she took him up to the Baron's Hall and to the great vaulted kitchen where two men cooks were at work. The other rooms he dismissed as 'Frenchifi'd – deal floor'd – and modernly glazed, without pictures,' and he saw in everything 'the fancy of a citizen, not the grandeur of a northern baron'. His eye became less jaundiced, however, when he met the young Lady Katharine Barnard, wife of the Darlingtons' son and heir, on horseback near the lodge. He 'was struck instantly in love by her white teeth and elegant bow! She is reckon'd the Dian of the North.'

Lady Katharine's husband, known to his family as Barney, was an amiable young man addicted to hunting and the fair sex. The alterations to the castle were completed in time for his coming-of-age celebrations in 1787, when the Baron's Hall was lit by thousands of tiny oil-lamps arranged in patterns on the walls. He married Lady Katharine, a daughter of the last Duke of Bolton, in the same year. She died in 1807 and he afterwards chose as his second wife the thirty-six-year-old daughter of a Yorkshire market gardener. However much raising of eyebrows this second marriage may have caused, it did not prevent him from being made Duke of Cleveland in 1833 (the title commemorated his descent, through his grandmother, from the Duke of Cleveland who was one of Charles II's natural sons by Barbara Villiers). His Duchess survived him by nearly twenty years and lived on at Raby, building up a collection of stuffed animals and birds, minerals and botanical specimens. With these she filled the Baron's Hall after it had been enlarged and shorn of most of its genuine medieval features by the fashionable architect William Burn, who was employed by her stepson, the 2nd Duke. Burn was also responsible for the grand and ornate early Victorian reception rooms in the south front of the castle, rebuilding this front in a hard and regular masonry which stood out rather too obviously against the medieval stonework. 'We made many attempts to destroy this unfortunate appearance of novelty,' the wife of the 4th Duke wrote in 1870 in her *Handbook to Raby Castle*, 'but always without result: stain the walls as we would the rain and storms of every winter washed them clean and bright again before spring.' Eventually an old Sussex mason gave her 'a recipe that was to be mixed with bullock's blood', which was used 'with entire success (except that the unfortunate man employed in laying it on became very sea-sick).'

The 4th Duke was over sixty when he inherited, but he lived to be eighty-eight, and he and his Duchess made the most of their years at Raby. During their reign, it was a friendly and hospitable house, while keeping very much an atmosphere of the past. 'When I and others who had arrived by the same train issued from the station doors', the writer W. H. Mallock recalls of a visit to Raby in their time, 'the carriages awaiting us in the twilight comprised old yellow chariots with postilions, like that of my grandfather in which I had swung myself when a child. When we approached the castle, whose towers were blots in the November evening, I felt we were approaching a castle in a child's fairy-tale.'

Mallock's fellow guest was Augustus Hare, that other literary spare-man of Victorian country house parties, who has also left an account of a visit to Raby in the time of the 4th Duke of Cleveland and his Duchess. The Duke would come and talk each morning and tell interesting stories about his past: 'He rises suddenly from his chair, walks rapidly backwards and forwards to the fire, and then sits down again; always with his sharp, fiery, restless look.' According to Hare, the Duke and Duchess had an insatiable love of stories; he himself told a story one evening and it was such a success that whenever he afterwards escaped to his room after 5 p.m., there came a knock at the door and a servant said: 'Their Graces want you to come down again.' It may have been a feeling that he was expected to sing for his supper which made Hare write a little sourly of his amiable hostess. He complained about her habit of making everybody play *petits jeux* after dinner, and he found it a bore having to write, before he left, in the Duchess's album, which was arranged in the form of a questionnaire. One column was headed 'Why you came': Hare remarked that the natural answer to this would seem to be 'Because I was asked.' Another column was for complaints, which were meant to take the form of a complaint that one's happy visit had come to an end. In fact it was not compulsory for the departing guests to answer the Duchess's questions; they could, if they preferred, adorn her album with a sketch or with some original verses. Mallock 'preferred to take refuge in the last', and wrote:

> Some scoff at what was, and some shrink from what may be
> Or is; but they all must be pleased at a place
> Where even what was looks enchanting in Raby,
> And where even what is is redeemed by Her Grace.

Another guest wrote in the album 'A pity at Raby there is no baby', which was all too true, for although the Duke had step-children – one of them was Lord Rosebery, the future Prime Minister – he had no children of his own. There was no heir to the dukedom or to the earldom of Darlington, though there was a distant kinsman who was able to succeed as the 9th Lord Barnard and who inherited Raby.

Raby Castle by James Miller, c. 1850.

Architecture and Contents

A great medieval castle, mainly of the fourteenth century, with no fewer than nine towers. It was given a series of Georgian rooms in the middle of the eighteenth century and more drastically remodelled in about 1783 when the carriage entrance was formed beneath the original Baron's Hall. This suffered further alteration in the 1840s at the hands of William Burn, who rebuilt the south front of the castle to provide a series of ornate reception rooms. The pictures at Raby include works by Claude, Sebastiano Ricci and the younger Teniers, as well as a collection of sporting paintings by artists such as Ben Marshall, John Wootton and the elder J.F.Herring; there are portraits by Lely, Amigoni, Pompeo Batoni, Reynolds, Hoppner and Sir Francis Grant.

ROUSHAM HOUSE
OXFORDSHIRE

Sir Robert Dormer, cadet of a family that had risen to prominence in Buckinghamshire and Oxfordshire in Tudor times, acquired Rousham and built the present house on the eve of the Civil War. His grandson, General James Dormer, a veteran of Marlborough's campaigns who at one time went as envoy-extraordinary to Lisbon, enlarged and remodelled the house a century later to the design of William Kent. General Dormer was a friend of Gay, Swift and Pope, a member of the Kit-Cat Club and a man of cultivated and indeed advanced tastes. Instead of making Rousham classical, as most of his contemporaries would have done, he showed an inclination for the Gothic, which Kent skilfully blended with the original Jacobean character of the house. The General was also at the forefront of fashion in being an admirer of the picturesque. He and Kent were largely responsible for the enchanting landscape garden at Rousham, which had been started by his two elder brothers, helped, according to tradition, by Pope, who often stayed here.

The General was a bachelor, and when he died in 1741, having not lived long to enjoy his improvements, he left Rousham to a cousin on his mother's side, Sir Clement Cottrell, who assumed the additional surname of Dormer. Sir Clement held the court appointment of Master of the Ceremonies, which had been held by his father and also by his grandfather, who while in exile during the Commonwealth was Steward to Charles I's sister, the 'Winter Queen'. The office was subsequently held by Sir Clement's son and grandson. His son, Sir Charles Cottrell-Dormer, was away in Hanover for George III's installation as Elector when Horace Walpole came to Rousham in 1760, causing him to remark: 'If I had such a house, so pretty a place, and so pretty a wife, I think I should let King George send to Herrenhausen for a Master of Ceremonies.' One has no doubt that Walpole, while considering the absent Sir Charles to be fortunate in both his wife and his house, envied him most for possessing 'so pretty a place', which he described enthusiastically as 'Daphne in little, the sweetest little groves, streams, glades, porticos, cascades and river imaginable ... as elegant and antique as if the Emperor Julian had selected the most pleasing solitude about Daphne to enjoy philosophical retirement.' The garden at Rousham had attracted visitors ever since it was first laid out. As early as 1740 Lord Chesterfield of the *Letters* called to see it, accompanied by Pope's friend Lord Bathurst. Kent even provided a visitors' entrance, a handsome classical doorway flanked by a battlemented lodge with an arch under which tourists could shelter from showers.

Such was the change in taste during the century following Walpole's visit

Kent's chimney-piece in the former library, with an overmantel portrait of General James Dormer.

that the Arcadian glories of the Rousham garden did not make much impression on Augustus Hare when he stayed here in 1859. He simply mentions 'long evergreen shrubberies, green lawns with quaint old statues, and a long walk shaded by yews, with a clear stream running down a stone channel in the midst', without any special praise, though the garden, when he saw it, must have been even more beautiful than it was a century earlier, now that the trees had grown. To this cultivated and sociable Victorian, Rousham was chiefly remarkable for its portraits, its manuscripts and a 'pedigree of the family from Noah'. According to Hare, his host, another Charles Cottrell-Dormer, would claim to be 'a Roman Catholic in disguise, chiefly to plague his wife', and would read through the entire works of Pope, 'in the large quarto edition', once a year. While he was thus engaged, his wife would look after the estate, riding about the place by herself.

If Hare was largely indifferent to the superlative work of art that is the Rousham garden, the 'capricious alcoholic' to whom Rousham was let for a period between the wars appears to have positively resented it. James Lees-Milne, who as an Oxford undergraduate was taken by friends one summer's evening to dine with this personage, tells of how his host, having at first amused himself after dinner by flicking the paint off the portraits with a hunting crop, then went outside with a rifle and fired at the private parts of the statues. 'I do not think that by then his aim can have been very accurate', Lees-Milne recalls. 'For all I remember he missed, and I sincerely hope that the manhood of Apollo, Pan and the Dying Gladiator remains unscathed to

A romantic view of Rousham.

this day. I have twice visited Rousham since, but on neither occasion could I bring myself to make a close inspection for fear of finding that some pudenda were missing, in which case I would hold myself partly responsible. For to my lasting shame I never raised a finger in protest against this hideous iconoclasm.'

The inebriate iconoclast fortunately did *not* shoot straight, and any other damage which the garden and the house may have suffered during his tenancy has been repaired since Thomas Cottrell-Dormer and his family came back to live here. Mr Cottrell-Dormer's love of Rousham is equalled only by his knowledge of its history, its architecture and its treasures, as any visitor fortunate enough to have been taken round the house by him would surely agree. As well as acting as guide, Mr Cottrell-Dormer has often, during the years since the house was first opened, sat at a table at the top of the front door steps selling admission tickets. One summer's afternoon when there were not many visitors, a party of Americans arrived to find him dozing peacefully at his table, his straw hat down over his eyes. 'How long have you been here?' one of them asked him, after he had awoken from his nap, to which he replied, 'Three hundred years.' The Americans were too much taken up with thoughts of Rip Van Winkle to listen while Mr Cottrell-Dormer courteously explained that three hundred years was not an unusually long time for an English family to have been at its ancestral home.

Mr Thomas Cotterell-Dormer sitting at the top of the front door steps of Rousham on a summer's afternoon in 1967, selling admission tickets.

Architecture and Contents

A house of 1635 with projecting wings and a three-storey porch, remodelled from 1738 onwards by William Kent, who added pavilions in the Palladian manner but maintained the house's Jacobean character, giving it a battlemented parapet and a cupola. The house was increased in depth in the Victorian period, so that the garden front of the main block is now Jacobean-Revival. To the right of the hall, in what had been the seventeenth-century kitchen, Kent created his ravishing Painted Parlour, with its ceiling of arabesques, its white marble chimney-piece by John Marden dominated by a Medusa head, and its elaborately carved overmantel framing a romantic scene by Pieter Van Laer. In one of his pavilions Kent made another glorious room, the Great Parlour, on a much grander scale and slightly Gothic in flavour, with a ribbed and vaulted ceiling. Originally a library, its bookshelves were removed in 1764 and the walls adorned with frames of rococo plasterwork by Thomas Roberts of Oxford which surround a series of resplendent portraits, one of them by Van Loo. The portraits at Rousham also include works by Cornelius Johnson, Dahl, Dobson, Lely, Kneller, Reynolds, Arthur Devis and Benjamin West, while among the other pictures in the house are works by Carlo Maratta, G.B. Pannini and John Piper. Of even greater importance than Kent's work in the house is his landscape garden, one of the earliest man-made romantic landscapes to have survived, with glades and vistas, statues and temples and arches, pools and cascades.

SALTRAM HOUSE
DEVON

The library at Saltram.

THE old Devon family of Parker acquired the estate of Boringdon through marriage to an heiress in 1582. In 1712 George Parker of Boringdon bought the neighbouring estate of Saltram, to which in the 1740s his son John decided to move on account of its more attractive landscape. The house at Saltram dated from the sixteenth and seventeenth centuries. John Parker and his wife Lady Catherine set about transforming it into a large

mid-eighteenth-century mansion, externally undistinguished but containing some magnificent plasterwork. Their son, another John, added to the interior glories of Saltram with the help of Robert Adam.

The younger John Parker was a well-known figure in his day. He was a Member of Parliament, moving in fashionable racing and card-playing circles, as well as a man of taste and a friend of Sir Joshua Reynolds, who was born close to Saltram at Plympton. Yet he had the outlook and manner of a backwoods country squire, even speaking with a Devon accent at a time when regional accents among the aristocracy aroused comment. 'I had the pleasure of finding Parker as dirty, as comical and talking as bad English as ever', Georgiana, Duchess of Devonshire (*see* CHATSWORTH) wrote after a visit to Saltram, where she was 'enchanted with the beauty of the place'.

The beauties of Saltram made as great an impression on Fanny Burney, who came here in 1789 when the house was lent to George III and Queen Charlotte. 'We followed immediately after the Royals and equerries', she wrote in her account of their arrival. 'So many of the neighbouring gentry, the officers &c were assembled to receive them, that we had to make our way through a crowd of starers the most tremendous, while the Royals all stood at the windows, and the other attendants in the hall.' While the King and Queen were at Saltram, no fewer than a hundred beds were made up for the guests.

By that time John Parker, who in 1784 had been raised to the peerage as Lord Boringdon, was dead, Saltram being then owned by his seventeen-year-old son. After he had come of age, the young Lord Boringdon was known, according to Harriet Wilson, as 'The Boring Don'. It may have been because she found him boring that his first wife, a daughter of the 10th Earl of Westmorland's runaway marriage to Sarah Child (*see* OSTERLEY PARK), left him in 1808 for Sir Arthur Paget (*see* PLAS NEWYDD), against whom, in the ensuing divorce proceedings, Boringdon was awarded £10,000 damages for *crim con*. The affair had a tragic sequel on which Mrs Henry Wood is said to have based her novel *East Lynne*, having been told the story by Thackeray. When she eloped with Paget, Lady Boringdon left her infant son, whom she did not see again until she returned nine years later to nurse him as he lay dying, the boy having swallowed a stalk of rye which caused a fatal illness. Her ex-husband was with her at their son's bedside, but he pretended not to recognize her.

Lord Boringdon had in 1815 been made Earl of Morley, having bought the small Devon village of Morley in order that he might take his title from it, and thereby give the impression of being descended from earlier Lords Morley whose surname was Parker – though they were in fact no relation. He was now happily married to his second wife, who came to Saltram as a bride in 1809, and wrote of it enthusiastically: 'The place is a thousand times more delightful than all the possibility of my imagination had conceived it; it is so gay, so riant, so comfortable and so everything that it ought to be that it is impossible to love and admire it enough.' She lost no time in performing the duties of her position. Later that same year the diarist Joseph Faringdon, on his way up to the house, noted with approval that her carriage was standing outside the local school, which she was visiting, and reckoned that this promised her husband 'more happiness than he could have enjoyed with His late divorced vicious wife'.

Robert Adam's magnificent saloon.

Two years after her marriage her clergyman brother came to stay at Saltram and was a little disappointed at the prevailing simplicity. 'The whole lower part of the house is abandoned, the library excepted', he complained. 'Our breakfast of the plainest description and the dinner the same ... bad port wine and claret ... no domestic attends, some three footmen, a Maitre d'Hotel and Valet de Chambre standing or laying on the great gallery of the staircase outside the door, till summoned by a hem or a whistle, his lordship performing by a Dumb Waiter the whole Ceremony himself.' When there was company, some of the grand rooms were used, though even then the footmen did not put on their gala livery of white trimmed with green and gold, but continued to wear 'plain green without the slightest relief or ornament to it'. One evening's entertainment described by the critical clergyman was 'a little Cards, a little Singing, a little Music and an infinitely little supper', but he appears to have been unlucky in his stay, for at other times his sister and brother-in-law entertained lavishly: in the previous autumn, for instance, they gave a ball for more than two hundred people, forty of whom were put up in the house.

Saltram.

As a sign of the 1st Earl of Morley's open-handedness, he left a mortgage of something like £250,000 on his estate when he died in 1840, with the result that his successor, the son of his second marriage, had to live very quietly. Towards the end of the 2nd Earl's life, Saltram was let, and it was not until 1883 that the 3rd Earl, who married into a very wealthy family, was able to return. The 3rd Earl was also able to play a part in public life, holding office in Liberal administrations and eventually becoming Deputy Speaker of the House of Lords. His two bachelor sons, the 4th and 5th Earls, who lived together at Saltram from 1905 until after the Second World War, kept the house in perfect condition while doing as little as they could in the way of modernization, so that in their time the saloon and other rooms continued to be lit only by candles.

Architecture and Contents

The exterior of Saltram, a mid-eighteenth-century rebuilding of an earlier house, is plain and of stucco, but inside are great riches. The hall and morning room have ceilings of vigorous Italian plasterwork contemporary with the rebuilding. The morning room is hung with Genoa velvet of a glorious faded red, covered with pictures arranged like postage stamps in an album in the authentic eighteenth-century manner, among them no fewer than five portraits by Reynolds. The dining-room and the saloon, dating from later in the century, are by Robert Adam, with plasterwork by Joseph Rose and decorative paintings by Antonio Zucchi. The saloon, a double-cube, predominantly light blue in colour with an Axminster carpet designed by Adam who may also have designed the giltwood chairs and settees, the picture frames and the stands (he is known to have designed the dining-room sideboard) is one of the most beautiful rooms in the west of England. The quality of the furniture and objects in the saloon and dining-room is maintained throughout the house, which passed into the care of the National Trust in 1957.

196

SHUGBOROUGH

STAFFORDSHIRE

THE Ansons, established as country squires at Shugborough by William Anson, a successful Staffordshire lawyer of the time of James I, rose into the higher aristocracy thanks to the career of the great eighteenth-century naval commander, Admiral Lord Anson. Anson is chiefly remembered for his epic four-year voyage round the world during which he and his men had all kinds of adventures and suffered unbelievable hardships – including three months of continual storm rounding Cape Horn – but he also has a place in history as a naval reformer as well as for his victory over the French off Finisterre in 1747 and for his successful blockade of Brest in 1758. When he died, in 1762, he was a very wealthy man, not least on account of his share of the booty of the voyage of circumnavigation, during the course of which a Spanish galleon was captured in the Pacific, worth with its cargo £400,000. Having no children, he left his fortune to his elder brother Thomas, who had inherited Shugborough in 1720.

Thomas Anson was a bachelor of romantic temperament and wide culture. He travelled in the Levant and was a founder member of the Society of Dilettanti, established in 1732 for the encouragement of Greek classical art. He was also interested in science, including among his friends the botanist and writer Benjamin Stillingfleet, the original 'Bluestocking', and he was to

An eighteenth-century view of Shugborough, with its park, gardens and neo-Grecian monuments, by Nicholas Dahl (d. 1777).

be associated with men like Josiah Wedgwood and Matthew Boulton in various industrial projects. Towards the end of the 1740s and early in the 1750s he enlarged the house at Shugborough and also began to improve its surroundings. For these schemes, he had financial help from his brother the Admiral, some of whose officers also helped him in other ways, such as by designing the Chinese House in the garden and supplying 'Indian paper of the Landskip kind' for the dressing-room used by Lady Anson when she stayed here. Thomas Anson was devoted to his sister-in-law, the Admiral's lady, who was charming, clever and high-spirited. He carried on a platonic flirtation with her, and when the two of them were together in the Arcadian surroundings of Shugborough they played at being a shepherd and shepherdess.

This innocent – and somewhat elderly – pastoral romance must have been an inspiration to Thomas Anson in creating his great landscape park, which he completed after he had become rich through his brother's death, by which time his Shepherdess had died also. His newly acquired wealth enabled him to embellish his park with buildings and monuments derived from *The Antiquities of Athens* by his friend James 'Athenian' Stuart, who helped him with their design: some of them commemorate the naval feats of his brother the Admiral. He also spent some of his money on amassing a splendid collection of pictures and classical sculpture.

A portrait of Admiral Lord Anson by Francis Cotes, at Shugborough.

Thomas Anson's successor at Shugborough was his sister's son George Adams, who changed his name to Anson. George's son, another Thomas Anson, employed Samuel Wyatt to carry out further additions and alterations to the house. He also extended the park, put up steam-heated greenhouses in which melons and cucumbers grew 'in perfection at all seasons', and built a model farm, being a keen agriculturalist like his father-in-law, Coke of Norfolk (*see* HOLKHAM HALL). Having represented the borough of Lichfield in Parliament, as his father and his great-uncle Thomas Anson had done before him, he was, through the influence of Charles James Fox, raised to the peerage as Viscount Anson in 1806. The 2nd Viscount, who was promoted to being Earl of Lichfield in 1831, had the distinction of being Postmaster-General when Sir Rowland Hill introduced penny postage. In other respects he was not a success. Charles Greville, while describing him as 'a fine fellow, with an excellent disposition, liberal, hospitable, frank and gay, quick and intelligent', writes of him as being 'without cultivation, extravagant and imprudent'. As well as being addicted to the Turf, he wasted £150,000 in fighting elections on behalf of various relations and political colleagues; he was also a gambler, using the upper room of the Tower of the Winds in the park – one of Thomas Anson's Athenian replicas – for play. As a result of all this improvidence, most of the contents of Shugborough, including Thomas Anson's collection, had to be sold, only the family portraits and a few other items being retained. The sale in 1842 lasted a fortnight. The 2nd Earl made good his father's depredations by acquiring French furniture worthy of the house, which is now in the care of the National Trust, part of it being occupied by the present Lord Lichfield, who is well known as a photographer.

*Lord Lichfield (top hat) and his family
on the steps at Shugborough in the
1860s.*

Architecture and Contents

A square block of about 1693 enlarged in the 1750s by the addition of bow-
fronted wings containing some fine rooms. It was enlarged again and
remodelled between 1794 and 1806 to the design of Samuel Wyatt, who gave
the entrance front its dramatic octostyle Ionic portico and added a projecting
centre with verandas on either side to the garden front. There is superb mid-
eighteenth-century plasterwork by Vassalli in the dining-room and library;
the red drawing-room has plasterwork of the later eighteenth century by the
younger Joseph Rose; the saloon, also dating from Wyatt's remodelling, is
lined with columns of scagliola. As well as the family portraits, the items
which survived the sale of 1842 include the Chinese porcelain acquired by
Admiral Lord Anson. The buildings and monuments in the garden and park
include a reproduction of the Arch of Hadrian in Athens, a Tower of the
Winds and a copy of the Choragic Monument of Lysicrates, all by 'Athenian'
Stuart and earlier than any other neo-Grecian architecture in England, with
the exception of Stuart's Ionic temple at HAGLEY.

STANFORD HALL
LEICESTERSHIRE

THE estate of Stanford, on both sides of the Avon which here forms the boundary between Leicestershire and Northamptonshire, was acquired by the Caves in the reign of Henry VIII. For the next 250 years they lived in a manor house on the Northamptonshire side of the river, but at the end of the seventeenth century Sir Roger Cave, 2nd Baronet, built the present house across the river in Leicestershire. Like other houses of its period, it has a dream-like quality. Its many-windowed façades of golden stone or pale orange brick seem not so much to be standing as floating, as though the house were moored in two opposite currents which are the two straight avenues running up to it from north and south. When Sir Roger died in 1703 the interior of the house was as yet unfinished. His son, Sir Thomas – who married into the ancient family of Verney – went on with the work, but it was not completed until the time of his grandson, another Sir Thomas, who also improved the park, notably by widening the river. 'As Sir Thomas has a very mechanical turn, and a particular taste for marine affairs,' a Northampton-shire clergyman wrote of him, 'he has by a lock swelled this rivulet to such an height, as to afford at once a fine prospect from his house, and also room for him to navigate a sloop or two of his own building upon it. This yields a most agreeable entertainment in a summer's evening.' As well as having 'a very mechanical turn', Sir Thomas was an antiquary and a bibliophile. He was also an MP who used his influence to save Rugby School, which was then almost defunct.

On the death of the childless 7th Baronet in 1792, Stanford passed to his sister, the wife of Henry Otway, of Castle Otway in County Tipperary. Otway, a brother of Admiral Sir Robert Otway who was with Nelson at Copenhagen, was of lethargic temperament. One day a messenger came to say that the Prince Regent, who was then staying a few miles away in Warwickshire, wished to come and stay at Stanford. The messenger waited for a reply, while Otway, who did not want to be bothered with a royal visit, tried to put his refusal into suitably conciliatory words. Having written and torn up letter after letter, he finally sent an excuse and the Prince never spoke to him again.

In 1839 the abeyance of the sixteenth-century barony of Braye was terminated in favour of Henry Otway's widow, who inherited her right to it through the Verneys, of whom she was now heiress. Three years later the septuagenarian Baroness visited Rome, where she bought the portraits and other relics of the Stuarts which are now at Stanford; they had belonged to the Young Pretender's brother Henry, the Cardinal of York. The Baroness lived until 1862, and her grandson and eventual successor, who was alive in

The ballroom at Stanford.

the 1920s, remembered her sitting at the head of the Stanford dinner table at the age of ninety, lamenting that the railway should have come so close to the house.

After the Baroness's death, the peerage again fell into abeyance between her four daughters, who became joint owners of the Stanford estate, the house being divided between three of them. By the end of 1879, however, all the sisters had died. Only one of them left children, of whom the surviving son succeeded as Lord Braye and came into Stanford outright. That year saw the death not only of the new Lord Braye's mother, but also of his aunt and of his elder brother, who was killed in the Zulu Wars, so that for several months there were no fewer than three hatchments or funeral escutcheons displayed over the principal doorway of Stanford.

The new Lord Braye, who was to reign until 1928, was a remarkable character: a soldier who became a pacifist, a strong upholder of aristocracy who ended by supporting the Labour Party, a poet and a writer of vigorous prose. He was also a very pious Catholic convert, who opposed legislation for easier divorce and campaigned for the abolition of the Declaration against Catholic doctrines which British sovereigns had been obliged to make since 1689. He was unusual for his generation in his love of classical architecture, and on succeeding to Stanford he set about restoring and embellishing the house in a very sympathetic manner, nothing having been done to it for over a hundred years, so that as he afterwards recalled, 'the windows and oak doors admitted the cold air freely'. He also added to the house a wing containing a dining hall and a richly Italianate chapel, where vespers used to be canonically sung, accompanied by his wife playing the harp in the tribune. The dining-hall was filled with music of a different sort when the band of Lord Braye's battalion played in the gallery during Pytchley Hunt dinners, occasions made colourful by the coats of scarlet and white worn by the twenty-five guests, who included the Master, the red-bearded Lord Spencer (*see* ALTHORP).

Other memorable occasions at late-Victorian Stanford included a visit by Cardinal Newman, who attended Benediction in the chapel. Then there was the ill-fated flight of the young pioneer aviator Percy Pilcher, who became airborne over the park in his bat-like glider on a windy afternoon in 1899. A shower of rain, which had fallen while he was having lunch in the house, had wetted the fabric of his flimsy machine and thereby made the tail too heavy. The tail snapped off in mid-air and Pilcher crashed – he was carried, mortally injured, to the house, where he died a day or so later.

Unlike his grandfather, Lord Braye was not averse to entertaining royalty. The Duke and Duchess of Teck, with their daughter and a party of friends, came to lunch at Stanford in 1891. The Duchess looked at the photographs which the Brayes had brought back from a recent trip to America, while the Duke wandered from room to room rearranging the china. Twenty-two years later, on the eve of the Great War, the 'Tecks' daughter returned to Stanford as Queen Mary. Lord Braye showed her the Stuart relics and also the chapel. He describes this visit in his memoirs as 'very likely a last occasion for the feudal touch in the reception of a Sovereign, at least at Stanford; the old blue and yellow of the family livery probably on its last display; and a line of hired constables in their uniform created a look of order and security along the park road.'

Writing these words in the 1920s, he had reason to feel depressed about the future of his ancestral home. His dining hall and his beloved chapel had been found to be riddled with dry-rot and there was nothing for it but to demolish them. 'So the house-breaker is summoned and pulls down the shrine where I have heard so many Masses and spent so many hours in long prayer', Lord Braye wrote while the work of destruction was going on. 'All of a heap, it will be levelled to the ground; a sad blow both to the brick wall and to the inside walls of my soul. The operators are called house-breakers: heart-breakers better.' This was not the only sorrow which Lord Braye had to endure in the closing years of his life. Some of the estate had to be sold, including a splendid beech avenue which the new owner insisted on felling. 'Scarcely had the poor chapel at Stanford crashed under the blows of the house-breaker, and St Thomas, portrayed on the vaulted ceiling, been hurled down from the clouds, from the sun rays, from the angels, pulverized, and the dust blown over into the contiguous county of Northampton only a few yards off, than

axes and hammers and saws and wedges were at work at venerable trees close by.'

As he contemplated all this ruin, Lord Braye would surely have been surprised if he could have known that now, nearly sixty years later and after a Second World War, Stanford is still the home of his descendants. With his somewhat radical views, he would probably have been pleased at the thought of the house being regularly open to the public.

Architecture and Contents

A dignified house with regular façades and a high roof, begun in 1697 by William and Francis Smith of Warwick, completed by Francis after William's death in 1724. Some of the rooms are late seventeenth-century in character; the grand staircase with its carved balusters dates from about 1730, while the two-storey hall – now known as the ballroom – has plasterwork of the 1740s by John Wright of Worcester and decorative paintings of the 1880s by a French artist named Joubert. In addition to family portraits by artists who include Cornelius Johnson, Kneller and Thomas Hudson, the house contains a collection of Stuart portraits and Jacobite relics which belonged to Henry, Cardinal of York. An aviation museum in the stables is dedicated to the memory of Percy Pilcher.

203

STONOR PARK
OXFORDSHIRE

WITH its martyrs and its medieval chapel which has known none but Catholic forms of worship, Stonor is the outstanding example of an ancient recusant house. Hidden among beechwoods in a fold of the Chilterns, it is older than COUGHTON or BADDESLEY CLINTON, and it has also passed by unbroken male-line descent for much longer than either of those two other famous old Catholic houses, having been the home of the Stonors at least since the time of Robert de Stanora who was living here in the twelfth century. And it is likely that Robert de Stanora was himself descended from the Herveys who held Stonor at the time of Domesday, and who were neither Normans nor Saxons but of ancient British stock.

From the time of Sir John de Stonore, Chief Justice under Edward III, the medieval Stonors were of considerable importance, and as a great quantity of their papers have survived, we know at least as much about them as we know about the Pastons. Their letters show them to have been courteous, affectionate towards their spouses, their parents and their children, and above all, pious. As a sign of their piety, they did not have just one chaplain at Stonor but six, who constituted what was in effect a small monastery, singing Divine Office regularly and occupying a cloister which still exists at the end of the house nearest to the chapel. As well as telling us what the medieval Stonors were like, the letters give us many details of their domestic life: for instance, we find even in the fifteenth century the familiar complaint: 'Servants be not so diligent as they were wont to be.'

From an inventory of 1474, drawn up by Thomas Stonor's wife Jeanne – who was the daughter of no less a personage than the romantic and tragic Jacqueline, Countess of Hainault – we learn that whereas the chapel at Stonor was then very richly appointed, the furnishings of the rest of the house were somewhat sparse. In the great hall there were black serge hangings, a turned chair and two plain chairs, a brass chafer, a pair of 'cob-irons' and a fire-fork. 'The chamber at nether end of the hall' – used this century as a study, but in those days doubling as the best bedroom and as a parlour for the ladies – had green worsted hangings and a white bed-hanging. It contained a bed with two coverlets, one 'green, with spots and ostrich feathers worked on it', a feather bed, a truckle bed, 'a tin basin' and an andiron. Beyond this room was 'the little chamber', hung with 'striped cloth, purple and green', and then three more bedrooms, hung with 'striped serge, red and green', in the wing leading towards the chapel. The domestic offices were, as now, on the other side of the hall. In the kitchen there was, in addition to the usual assortment of pots and pans, 'a great spit', 'a medium-sized spit' and 'a bird spit'; the bakehouse contained 'an eel tub' and also 'a vat for mashing malt' and nine barrels, which would suggest that it was also used as a brewhouse. The inventory mentions two halberds and a boar-spear which have remained in the house to this day.

Writing to her husband when he was away, Jeanne reminds him to bring her 'gentian, rhubarb, baize, caps, pots, cheverel-laces, an ounce of flat silk, laces, treacle'. As an indication of the hospitality which fifteenth-century Stonor was able to provide, we have an account of the dinner given to all those who attended Thomas's funeral. This did not take place at Stonor itself but six miles away at Pyrton, where the then parish church was situated. However, the servants, cooking utensils, 'wode and colis' for the fire, 'cuppis and bollis and pottis' for the ale, 'sponys of silver and salt selers of silver for the most worshipful men' were all sent up from Stonor, as though for a grand shooting-lunch in the reign of the seventh rather than the fourth Edward. For the first course, the priests and gentry were given capon broth, mutton, goose and custard, while the poor – who were provided with tables, table-cloths and 'sytting plasis' just as the gentry were – had a soup made from the umbles of deer, and stewed beef and roast beef in a dish together. For the second course, the gentry were served with a 'jostle' or hotch-potch of 'capons, lambe, pigge, vele, peiouns rosted, baken rabettes, ffesauntis, venison, gelie, etc' while the poor had roast pork. The dishes were flavoured and garnished with saffron, pepper, cloves, mace, Corinth raisins, dates, ginger and cinnamon; the geese were cooked in wine.

Thomas's and Jeanne's son, Sir William Stonor, enjoyed the favour of Edward IV and at that monarch's funeral was one of the four knights in full armour who carried the canopy over the corpse. Sir William's nephew and eventual successor Sir Walter Stonor, who enlarged the house, had a long career as a courtier under Henry VIII, and it seems likely that the family star would have continued to rise had it not been for the Reformation and the Stonors' staunch adherence to the Old Faith. In 1581 Sir Walter's widowed daughter-in-law, Cecily Lady Stonor, allowed the Jesuit priest and Oxford scholar Edmund Campion and his fellow Jesuit Robert Persons to set up a

House party for the shoot at Stonor,
19 November 1911.

secret printing press at Stonor, which was then unoccupied. Here, 400 copies of Campion's *Decem Rationes* were printed for circulation at Oxford. Campion and Persons stayed in the house for some time, to supervise the work and 'take counsel on their affairs'. They probably occupied the bedroom known as Mount Pleasant in the gable over the porch, from which it was possible to escape into the attics by way of a concealed opening. According to tradition, when Campion and Persons heard that the authorities were after them, they said Mass not in the chapel but in a space among the rafters. Towards the middle of July, the two Jesuits left and a few days later Campion was arrested. Stonor was raided, the press seized and the printers sent to the Tower. Cecily Stonor's younger son John was also imprisoned, though he was released after eight months and went into exile abroad. By 1592 Cecily had herself been put in prison, where she remained for the rest of her life.

Campion, who was executed at Tyburn towards the end of 1581, was not the only Catholic martyr associated with Stonor. No fewer than seven others were close connections of the family, including the Carthusian Sebastian Newdigate, Cecily's uncle; Margaret Pole, the last of the Plantagenets, Sir William Stonor's first cousin by marriage; and Adrian Fortescue, Sir William's son-in-law. Fortescue, a soldier and courtier who became a Knight of St John after his wife's death, lived for many years at Stonor which his family claimed on the grounds that his wife was Sir William Stonor's heiress, but after a lawsuit that lasted for thirty-four years it was recovered by the male heir, Sir Walter Stonor.

The following century saw the ten-year imprisonment of Elizabeth Lady Stonor in the reign of James I, the death in action of her son William in the heroic defence of Basing House during the Civil War, and the sale of most of the family estates outside Oxfordshire to pay the recusancy fines under the Commonwealth. The Restoration brought a turn for the better, though the fourth Thomas Stonor was one of the many prominent Catholics informed against during the Titus Oates frenzy. The eighteenth-century Stonors were able to live more peacefully, though in 1705 Stonor was searched for arms and the fifth Thomas had to promise to hand over a grey mare which he 'used a-hunting for his health'. Like other eighteenth-century recusants, the Stonors sent their children to be educated abroad; some of them became priests or nuns. The fifth Thomas's brother, John Talbot Stonor, became a bishop, and during the last three years of his life he lived at Stonor with his nephew. To avoid quarrels between their respective servants, they kept separate establishments – even the bishop's firewood was separate from that used by his nephew's household. The bishop, together with his chaplain, his manservant and his housekeeper, occupied the warm rooms above the kitchen and buttery as well as Mount Pleasant, which he nicknamed 'The Mountain of Misery'. Thirty years earlier, during his nephew's minority, the bishop had supervised the estate, and it may have been thanks to his good management that his nephew, the sixth Thomas, felt sufficiently well-off by the 1750s to carry out various alterations to the house.

The seventh Thomas Stonor's sister Mary was one of the English Augustinian canonesses who, at great peril to their lives, stayed in Paris throughout the Revolution. She eventually became prioress of her convent.

Stonor in the late seventeenth century.

We have an endearing glimpse of the future prioress as a girl of nineteen in 1787. She went up from Stonor to London for a party, and sent a messenger to ask the family chaplain, Doctor Joseph Strickland – who was also her great-uncle – to look for a bodkin which she had left behind. 'The bodkin was found in Miss Mary's room, which on account of the quantity of grease and powder that besmears the floor and all the furniture looks more like a barber's shop than a young lady's bedchamber', Doctor Strickland reported in a letter. 'I am at a loss to know how they manage in great homes, where the furniture is for the most part very valuable, for certainly no furniture whatever can stand the modern method of ladies making so much use of powder and pomature. This, however, is not meant as the least reflection upon Miss Mary, who must do and dress like other people. It only says that she has the misfortune to be born in a very flashy and dirty age.' The old priest's remark about 'very valuable furniture' in 'great homes' is a reminder that Mary's mother had selfishly sold all the furniture out of Stonor to pay the debts of her second husband, whom she married soon after her Stonor husband's premature death in 1781. It was not until the 1790s that Mary's brother, the seventh Thomas (who came of age in the year of the bodkin episode) was able to make good his mother's depredations.

The passing of the Catholic Emancipation Act enabled the Stonors once again to play a part in English public life. The eighth Thomas Stonor became an MP and in 1839 the medieval barony of Camoys, of which he was a co-heir through his great-grandmother, was called out of its 400-year abeyance in his favour. While one cannot but regret that the proud designation of Stonor of Stonor should have been superseded by a title which has no historical connection with the family, it was none the less fitting that the Stonors should have a peerage, since they would almost certainly have acquired one a century or two earlier but for their religion. The peerage also brought the Stonors back to Court, from which they had been absent since the time of Sir Walter (unless one counts the eighteenth-century Monsignor Christopher Stonor's service in the household of the exiled Stuarts). The eighth Thomas was a lord-in-waiting to Queen Victoria almost continuously from 1846 to 1874; his daughter-in-law was Woman of the Bedchamber to the Princess of Wales, the future Queen Alexandra; his grandson Sir Harry Stonor (one of the best shots of his time) was Gentleman Usher and Groom-in-Waiting to no fewer than five sovereigns, from Queen Victoria to George VI. Sir Harry and his sister Julia were lifelong and very close friends of George V, with whom they more or less grew up, and they and their two brothers were virtually adopted by the Prince and Princess of Wales after their parents' death.

Architecture and Contents

A long, rambling house of brick and flint, enclosing several small inner courts, its oldest parts medieval, but enlarged and remodelled at various periods so that it now has a front of eighteenth-century sash windows with a hipped roof on a timber cornice. At the centre, however, is an Elizabethan porch gable, and attached to the right-hand end of the front is the medieval chapel, like a small parish church. The interior of the chapel is Georgian Gothic of about 1800, with a plaster vault and a painted window based on a picture by Carlo Dolci. The great hall was also redecorated in Georgian Gothic, but some fifty years earlier. This work survives in an attenuated form, the hall having been divided lengthwise in 1834, the front part being turned into the present drawing-room. Upstairs there is a long library with a barrel ceiling, which contains a notable collection of recusant books. These, and the family portraits, are among the contents of the house which survived the sales of 1938 and 1975. Despite these unfortunate sales, Stonor is still full of treasures, some of them inherited by the present Lord Camoys from his cousin, the late Francis Stonor, others lent by Mrs Eyre Huddleston, who is also a cousin of the family. There are pictures by Tintoretto, the three Carracci and Giambattista and Domenico Tiepolo. The furniture ranges from early productions of the firm of Gillow to an exotic shell-shaped bed supported by mermaids and dolphins which is thought to be Italian, and from 'New York' mahogany chairs to Venetian celestial and terrestrial globes by Coronelli.

STOURHEAD

WILTSHIRE

Sir Henry and Lady Hoare with their son Henry and Sweep, the dog, October 1912. Young Henry was fatally wounded in the Great War, but his parents survived him by almost thirty years; they both died on the same day in 1947.

THE estate of Stourton was bought in 1718 from the ancient Catholic family of that name by Henry Hoare, son of the founder of Hoare's Bank in Fleet Street, who renamed it Stourhead and commissioned Colen Campbell to build him a new house here. His son, another Henry, spent forty years in making the landscape garden for which the place became famous – an enchanted valley with lakes, hanging woodlands, temples, a bridge and a grotto. So numerous were the visitors who flocked to see his grounds that Henry Hoare built an inn to accommodate them. Mrs Lybbe Powys and her husband, who had planned to celebrate their fourteenth wedding anniversary in August 1776 by seeing Stourhead, arrived here at ten o'clock on the previous night only to find it full. They had to go to Mere, 'a shocking little town three miles off', where the best inn was also full. In the end they had to make do with a place that was little better than an ale-house. Next day they agreed that the beauties of Stourhead were well worth the discomforts of the night before. Mrs Lybbe Powys noted that fifty men were employed to keep the grounds in order, and particularly admired the 'Turkish Tent', which being of painted canvas remained up all the year round.

On Henry Hoare's death in 1785, Stourhead passed to his great-nephew Richard Colt Hoare, who afterwards inherited a baronetcy. In 1791, on his return from Italy, Sir Richard Colt Hoare added the wings to the house, containing respectively, as was fitting, a picture gallery and a library; for as well as being a dilettante and a great collector like other members of his family, he was also a scholar. A visitor to Stourhead in his day was the painter John Constable; another was Sir Robert Walpole's biographer the Reverend William Coxe, who was 'remarkable for his love of good eating'. When he left, Sir Richard said 'He is gone away well filled, as I have given him Venison every day.'

Sir Henry Hoare, the 6th Baronet, rebuilt the central block after it was gutted by fire in 1902 – most of the contents having fortunately been saved. When he was an old man during the Second World War, Sir Henry was visited by James Lees-Milne, who described him as 'an astonishing nineteenth-century John Bull, hobbling on two sticks . . . wearing a pepper and salt suit and a frayed grey billycock over his purple face'. He met Lees-Milne in Salisbury and took him to Stourhead in his car, driven by 'an old chauffeur of immense, overlapping fatness who had an asthmatic wheeze, like a blacksmith's bellows'. At Stourhead they were greeted by Lady Hoare, 'an absolute treasure and unique . . . tall, ugly and eighty-two; dressed in a long black skirt, belled from a wasp waist and trailing over her ankles. She had a thick net blouse over a rigidly upholstered bosom, complete with stiff, whaleboned high collar round the throat.' They dined that evening in the small dining-room, with its screen of columns. Despite the wartime shortages the meal consisted of soup, fish, pheasant, pudding and dessert, accompanied by Rhine wine and port. The Hoares had no housemaids, but they still had a cook and butler. Lady Hoare said with satisfaction, 'The Duchess of Somerset at Maiden Bradley has to do all her own cooking.' She also asked Lees-Milne if he did not find the food better in the present war than in the one previous, to which Lees-Milne replied that he was rather young during the previous war, but remembered the rancid margarine at his preparatory school. 'Oh!' said Lady Hoare. 'You were lucky. We were reduced to eating rats.' 'No, no, Alda', interspersed Sir Henry, looking up from his plate. 'You keep getting your wars wrong. That was when you were in Paris during the Commune.'

A view across the stone bridge to the Temple of Apollo.

North-east View of Stourhead House
by John Buckler.

Architecture and Contents

The centre of Stourhead is a square Palladian mansion built in about 1720 to the design of Colen Campbell. The projecting portico was added to the east front in 1841 in accordance with Campbell's original design. This front was extended with wings in 1791, one of them containing a picture gallery, the other a library with a painted lunette window by Francis Eginton. The central block was rebuilt, with alterations to the west front, after a fire in 1902, the architects of the rebuilding being Sir Aston and Dorian Webb. Stourhead contains one of the great art collections of eighteenth-century England, mainly built up by the second Henry Hoare and by Sir Richard Colt Hoare. The pictures include important works by Nicolas and Gaspard Poussin, Carlo Maratta, Vernet, the younger Teniers and Anton Mengs; there is sculpture by Le Sueur and Rysbrack, an Italian *pietre dure* cabinet which once belonged to Pope Sixtus v, and a wealth of fine English furniture. But even more famous than the treasures of Stourhead is its landscape garden, with temples around the great lake by Henry Flitcroft. Stourhead is now in the care of the National Trust.

STRATFIELD SAYE

HAMPSHIRE

AFTER the Battle of Waterloo, Parliament voted to buy a country seat for Europe's hero, the Duke of Wellington, who, having been offered a choice of several, including UPPARK and HOUGHTON HALL, settled for Stratfield Saye, which had formerly belonged to a branch of the Pitts. His choice appears to have been influenced by the surroundings rather than by the house, a long, low stuccoed mansion dating from the reign of Charles I and much altered in the eighteenth century, and the original plan was that the old house should be demolished and replaced with a neo-classical BLENHEIM. Various architects produced designs for a 'Waterloo Palace' which, however, was beyond both the nation's generosity and the Duke's resources – his cash grant of £200,000 was enough to support him in a suitable style and enabled him to buy Apsley House in London, but certainly would not have stretched to the building of a new and palatial country house. So with characteristic good sense, the Duke decided to make do with the old house, to which he afterwards made various additions, though he was apt to complain that it had been 'a bad investment', and many of his contemporaries echoed the sentiments of his friend Mrs Arbuthnot who thought it 'an indifferent one for him'. His son and successor used to say that it was 'like a great cottage'.

During the years when he was active in politics the Duke spent little time at Stratfield Saye, though the house was much used by the Duchess, 'poor Kitty Pakenham' as she was generally known. Their sad, distant relationship is reflected in the distance between their respective bedrooms – the Duchess's on the first floor at the northern end of the garden front, the Duke's on the ground floor next to his study at the southern end of the entrance front. The footman who carried a message from one to the other had to walk nearly a hundred yards. The Duke's bedroom was part of a self-contained suite which included a somewhat gloomy bathroom. His ideas of plumbing were very much in advance of his time, for in 1841 he installed water-closets in eight bedrooms, concealed in large cupboards which had a complicated mechanism to prevent the occupant from being accidentally locked in. Another of the Duke's innovations was central heating; two of his radiators are still in use. The Duke was as much concerned with the aesthetic side of the house as with its comfort: he bought Buhl furniture and other works of art, and wrote out minute instructions for hanging the pictures in the drawing-room. Attracted by the existing decoration of the long gallery with prints applied to the walls, he decorated many of the bedrooms in this way, marshalling the prints with military precision and pasting them up with his own hands, 'signing' each room with a print of himself.

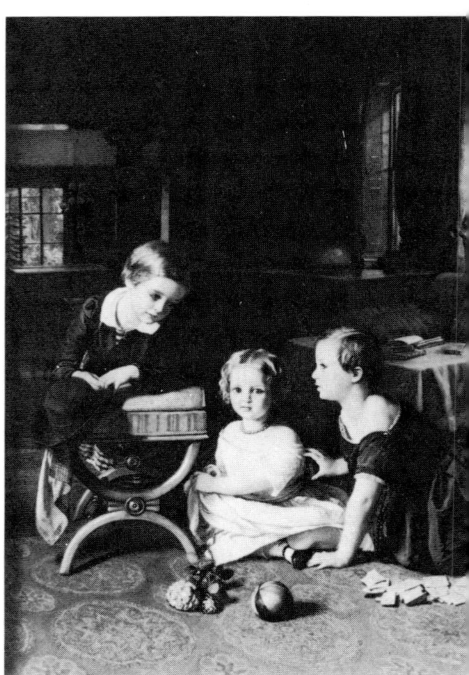

The Great Duke of Wellington in the library at Stratfield Saye in 1852, the last year of his life, with his grandchildren Henry, Mary Angela, Arthur and Victoria. Henry (left) *and Arthur became successively the 3rd and 4th Dukes; Arthur lived until 1934. (A miniature on ivory by Robert Thorburn.)*

The 2nd Duke of Wellington, though very much overshadowed by his father, to whom he bore a strong likeness, was nevertheless a personality in his own right. He rose to the rank of lieutenant-general in the army and was renowned among his friends for his wit. When a lady of his acquaintance wrote asking him to contribute £100 towards the restoration of her family church, he replied that he would be very happy to give her £100 and added that he was himself about to restore the church at Stratfield Saye and had no doubt that she would gladly send him a similar sum. 'In that case', he remarked drily, 'I think no money need pass between us.'

A favourite amusement of his was making translations from Horace, and he once, in the Stratfield Saye library, gave a young lady guest a practical lesson in public speaking. He had a fund of stories about his father, treasuring up every reminiscence of him just as he carefully preserved every relic and memento – even the last pheasants shot by the Great Duke were stuffed and on display in his little sanctum. He felt he owed it to his father's memory to entertain any distinguished foreign soldier who came to England. When that rough old warrior the Duc de Malakoff was in London as French Ambassador, he invited him down to Stratfield Saye in September for the partridge shooting. There were some cock pheasants strutting about in a field, and Malakoff was 'seized with an uncontrollable desire to slay one', though it was still the close season for pheasants. The Duke conferred with Smith the keeper, who reckoned that they could 'put it down as a partridge'. So the Ambassador stalked a pheasant on the ground, shot at it and missed. He fired a second time and wounded the bird, which tried to run away, but he gave chase, caught it and dashed its brains out against a tree, exclaiming triumphantly: 'Enfin, brigand! Je te tiens!' 'That' said the Duke to Smith, as they watched this performance, 'is the great Marshal Duke of Malakoff, who smoked out four hundred Arabs in a cavern in Algeria.' 'Well, Your Grace' answered the keeper contemptuously, 'a man who would treat a cock-pheasant like that, and in September too, there is no saying what he might not do to an Arab.'

The 4th Duke, the younger of the Great Duke's two surviving grandsons, lived until 1934. In his time the open balustrade of the gallery which runs across the hall at first-floor level was boxed in so that people below might no longer be offended by the sight of the servants' posteriors passing along it as their owners stooped to avoid being seen. Since the 4th Duke preferred to live at Ewhurst, a few miles to the west, Stratfield Saye was empty during much of his reign. It eventually became the home of his eldest son, afterwards the 5th Duke. The latter was more interested in the sporting amenities of the estate than in the house itself: he installed baths in the bedrooms with unsightly pipes going up to the ceiling, and his wife's dogs scratched the paintwork off the doors.

After the gallant death in action of the young 6th Duke in 1943, Stratfield Saye passed to his uncle, the late Duke, who as Lord Gerald Wellesley was well known as an architect. He was also a notable connoisseur. Having moved into the house before the end of the war when it had no electric light and little heating, he set about arranging the rooms with more elegance and comfort, so that they were eventually seen to better advantage than they had been at any time under his forebears.

The long, low façade of Stratfield Saye.

The hall at Stratfield Saye, hung with Napoleonic banners and, in the centre, the standard of the Duke of Wellington. Roman mosaic pavements excavated from nearby Silchester are set into the floor.

Architecture and Contents

Basically a Carolean house of which the original curved and pedimented gables can still be seen on the entrance front. It was enlarged and remodelled in the eighteenth century when its façades were lengthened, its brickwork stuccoed and its mullions replaced with sash windows. Predominantly eighteenth-century interior: a two-storey hall with a screen of Ionic columns, a long gallery decorated with prints against a background of gold leaf, a drawing-room with a rococo ceiling and a library with a ceiling very much in the manner of William Kent. The house is full of pictures and objects associated with the Great Duke of Wellington, his campaigns and his subsequent career. The rooms also contain some magnificent French furniture and other works of art. Much of it was bought by Wellington from the collection of Napoleon's uncle, Cardinal Fesch, though there are also gifts from European monarchs, notably porcelain from the King of Prussia, the Austrian Emperor and the Tsar, who also gave the Duke the malachite *tazza* now in the hall. Some of the pictures from the Spanish royal collection, which the King of Spain generously insisted that Wellington should keep after he had captured them from Joseph Bonaparte's baggage-train, are at Stratfield Saye, the rest being at Apsley House. There are works by Hogarth, Hoppner and Lawrence among the family portraits.

SUDELEY CASTLE
GLOUCESTERSHIRE

THE great medieval and Tudor castle of Sudeley, once the home of Queen Catherine Parr who lies buried in its chapel, was in ruins for nearly two centuries before it was bought in the 1830s by the brothers John and William Dent of Worcester, whose wealth was derived from the manufacture of gloves. These two bachelors were antiquarians, and their restoration of the castle was gradual and restrained. They confined themselves to making the Tudor ranges habitable, leaving the medieval buildings in a state of picturesque ruin, a background to the gardens which were laid out around and inside the castle walls. The Dents also collected furniture, pictures and historical relics for the rooms which they were reinstating, including many things associated with previous owners of the castle, or which had actually been in the castle in former times. The latter were mostly acquired at the Strawberry Hill sale of 1842, having belonged to Horace Walpole.

The nephew and heir of the brothers, John Coucher Dent, restored one side of the medieval inner court in the 1850s; his wife Emma carried out more work in 1887 after his death. Mrs Dent, who came of the old Cheshire family of Brocklehurst, shared the antiquarian interests of her husband and his uncles, as testified by her book, *The Annals of Winchcombe and Sudeley*. She was at home when Augustus Hare and some friends looked in at the castle in the autumn of 1876, and as they were coming out of the chapel she appeared, 'a picturesque figure in a Marie Antoinette hat' and invited them in to tea. 'The Dents made their fortune as glovers,' Hare observed, 'and in their present magnificence a parcel of their gloves, as from the shop, is always left in a conspicuous place in the hall, "to keep them humble".'

While subsequent owners of Sudeley have remembered the founders of

An eighteenth-century prospect of Sudeley Castle when it was ruinous.

Emma Dent sitting by the fire at Sudeley.

the family fortunes by bearing the additional surname of Dent, they have not in fact been related to them by blood. John Coucher Dent had no children, and after his death in 1885 Sudeley passed first to his widow and then to her nephew, Henry Dent Brocklehurst, whose wife was Marion Lascelles, a granddaughter of the 3rd Earl of Harewood (*see* HAREWOOD HOUSE). Their son, Major John Henry Dent-Brocklehurst, remodelled and redecorated the interior of the castle in the 1930s, the Dent brothers having panelled most of the rooms in dark oak, which made them rather sombre.

Architecture and Contents

A castle built in 1442 and remodelled about 1572. It was abandoned after the Civil War and fell into decay, but was restored from 1837 onwards partly under the supervision of Sir George Gilbert Scott, the inner court being left ruinous and made into a garden. The nineteenth-century interior was remodelled and redecorated in the 1930s. Sudeley contains a notable collection of pictures, including works by Claude, Van Dyck, Greuze, Hogarth, Constable and Turner. There are many relics connected with the history of the castle and a collection of letters and autographs started by Emma Dent and continued by the family after her death.

UPPARK
WEST SUSSEX

IN 1746 the wealthy London merchant Sir Henry Fetherston died, leaving his fortune, estimated at the then vast sum of £400,000, to a distant kinsman, Matthew Fetherstonhaugh, the thirty-year-old son of a mayor of Newcastle-upon-Tyne. Sir Henry attached two conditions to this bequest: that his heir should acquire a baronetcy and also a country estate. Fetherstonhaugh lost no time in fulfilling both conditions. He was made a baronet in 1747 and in the same year bought Uppark, with its dream-like rose-coloured house on the crest of the South Downs built in the reign of William and Mary by Forde Grey, Earl of Tankerville, a somewhat disreputable character but an expert in the art of pumping water uphill which enabled him to establish himself on so elevated a site. Having acquired their new home, Sir Matthew and his wife Sarah, the daughter of a rich London merchant of Huguenot stock, set off on a Grand Tour to buy works of art with which to embellish it, and they redecorated most of the interior of the house in the taste of their time, with ceilings of ravishing plasterwork. Sir Matthew was determined to make the most of his inheritance, but like so many other very rich men he was careful with his money and kept detailed accounts of his expenditure (the journey to Uppark when he and Sarah came here in 1747 cost £9 5s and he gave a guinea to the ringers of Harting who welcomed them with their bells). In 1755, he refused to spend more than £600 on his campaign for election to Parliament, but nevertheless managed to win a seat that he retained for the rest of his life. His other interests included a scheme in which Benjamin Franklin was also involved for founding a new American colony to be called Vandalia. It came to nothing, but is commemorated at Uppark in a Gothic folly known as the Vandalian Tower. He was also a scientist and wrote two manuscript volumes on 'natural philosophy', including a chapter on electricity.

Sir Matthew's son, Sir Harry, who succeeded at the age of twenty in 1774, was, like him, a man of exquisite taste. He bought French furniture and *objets d'art*, and made improvements to Uppark and its grounds. But in other respects he differed from his serious-minded father: he was extravagant and liked entertaining in grand style, he hunted, raced and played for high stakes in the company of the Prince of Wales, who in 1785 stayed with him at Uppark for three days, when the party also included the Duc de Chartres, afterwards Duc d'Orleans and notorious as Philippe-Égalité. 'They had races of all sorts', Mrs Elizabeth Montagu wrote of this royal visit. 'Fine horses, ponies, cart-horses, women, and men in sacks, with various other divertimenti fit for children of six foot high.' Each morning at breakfast the company was served with 'three hot dishes of meat' which had to be carried a

Benjamin West's portrait of Sir Harry Fetherstonhaugh.

hundred yards along the underground passage joining the kitchen wing to the main block of the house. Despite the distance from the kitchen to the dining-room, the food cooked by Sir Harry's chef, Moget, was so renowned that neighbours preferred to have guests to stay on their way *to* Upark rather than from it.

Magnificent though the entertainment for the Prince may have been, it was not attended by any fashionable ladies from London. Sir Harry's mother, the widowed Sarah, Lady Fetherstonhaugh, who lived with him as he was unmarried, 'fled from the riot' to the house of her half-brother, whose daughter has left a record of quieter times at Upark, when she and Sarah 'drove in the harvest fields by moonlight in an open carriage, and supped on our return by the same light without candles'. For more than a year Sarah had to endure the presence at Upark of Emma Hart, who having been the eighteenth-century equivalent of a showgirl in London, became her son's mistress. The beautiful Emma is said to have entertained Sir Harry and his friends by dancing on the dining-room table. But then, at the end of 1781, when she was about to become a mother for the second time – not, it would seem, on Sir Harry's account – she was sent packing with hardly any money and would have been destitute had she not been rescued by Charles Greville, a kinsman of the diarist, who had met her while staying at Uppark for the shooting. Greville subsequently introduced her to his uncle and her future husband, Sir William Hamilton. Thirty years later, when Emma's most famous lover Nelson was dead, and she and her daughter Horatia were once again homeless, Sir Harry, still a bachelor, lent her money. He also wrote her some friendly letters, sent her presents of game and promised to invite her to stay, or as he put it, to let her have 'a view of old Uppark *dans la belle saison*'.

Emma died in 1815 and in the following year Sir Harry appears to have considered selling Uppark to the nation as a country seat for the Duke of Wellington, who in the event preferred STRATFIELD SAYE. Sir Harry remained at his old home and in 1825, when he was over seventy, he married his dairy-maid, Mary Ann Bullock, who was then eighteen, sending her to be educated in France to fit her for her new position. She made him an excellent wife, and when he died, childless, at the age of ninety-one in 1846, he left Uppark to her. She survived her husband by thirty years, keeping the house exactly as it was in Regency times – or as her younger sister Frances, who lived with her, used to say, 'as Sir 'Arry 'ad it'. Frances's difficulty with her aspirates is surprising, for her sister had engaged a governess to educate her. As she never married, the governess stayed on at Uppark making a trio of old ladies who would vary their life by going up to London to stay at Claridge's.

When Mary Ann died she left Uppark to Frances, who assumed the name of Fetherstonhaugh and carried on her sister's late Georgian *ménage*. In 1880 the mother of H.G.Wells, who had been Frances's maid, became her housekeeper. 'Except that she was thoroughly honest, my mother was perhaps the worst housekeeper that was ever thought of', Wells writes in his autobiography.

She had never had the slightest experience in housekeeping. She did not know how to plan work, control servants, buy stores or economise in any way. She did not know clearly what was wanted upstairs. She could not even add up her accounts with assurance and kept them for me to do for her. All this came to light. It dawned slowly upon Miss Fetherstonhaugh; it became clearly apparent to her agent ... it was manifest from the first to the very competent, if totally illiterate, head housemaid Old Ann, who gave herself her own orders more and more. The kitchen, the laundry, the pantry, with varying kindliness, apprehended this inefficiency in the housekeeper's room. At length I think it dawned even upon my mother. Not at first. She was frightened, perhaps, but resolute and she believed that with prayer and effort anything can be achieved. She knew at least how a housekeeper should look, and assumed a lace cap, lace apron, black silk dress and all the rest of it, and she knew how a housekeeper should drive down to the tradespeople in Petersfield and take a glass of sherry when the account was settled.

Wells, who was a youth at the time, would stay with his mother at Uppark when he was on holiday or out of work. He afterwards depicted the house as Bladesover in his novel *Tono Bungay*, and in his autobiography he describes it as 'a handsome great house looking southward, with beechwoods and bracken thickets to shelter the dappled fallow deer of its wide undulating

On the steps at Uppark. This is the only picture in existence of Frances Bullock-Fetherstonhaugh (centre), *the younger sister of the former dairy-maid who married Sir Harry Fetherstonhaugh, Uppark's owner in Regency days. She was in mourning for her companion Ann Sutherland – Sir Harry's natural daughter – who died in 1893. The girl in the bottom left-hand corner is Beatrice Winterton Turnour, daughter of Colonel Keith Turnour, a Sussex neighbour to whom Frances left Uppark for life.*

downland park'. But what made a greater impact on his memory than the beauty of the house and its surroundings was a dance in the servants' hall one Christmas, an occasion when the élite of the housekeeper's room – of which the young Wells, by right of his mother, was a member – mixed freely with the lower servants.

There was a kitchen maid whom I suddenly discovered was pretty beyond words and I danced and danced again with her, until my mother was moved to find other partners for me ... Her name was Mary and that is all the name I ever had for her. And afterwards in one of the underground passages towards the kitchen, where perhaps I was looking for her, she darted out of a recess and kissed and embraced me. No lovelier thing had ever happened to me. Somebody became audible down the passage and she made a last dash at me, pressed her lips to mine and fled. And that is all. Next morning I trundled off in the dog-cart on the frosty road to Rowlands Castle station for Portsmouth, before sunrise, and when I next went to Uppark for a holiday, Mary had gone.

Wells's mother became even less effective as a housekeeper owing to increasing deafness. Miss Fetherstonhaugh was deaf also, so 'they were two deaf old women at cross purposes'. Miss Fetherstonhaugh was forbearing until she heard that her housekeeper was gossiping about some imaginary incidents in her and her sister's early life, which brought retribution in the form of a month's notice. 'The fallen housekeeper, with all her boxes and possessions, was driven to Petersfield station on February 16th 1893, and the hospitable refuge of Uppark was closed to her and her needy family for ever.'

Two years later Miss Fetherstonhaugh died. She left Uppark for life to the younger brother of Earl Winterton, another Sussex landowner, and then to a younger son of the Earl of Clanwilliam, an Irish peer who leased a neighbouring country house for the shooting. Lord Clanwilliam's son, Admiral Sir Herbert Meade, who took the additional surname of Fetherston-haugh, came into Uppark in 1930, by which time this sleeping beauty of a house was suffering from the effects of having had nothing done to it for a hundred years and more; the roof was in a bad way, the pictures were black, the eighteenth-century curtains were faded and in tatters. During the decade that followed, the Admiral and his wife restored the house and its contents with painstaking care. Lady Meade-Fetherstonhaugh repaired all the curtains and hangings herself, bringing their faded colours to life by washing them in an infusion of the herb *saponaria*, which grows in the park. Thanks to this labour of love, some of the most complete and unaltered eighteenth-century interiors in England have been preserved for posterity, while keeping the atmosphere and patina which makes Uppark one of the most magical of country houses.

Architecture and Contents

A late seventeenth-century house of brick and stone with a high hipped roof carried on a bold modillion cornice. Although some of the rooms keep their original painted panelling, most of the interior was redecorated in the middle of the eighteenth century, with ceilings of magnificent plasterwork.

Humphry Repton was employed to carry out various alterations in about 1810, notably the addition of a portico and Doric colonnade on the north front. The pictures at Uppark include works by Luca Giordano, Vernet and Zuccarelli, together with portraits by Arthur Devis and Pompeo Batoni. There is English and French furniture of the highest quality, Meissen, Sèvres and Chelsea porcelain. From the time of Sir Harry Fetherstonhaugh down to the present, the house has remained remarkably unchanged, even to the early nineteenth-century wallpapers and the eighteenth-century curtains and hangings, many of which were painstakingly restored by the late Lady Meade-Fetherstonhaugh, whose husband gave Uppark to the National Trust in 1954.

An early eighteenth-century view of Uppark by the Dutch painter Pieter Tillemans.

WALLINGTON HOUSE
NORTHUMBERLAND

WALLINGTON was inherited in 1728 by Walter Calverley from the wealthy Newcastle merchant and coal-mining family of Blackett. Calverley, who became Sir Walter Calverley Blackett, was a powerful figure in the north-east, a great benefactor to the city of Newcastle of which he was five times mayor, and which he represented for over forty years in Parliament. In 1770, towards the end of his life, he surprised his fellow members in the Commons by getting up and making a quite irrelevant statement in order, as he said, to salve his own conscience. In the 1740s he remodelled the late seventeenth-century house at Wallington. His improvements were admired by that inveterate country house visitor, the first Duchess of Northumberland (*see* ALNWICK CASTLE), though she commented on the lack of pictures and criticized the siting of the kitchen, which, as she recorded, 'unluckily regales two of your senses, your sight and your smell, before it gratifies the third . . .'

Wallington from the north.

Dying childless in 1777, Sir Walter Calverley Blackett left Wallington to

his nephew, Sir John Trevelyan, of an old Cornish and Somersetshire family, whose descendants, from the middle of the nineteenth century onwards, gave the house the intellectual flavour for which it is now well known. This originated with Sir Walter Trevelyan, who succeeded in 1846, and even more so with his fascinating wife Pauline, whom he met at a conference in Cambridge organized by the British Association for the Advancement of Science. Pauline Lady Trevelyan was an artist who attracted such people as Ruskin, Millais and Swinburne to Wallington. Ruskin, his wife Effie, and Millais came to stay in the summer of 1853. 'This is the most beautiful place possible', Ruskin wrote to his father: 'A large old seventeenth-century stone house in an old English terraced garden, beautifully kept, all the hawthorns still in full blossom ... undulating country with a peculiar Northumberlandishness about it – a faraway look which Millais enjoys intensely ... We are all very happy, and going this afternoon over the moors to a little tarn where the seagulls come to breed.' For his part, Millais was no less enthusiastic, and wrote to Holman Hunt: 'The country is glorious like the Isle of Wight from the sea ... Today I have been drawing Mrs Ruskin who is the sweetest creature that ever lived; she is the most pleasant companion one could wish ... Ruskin is benign and kind.' In two subsequent letters to his father, Ruskin described the Trevelyans as 'two of the most perfect people I have ever met with'. Their pleasantness, he wrote, consisted in 'very different qualities: in Lady Trevelyan in her wit and playfulness, together with very profound feeling: in Sir Walter in general kindness, accurate information on almost every subject, and the tone of mind resulting from a steady effort to do as much good as he can to the people on a large estate.'

Augustus Hare, who stayed at Wallington nine years later, was less complimentary, perhaps because Lady Trevelyan, like so many Victorian intellectuals, was oblivious of creature comforts. She and her husband had roofed over the courtyard to make a lofty central hall which was being painted with scenes from Northumbrian history by their friend, the Pre-Raphaelite William Bell Scott; but she did not, according to Hare, pay much attention to the rest of the house, which was 'only partly carpeted and thinly furnished with ugly last-century furniture'. Besides Sir Walter and his wife, Hare found 'another strange being' at Wallington – a Mr Wooster, 'who came to arrange the collection of shells four years ago and has never gone away ... what he does here, nobody seems to know; the Trevelyans say he puts the shells to rights, but the shells cannot take four years to dust.'

Sir Walter Trevelyan was succeeded at Wallington by his cousin Sir Charles Trevelyan, a brilliant civil servant who in 1859 became Governor of Madras, only to resign a year later owing to a violent quarrel with the Government of India. He afterwards played a part in reforming the Indian finances. He married a sister of Macaulay, whose talents were inherited by his son, the historian and politician Sir George Otto Trevelyan, as well as by his grandson, the historian George Macaulay Trevelyan, both of whom received the Order of Merit. George Macaulay Trevelyan was the youngest of three brothers of whom the eldest, Sir Charles Philips Trevelyan, was President of the Board of Education in the Labour Governments of Ramsay MacDonald, while the second, Robert Calverley Trevelyan, was a poet and a translator from the Greek.

The three brothers,
Sir Charles, Robert Calverley
and George Macaulay Trevelyan, with
their 'beloved old nurse' Mrs Prestwich
on the parlour steps at Wallington.

Architecture and Contents

A solid late seventeenth-century house built round a courtyard, remodelled in the 1740s and given some splendid rooms with rococo plasterwork by Pietro Francini. In the nineteenth century the courtyard was roofed over to form a central hall, which was decorated with paintings by the Pre-Raphaelite William Bell Scott. The family portraits include works by Gainsborough, Reynolds, Romney and Hoppner. The house is rich in porcelain, European as well as Oriental. Other treasures include the desk at which Macaulay wrote his *History of England*, a collection of dolls' houses and an *omnium gatherum* of objects ranging from fossils to stuffed birds known as Lady Wilson's Cabinet of Curiosities. Sir Charles Philips Trevelyan gave Wallington to the National Trust in 1941.

WILTON HOUSE

WILTSHIRE

WITH its Inigo Jones front, its Double Cube room and its Palladian bridge set in an Arcadian landscape, Wilton is without doubt the most likely candidate for the title of the most beautiful country house in England. But even before the time of Inigo Jones, this seat of the Herberts, Earls of Pembroke, had acquired a unique reputation among English country houses. As the home of the Elizabethan 2nd Earl and his Countess, and of their elder son, the 3rd Earl, it was, in the words of John Aubrey, 'an academie as well as a palace', the centre of a brilliant court of painters, musicians, engineers and poets, the latter including the Countess's brother, Sir Philip Sidney and Shakespeare (*see* CHARLECOTE PARK) who gave the first performance of *As You Like It* at Wilton and described the 3rd Earl and his brother, the future 4th Earl, as 'incomparable'. Wilton was nothing less than the nursery of the English Renaissance. It stood for the concept of the Complete Man which was personified by the Herberts themselves, not just then but in subsequent generations.

The former abbey of Wilton was granted by Henry VIII to Sir William Herbert, 1st Earl of Pembroke of the present creation, an illegitimate scion of the great Norman–Welsh family represented in the female line by the Dukes of Beaufort (*see* BADMINTON) and the Earls of Powis (*see* POWIS CASTLE). The monastic buildings were transformed into a Tudor mansion built round a courtyard, of which the southern side was rebuilt in the latest Renaissance style from 1633 onwards by the 4th Earl with, as his advisers, Inigo Jones and the French architect, Isaac de Caus. Jones was recommended by Charles I, who, as Aubrey tells us, 'did love Wilton above all places and came thither every summer'. Having been very much a courtier, the 4th Earl sided with Parliament in the Civil War. He does not appear to have been a very attractive character, for all his taste and connoisseurship; he and his second wife, the celebrated Anne Clifford, Countess of Dorset (*see* KNOLE) parted after four years of marriage. He is said to have become a Roundhead in order to keep Wilton and his art collection; if so, it is poetic justice that his new building should have been partially gutted by fire soon after the Royalist collapse. Despite the uncertainty of the times, he immediately set about repairing the damage, advised once again by Jones who being by then old and infirm left much of the work to John Webb, his nephew by marriage. The sumptuous state rooms date mostly from this period. It comes as a shock to find that the Double Cube, so evocative of the halcyon years of Charles I's reign, with its gilded carving and portraits by Van Dyck, was in fact largely created under the Commonwealth.

The 4th Earl died in 1650, leaving his splendid rooms to be completed by

Wilton : the east front, which was the entrance front until 1801, with the Tudor gate tower in the centre.

his son. The new Lord Pembroke, who dissociated himself from his father's politics, survived the Restoration by only a few years and was followed by three of his sons in succession, of whom the second was the one notorious black sheep among the 'incomparable' Herberts; a young man 'chiefly known for deeds of drunkenness and manslaughter', as Aubrey recorded. Though he only lived to be thirty, the misdeeds of this homicidal Earl of Pembroke were legion. He was found guilty of manslaughter in 1678 and convicted of murder three years later, but on the first occasion he got off through a technicality and on the second he was pardoned by the King. Fortunately for Wilton, his younger brother, the 8th Earl, was true to the Pembroke form: a great connoisseur, who acquired collections of antique sculpture, books, manuscripts, coins and paintings – including the Wilton Diptych. Lord Hervey of the *Memoirs* breakfasted at Wilton towards the end of 1731, when the 8th Earl was in his seventies. He had a few years previously been married for the third time, to a wife much younger than himself. As Hervey reported to the Prince of Wales:

Old Pem received us with great civility and courteousness . . . My Lady was sent for down; and we were carried with great form and method through every room of a very fine old house. It is directly like an Italian Palace. There are a great many very fine statues, and a great many more with only very fine names, to which I believe his Lordship stood sole godfather. He was dressed in a pale blue damask night-gown and a black velvet night cap, which I suppose in the Antiquaries' style was emblematically to signify the youth of his body and the maturity of his head. Whether my Lady Countess will allow of this interpretation I cannot tell . . . She knew the history of

227

every busto as well as his Lordship. I do not wonder at his having endeavoured to bring her into a taste for antiques; but I question much whether her taste is so established, that if the antique in her bedchamber was to be exchanged for a modern, she would be much afflicted.

An exchange such as Hervey envisaged did in fact take place, for 'Old Pem' died a year later and his widow soon afterwards consoled herself with a second husband nearer to her in age. Old Pem's son, one of three successive Earls of Pembroke to become Generals, is remembered as the 'Architect Earl'. He designed many buildings in collaboration with his clerk of works, Roger Morris, notably that superb adjunct to Wilton's Inigo Jones front, the Palladian bridge. His son, the 10th Earl, who succeeded in 1750, continued his work of embellishing the Wilton landscape, employing Sir William Chambers as architect.

The 10th Earl's marriage to the beautiful Lady Elizabeth Spencer, a daughter of the 3rd Duke of Marlborough (*see* BLENHEIM PALACE), was not a success, and he eloped with Miss Kitty Hunter who was reputed to have 'the face of a Madonna'. Lady Pembroke, who was in high favour with George III and Queen Charlotte, eventually set up house on her own in Richmond Park. In 1778 she was faced with the prospect of receiving the King and Queen at Wilton, where she still went for periodic visits. She was, according to Lady Louisa Stuart, 'quite miserable' at the thought of their coming, and at 'the want there would be of everything necessary to entertain them, which people would charge to her, though she knew no more of her own house than anybody she met in the street. She said they had no plate and no furniture, that the State Room, which was hung with red damask, had no bed; but that want, I hear, his Lordship has supplied (to their Majesties' use) by hiring a green one at Salisbury.'

Wilton by that time had become more of a museum than a house for living in and entertaining royalty, its rooms crammed with sculpture, so that they reminded Mrs Lybbe Powys of 'a statuary's shop'. She and her husband called in here as tourists in 1776, on their way to STOURHEAD; they were asked to write their names in a book at the porter's lodge, from which they saw that 2,324 people had visited the house during the past year. 'Merely to *see*, 'tis certainly one of the finest sights in England,' was her verdict. 'But to reside at, 'tis too grand, too gloomy, and what I style *most magnificently uncomfortable*.' It was to make the house easier to live in that the 11th Earl called in James Wyatt in 1801. This Wyatt certainly achieved, though at the cost of destroying the seventeenth-century Grecian Hall and other rooms. His Gothic cloister-corridor round the inside of the courtyard not only served as a gallery for the sculpture but also made it possible to circulate without having to pass through the rooms themselves.

The 11th Earl married as his second wife the beautiful and charming Catherine Woronzow, daughter of the Russian Ambassador. The Russian Lady Pembroke lived on at Wilton for many years after her husband's death, the house being leased to her by her stepson, the 12th Earl. Her own son, the high-minded Victorian statesman Sidney Herbert, afterwards Lord Herbert of Lea, who as Secretary for War was responsible for sending Florence Nightingale to the Crimea, also lived at Wilton with his wife and children, of whom two of the sons eventually succeeded as the 13th and 14th Earls. The

The Double Cube room at Wilton, which remains exactly as Inigo Jones designed it.

13th Earl and his wife were prominent in that intellectual but light-hearted coterie of the 1880s known as the Souls, which also included George Curzon, George Wyndham (*see* PETWORTH HOUSE), Lady Elcho, Lady Granby (*see* BELVOIR CASTLE), Harry Cust (*see* BELTON HOUSE) and Alfred Lyttelton (*see* HAGLEY HALL).

The 14th Earl, like his father, followed a political career. It was in his time that the Russian Ambassador and Ambassadress, Count and Countess Benckendorff, to whom he was connected through his Russian grandmother, came to a Whitsun house party at Wilton, bringing their daughter and their son Constantine, a young officer in the Imperial Navy just back from the war against Japan. When they arrived, tea was in progress on the lawn between the house and the Palladian bridge. Constantine Benckendorff afterwards recalled how he was left to fend for himself 'amongst an assembly of strangers so indifferent, in manner at least, to my presence, that they seemed calmly hostile. My distress began then and there and continued the rest of the day, culminating at dinner: my neighbours were two young females, very attractive indeed, but whose halting French was only equalled, if not surpassed, by a sort of stutter emitted by me in lieu of English.'

After 'an interminable session with port', the young Russian was rescued by the daughter of the house, Lady Muriel Herbert:

she promptly engaged me in, oh blessed relief, perfect French. Contact of the most animated kind was speedily established and soon we somehow drifted out of the drawing room to find ourselves eventually on the imposing staircase of the house, at that hour completely deserted. Proposing to sit down for a while on the steps, Lady Muriel asked me for a cigarette: two shocks for me because (a) I had been told that smoking was not allowed anywhere in the house, except in the billiard room . . . and (b) because I was not yet aware of the custom of choosing a preferably deserted staircase for a conversation of any degree of intimacy: a habit, as I since discovered with ever increasing satisfaction, prevailing in this country, if hardly anywhere else in the world. But my qualms were soon allayed when Lady Muriel proceeded to give me a fascinating lecture on the habits, manners and idosyncrasies of the mysterious islanders, by whom I was surrounded; and such was the verve and the wit she displayed that I completely lost my heart to her then and there – as a teacher at least. She did not seem to mind that, because when we parted everyone else had gone to bed.

Architecture and Contents

Of the Tudor mansion built round a courtyard which took the place of the former abbey here, the chief exterior feature to have survived is the gate tower in the centre of the east front. The southern range was rebuilt from 1633 onwards with the help of Inigo Jones, Isaac de Caus and John Webb. Its façade, with the two raised roof pavilions, is one of the most beautiful in Britain, just as it contains some of Britain's most beautiful country house interiors. Of these, the Double Cube room is the best known, with its walls of white and gold, adorned with carved swags of fruit, flowers and classical masks, and its coved painted ceiling. The ceiling paintings in the Double Cube have been attributed to Emanuel de Critz and also to Francis Cleyn;

other rooms in the southern range have ceiling paintings by Giuseppe Cesari, Andien de Clermont and Luca Giordano. Subsequent alterations gave the house some eighteenth-century rooms and James Wyatt's spectacular vaulted cloister-corridor which contains what is left of the 8th Earl of Pembroke's collection of sculpture. The north or entrance front, approached through William Chambers's triumphal arch, was also rebuilt in Gothic by Wyatt, but was remodelled in a plainer style early this century. The famous portraits by Van Dyck in the Double Cube represent only a small part of Wilton's picture collection: there are also works by Claude, Rembrandt, Rubens, Lorenzo Lotto and Andrea del Sarto, seascapes by the younger Van de Velde and views of Wilton by Richard Wilson. The portraits, in addition to the Van Dycks, include works by Dahl, Mytens, Lely, Reynolds and Lawrence. The superb gilt settees and side tables by William Kent in the Double Cube have pride of place among the furniture. Wilton stands in a landscape of lawns and cedar trees, its south front facing towards the 'Architect Earl's' Palladian bridge.

A house party for King Edward VII and Queen Alexandra. The Queen stands behind the King, between her host and hostess, the 14th Earl of Pembroke and his wife. Standing on the right is the Pembrokes' younger daughter, Lady Muriel Herbert.

WOBURN ABBEY

BEDFORDSHIRE

THE former Cistercian abbey of Woburn, granted to Henry VIII's courtier John, Lord Russell, afterwards 1st Earl of Bedford (one of the most successful of the Tudor 'New Men'), was demolished by the Puritan 4th Earl of Bedford who replaced it with a Carolean mansion on the same site. This house was transformed into the present mid-eighteenth-century ducal palace by John Russell, 4th Duke of Bedford. His architect was Henry Flitcroft, who incorporated parts of the earlier building in the new structure, notably the northern wing containing the grotto which in the 1630s had been remarkable in having water piped to it. No less advanced for its time was the plumbing of the 4th Duke's palace, which had cold and hot baths adjoining each other in the basement, as well as a water-closet in the garden for the Duke's exclusive use. Unfortunately, the water supply was inclined to run short.

Another modern feature of Woburn as remodelled by Flitcroft was the use of earthenware stoves imported from France to warm the corridors and staircases. As further evidence of the 4th Duke's Francophile tendencies, there was at Woburn in his day a French chef, who received £60 a year, twice as much as was paid to the English cook who assisted him. The 4th Duke's household included a butler, under-butler and groom of the chambers, together with ten footmen whose annual wage ranged from £6 to £8; there were four or five kitchen-maids who received £8, a confectioner who was paid £52 10s – almost as much as the chef – and a confectioner's maid who only got £5. At the head of the hierarchy was Mr Butcher, the agent-in-chief, who received a salary of £700 a year.

The 4th Duke was succeeded in 1771 by his six-year-old grandson who, from the time he came of age until his death while still in his thirties, lived life to the full. He raced, he hunted, he gambled, he moved in the Prince of Wales's set; he kept several mistresses of whom the reigning favourite was thirty years his senior. On a less frivolous plane, the young 5th Duke gave the abbey its delightful family rooms designed by Henry Holland. He took a keen interest in agriculture, his annual sheep-shearings at Woburn rivalling those of Coke of Norfolk (*see* HOLKHAM HALL). He played a part in politics under the leadership of Charles James Fox, becoming an effective speaker in the Lords, though he was said to have reached the age of twenty-four without ever opening a book. He was, as it turned out, the last Duke of Bedford to be active in public life, subsequent Dukes being more concerned with their estates than with the nation at large. The most distinguished later members of the Bedford family were all younger sons or cousins, such as the Prime Minister Lord John Russell and his grandson Bertrand Russell.

Lord John Russell was a frequent guest at Woburn during the reign of his brother the 7th Duke, whose Duchess made social history by introducing the custom of five o'clock tea. The 7th Duke's reign, which coincided with the first two decades of the reign of Queen Victoria, can be said to have marked Woburn's zenith as a centre of ducal hospitality. In one year alone 1,129 persons ate at the 7th Duke's table, while in the same period 2,596 were fed in the steward's room and 8,217 in the servants' hall – a total of nearly 12,000. The Christmas and New Year celebrations were prodigious, with 'small items of jewellery' and French fans on the Christmas tree as presents for the women of the party and silk or velvet waistcoats for the men, while the poor of the neighbourhood gathered outside the dining-room windows after dinner on Christmas day and scrambled for the cutlets, mince-pies and sweets thrown to them from the ducal table. The celebrations usually culminated in a theatrical performance. The New Year of 1857 was ushered in with *Golden Eggs or Trees to Roost in*, 'An Extravaganza', of which the cast included the Comte de Jarnac, Lord Francis Russell, Viscount Hamilton, Lord Gerald FitzGerald, Lady Rachel Butler, Lady Jane Repton and Lady Alexander Russell, with the Earl of Lichfield as prompter (*see* SHUGBOROUGH).

Between 1861, when the 7th Duke died, and 1953, when the present Duke succeeded, Woburn saw little or nothing of normal happy life, being owned by a succession of shy, remote, rather tragic figures. There was the hypochondriac 8th Duke, and the 9th Duke who built his own private crematorium; there was the short-lived 10th Duke whose marriage to a daughter of the 3rd Earl Somers (*see* EASTNOR CASTLE) was loveless and

Visit of Queen Victoria to Woburn Abbey.

childless; there was his brother Herbrand, the 11th Duke, who reigned at Woburn from 1893 to 1940 in an atmosphere of cold formality and antiquated grandeur. Up to 1937, the abbey had an indoor staff of nearly seventy, although on account of the Duke's shyness and his wife's deafness there was not much entertaining. Beer was specially brewed for washing the oak floors and bringing out the colour of the wood. Although there was an attempt to install electric light in the abbey at the beginning of the century, this was abandoned after part of the wiring had caught fire, and it was not until about 1930 that electricity finally came. Even after that oil lamps continued to be used, with a man employed full time in trimming and filling them. To remind his guests of the existence of the novel method of lighting – one of them, knowing nothing about it, having made do with the candle on the desk in his room which was meant for sealing letters – the Duke had plaques bearing the legend 'Electric Light' put up above the switches. His sister, Lady Ermyntrude Malet, came to terms with electricity rather sooner than he did. 'My dear boy,' she said to her young cousin, Edward Sackville-West (*see* KNOLE), who was having tea with her shortly after the outbreak of the First World War, 'now there's a war on, we must learn to do things for ourselves.' And she switched off the light.

The 11th Duke became even more withdrawn after the death of his wife, who having taken up aviation in her old age achieved fame as the 'Flying Duchess' and was lost on a solo flight over the North Sea. His cousin, Conrad Russell, who came to stay with him and his elderly housekeeper-companion, Miss Flora Greene, not long after the Flying Duchess's death, has left an entertaining account of life at Woburn on the eve of the Second World War:

At 9 minutes to 9 we all assemble in the Canaletto Room. At 9 the butler knocks loudly at the door, comes in and bawls: 'Breakfast on the table, Your Grace.' Herbrand says: 'Well, shall we go to breakfast?' We all file in then. There are five men to wait on us, one for each. Everyone has their own tea or coffee pot. You help yourself to eggs and bacon. The butler takes your plate from you and carries it to

Right *The Flying Duchess, and* far right *her husband Herbrand, 11th Duke of Bedford.*

your place. You walk behind him. It makes a little procession. . . . Later a comic opera Rolls dating to 1913 picked us up. Man on box as well as driver and the back wheels fitted with chains as if for snowy weather. Miss Greene held a small butler's tray on her lap and on the tray stood a small Pekinese the size of a basset hound. The tray was supported by a single leg and hitched to the front of the car by green baize straps. By this means the dog's behind is brought to within a half-inch of one's nose. There's no escape.

The 11th Duke was well known for his zoological collections, establishing herds of bison, Père David deer and other wild animals in the park at Woburn, but Conrad Russell, after staying with him, was inclined to believe that the strangest specimens were to be found within the Abbey itself. 'My family is a zoo,' he wrote, 'only instead of lions and bears in the cages there are unicorns, chimaeras, cockatrices and hippogriffs.'

Architecture and Contents

A great Carolean house, built round a courtyard in accordance with the plan of the abbey which it replaced, Woburn was remodelled in the mid-eighteenth century by Henry Flitcroft, who gave it a Palladian west front with a pediment carried on engaged Ionic columns. Flitcroft also designed the twin stable blocks flanking the east front which was demolished in 1950, so what was formerly an enclosed quadrangle has become a three-sided court. The southern range was rebuilt from 1787 onwards to the design of Henry Holland, who provided a series of family rooms including the superb library. The state rooms, decorated by Flitcroft, extend along the principal storey of the western range backed by a long gallery. The treasures of Woburn are unending: an outstanding collection of sixteenth- and early seventeenth-century portraits, which includes the famous 'Armada' portrait of Elizabeth I, and later portraits by Van Dyck, Reynolds and Hoppner; a series of self-portraits by great masters such as Hals, Rembrandt, Tintoretto, Murillo and Hogarth; pictures by Claude, Teniers, Poussin and Vernet; a wealth of fine seventeenth- and eighteenth-century English and French furniture; eighteenth-century English and Sèvres porcelain and services of silver, silver gilt and gold plate. Woburn is also famous for its collection of exotic animals in the park, largely built up by the 11th Duke and his wife, the 'Flying Duchess', to whose memory a room in the abbey is dedicated.

SELECT BIBLIOGRAPHY

ADDISON, WILLIAM, *Audley End* (London 1953)

ASKWITH, BETTY, *The Lytteltons* (London 1975); *Piety and Wit* (London 1982)

ASQUITH, CYNTHIA, *Remember and be Glad* (London 1952)

BENCE-JONES, MARK and MONTGOMERY-MASSINGBERD, HUGH, *The British Aristocracy* (London 1979)

BLAKISTON, GEORGIANA, *Woburn and the Russells* (London 1980)

BRAYE, LORD, *Fewness of my Days* (London 1927)

CECIL, DAVID, *The Cecils of Hatfield House* (London 1973)

CLIVE-PONSONBY-FANE, CHARLES, *We Started a Stately Home* (Brympton d'Evercy, Yeovil 1980)

COMPLETE PEERAGE ed. G.E.C. *et al*, new edn., 13 vols (London 1910–59)

COOPER, DIANA, *The Rainbow Comes and Goes* (London 1958)

COUNTRY LIFE articles by Clive Aslet, John Cornforth, Mark Girouard, Christopher Hussey, Gervase Jackson-Stops, James Lees-Milne, Gordon Nares, Arthur Oswald, Alistair Rowan, H. Avray Tipping, *et al.*

DEVONSHIRE, DUCHESS OF, *The House* (London 1982)

DOUGLAS-HOME, MARGARET, *Althorp's Special Ghosts* (*Country Life*, 18 March 1982)

EGREMONT, LORD, *Wyndham and Children First* (London 1968)

FAIRFAX-LUCY, ALICE, *Charlecote and the Lucys* (London 1958)

FEDDEN, ROBIN and JOEKES, ROSEMARY, *The National Trust Guide* (London 1977)

FEDDEN, ROBIN and KENWORTH-BROWNE, JOHN, *The Country House Guide* (R.R. Guide Books 1979)

FLOWER, SIBYLLA JANE, *Bulwer Lytton* (Aylesbury 1973)

FOSS, ARTHUR, *Country House Treasures* (London 1980)

GIROUARD, MARK, *Life in the English Country House* (New Haven and London 1978)

HAMPDEN, ANTHONY, *Henry and Eliza* (Haywards Heath – privately printed)

HARDWICK, MOLLIE, *Mrs Dizzy* (London 1972)

HARE, AUGUSTUS, *Memorials of a Quiet Life* (3 vols, London 1872–6); *The Story of My Life* (6 vols, London 1896–1900)

HENLEY, DOROTHY, *Rosalind Countess of Carlisle* (London 1958)

HUNN, DAVID, *Goodwood* (London 1975)

KENNEDY, CAROL, *Harewood* (London, Melbourne, Sydney, Auckland and Johannesburg 1982)

LEES-MILNE, JAMES, *Another Self* (London 1970); *Ancestral Voices* (London 1975); *Prophesying Peace* (London 1977)

MILLER, GEORGE C., *Hoghton Tower* (Preston 1948)

NATIONAL TRUST GUIDE BOOKS: Guide books to all National Trust houses included in this book are currently in print, as are those to the houses in private ownership.

POWELL, VIOLET, *Margaret Countess of Jersey* (London 1978)

PÜCKLER-MUSKAU, PRINCE, *Tour of England, Ireland and France in 1828 and 1829 by a German Prince* (4 vols, London 1832)

ROBINSON, JOHN MARTIN, *The Dukes of Norfolk* (Oxford and New York 1982)

ROWSE, A.L., *The Later Churchills* (London 1958)

SACKVILLE-WEST, V., *Knole and the Sackvilles* (London 1923)

STONOR, ROBERT JULIAN, OSB, *Stonor* (Newport Mon. 1951)

SYKES, CHRISTOPHER SIMON, *The Visitors Book* (London 1978)

TORRINGTON DIARIES ed. C. Bruyn Andrews (4 vols, London 1934–8)

VICKERS, HUGO, *Gladys Duchess of Marlborough* (London 1979)

WALPOLE, HORACE, *Letters* (Yale Edition ed. W.S. Lewis, London 1937)

WATERSON, MERLIN, *The Servants' Hall* (London 1980)

ACKNOWLEDGEMENTS

The publishers would like to thank the following for kindly supplying photographic material for reproduction:

By gracious permission of Her Majesty the Queen, from the Royal Archives, Windsor: 101, 122–3, 142–3, 186–7, 187R; by kind permission of the Duke of Beaufort: 31, 32–3; by kind permission of the Viscount and Viscountess Cobham: 109; by kind permission of Viscount Hampden: 97; by kind permission of the Earl of Harewood: 115; by kind permission of the Duke of Norfolk: 18, 20–1 (photo: National Monuments Record); by kind permission of the Marquess of Northampton: 61, 62; by kind permission of the Marquess of Salisbury: 118, 120; by kind permission of the Marquess of Tavistock and the Trustees of the Bedford Estates: 232, 233; by kind permission of His Grace, the Duke of Wellington, Stratfield Saye: 212–3 (photo: Courtauld Institute of Art).

Aerofilms: 100–1
BBC Hulton Picture Library: 15, 45, 69, 116, 140–1, 144, 205
Mark Bence-Jones: 192
John Bethell: 11, 87, 114, 177, 195
Bridgeman Art Library: 59, 99, 189
Brympton Estate Office: 53, 55
Castle Howard Collection: 64
Country Life: 27, 28, 29, 85L & R, 88–9, 154–5, 155, 163L, 177L, 190 191
Courtauld Institute of Art: 57, 138–9 (Hermione Cobbold Collection)
Christopher Dalton: 50, 51
Devonshire Collection, Chatsworth, reproduced by permission of the Chatsworth Settlement Trustees: 72–3, 75, 76, 77
English Life Publications Ltd: 9, 96–7, 98, 103, 132, 141, 147, 181T & B, 182, 201, 203
Fitzwilliam Museum: 60

The Garland Collection, West Sussex Record Office: 174–5B
Hoghton Tower Preservation Trust: 125 (photo: Colourmaster Ltd) 126
Michael Holford: 22–3, 58
Illustrated London News: 153
Jarrold & Sons Ltd: 157, 158
A.F. Kersting: endpapers, 41, 47, 106, 110, 119, 150, 151
Lucinda Lambton/Arcaid: 214, 215
Lamport Hall Trust: 148–9
National Monuments Record: 24–5, 25T, 83, 149
National Portrait Gallery: 183
The National Trust: 48, 49, 68, 71 (John Bethell), 79T & B, 82–3, 94 (John Bethell), 95 (John Bethell), 135 (Edward Sweetland), 137 (Jeremy Whitaker), 146 (John Bethell), 161 (John Bethell), 162 (Alex Morwood), 163R, 165 (John Bethell), 168 (John Bethell), 169 (Nicolette Nalette), 171, 172 (Jeremy Whitaker), 173, 193, (John Bethell), 197 (Erik Pelham), 209, 210 (Martin Trelawney), 211 (Angelo Hornak), 219 (John Bethell), 222 (John Bethell), 223 (Turner), 225
Sydney Newbery: 139
Lady Rachel Pepys: 19
William Proby: 90, 92
Stan Smith: 220–1
Terence Spencer: 159
Stonor Park: 207
Sudeley Castle: 216, 217
Baroness von Twickel: 80–1
Victoria & Albert Museum: 112, 113
John Webb: 128
Weidenfeld & Nicolson Archives: half-title, frontispiece, 10, 13, 14–15, 16, 17T, 17B, 34–5, 35T, 36, 39L & R, 42–3, 44, 65, 67, 104L & R, 105, 108, 124–5, 127, 129, 130, 131, 133, 174–5T, 178L, 178–9, 185, 198, 227, 228–9, 230
Jeremy Whitaker: 43